Urban Forest Landscapes:
Integrating Multidisciplinary Perspectives

URBAN FOREST LANDSCAPES

Integrating Multidisciplinary Perspectives

Edited by GORDON A. BRADLEY

University of Washington Press

SEATTLE AND LONDON

The following chapters were written and prepared by U.S. government employees on official time, and are, therefore, in the public domain: "Toward Ecosystem Management: Shifts in the Core and the Context of Urban Forest Ecology" by Rowan A. Rowntree; "The Role Economics Can Play as an Analytical Tool in Urban Forestry" by John F. Dwyer; "Energy-Efficient Landscapes" by E. Gregory McPherson, Rowan A. Rowntree, and J. Alan Wagar; and "Net Benefits of Healthy and Productive Urban Forests" by E. Gregory McPherson

Library of Congress Cataloging-in-Publication Data
Urban forest landscapes: integrating multidisciplinary perspectives / Gordon A. Bradley, editor.
    p.   cm.
  Includes bibliographical references and index.
  ISBN 0–295–97438–9 (cloth) — ISBN 0–295–97439–7 (pbk.)
  1. Urban forestry. 2. Urban ecology (Biology) 3. Forest landscape design.
4. Urban forestry—United States. 5. Urban ecology (Biology)—United States.
6. Forest landscape design—United States. I. Bradley, Gordon A.
SB436.U7   1995   94–23781
333.75'09173'2—dc20   CIP

The paper used in this publication meets the minimum requirements of American National Standard for Information Sciences—Permanence of Paper for Printed Library Materials, ANSI Z39.48–1984.

Institute of Forest Resources Contribution No. 76

Contents

PART 1: INTRODUCTION AND HISTORICAL PERSPECTIVE

1   Urban Forest Landscapes:
Integrating Multidisciplinary Perspectives   3
Gordon Bradley

2   Urban Forestry: A National Initiative   12
Gary Moll

3   Changing Forms and Persistent Values:
Historical Perspectives on the Urban Forest   17
Henry W. Lawrence

PART 2: THE ENVIRONMENTAL SETTING

4   Toward Ecosystem Management: Shifts in the Core
and the Context of Urban Forest Ecology   43
Rowan A. Rowntree

5   Informational Issues: A Perspective
on Human Needs and Inclinations   60
Rachel Kaplan

6   Land Use Control as a Strategy for Retaining
and Integrating Urban Forest Landscapes   72
Konrad Liegel

7   Keeping It Green: Political and Administrative Issues
in the Preservation of the Urban Forest   78
Gene Duvernoy

8   The Role Economics Can Play as an Analytical Tool
in Urban Forestry   88
John F. Dwyer

9   The Urban Forest as a Source of Psychological Well-Being   100
Stephen Kaplan

PART 3: SPECIAL PURPOSE LANDSCAPES

10   Scenic Value in the Urbanizing Landscape   111
     Patrick A. Miller

11   Management of Greenbelts and Forest Remnants
     in Urban Forest Landscapes   128
     James K. Agee

12   Wildlife Habitat Design
     in Urban Forest Landscapes   139
     Dorothy A. Milligan Raedeke and Kenneth J. Raedeke

13   Energy-Efficient Landscapes   150
     E. Gregory McPherson, Rowan A. Rowntree, and J. Alan Wagar

14   Water Conserving Landscapes   161
     Robert C. Perry

15   Fire-Safe Landscapes   164
     James R. Clark

PART 4: INTEGRATION: TRADEOFFS AND BENEFITS

16   Sustainability in Landscaping   175
     Robert C. Perry

17   Net Benefits of Healthy and Productive Urban Forests   180
     E. Gregory McPherson

18   Bellevue, Washington: Managing the Urban Forest
     for Multiple Benefits   195
     Lee Springgate and Roger Hoesterey

19   Tiger Mountain State Forest: A Working Forest
     in an Urban Environment   201
     Doug McClelland

20   Some Thoughts on Integrating Multiple Objectives
     for Urban Forest Landscapes   208
     Gordon A. Bradley

Contributors   213

Index   217

Preface

In recent years there has been considerable interest in community tree planting projects. While the underlying motives for such endeavors are commendable, many individuals have expressed concern about the ultimate results. Has sufficient consideration been given to species selection, long-term maintenance costs, the mix and arrangement of plants used in the landscape, and their effects on people and wildlife? These questions have tended to refocus attention so that urban forestry is now seen less as an effort to plant single trees and more as an opportunity to create diverse urban landscapes that will produce an ongoing flow of benefits to people, wildlife, and their respective communities. Conversations with many people who have varied interests in urban forestry showed that an examination of urban forest landscapes by experts representing different disciplinary perspectives should be very useful. This book presents the papers and discussions that resulted from a symposium that took that approach to the subject of urban forestry.

Prior to convening the symposium, a group of experts met at the Center for Urban Horticulture at the University of Washington in Seattle for two days in the spring of 1991 to discuss the idea of special purpose landscapes. The concern was that in our efforts to develop landscapes that address specific goals such as fire safety, energy conservation, aesthetics, and wildlife we may in fact be creating more problems than we are solving—or at least we may be achieving the purpose of one landscape at the expense of the purpose of another. After much discussion, it became obvious that we were really talking about the need to focus multidisciplinary attention on the development of urban forest landscapes. This includes not only the need to bring this expertise to bear on the development of urban landscapes but also to recognize the social and political settings from which urban forestry programs emerge. As the meeting concluded it was agreed that there was sufficient material and interest to proceed with a more formal program that would be made available to a much wider audience, hence the development and convening of a symposium in the spring of 1992 entitled Urban Forest Landscapes: Integrating Multidisciplinary Perspectives. The organization of this book essentially follows the flow of presentations at the symposium.

ORGANIZATION OF THE BOOK

This book has four parts. Part 1 introduces the subject and provides a discussion of how various disciplines may contribute to the development of urban forest landscapes. The social-political context is outlined along with the notion of the urban forest as a gradient extending from the city center to the urban fringe. Part 1 also offers insights on urban forestry as a contemporary national initiative in the United States. In addition, it provides an extensive history that draws on the experience of European cities over the centuries and shows how many European ideas have influenced urban forestry in the United States.

Part 2 examines the setting from which urban forestry programs emerge, starting with those aspects of landscape ecology, plant succession, and dynamics of disturbance that are significant in creating and maintaining urban forests. Discussion then shifts to informational issues that deal with how knowledge is shared and how we evaluate various claims to expertise regarding urban forestry.

Institutional issues are treated next. These include legal, political, and economic considerations with an emphasis on grassroots organizations, legal and administrative mechanisms to facilitate program development, and economic aspects of program viability. Part 2 concludes by focusing on the relationship between people and plants and the restorative benefits that urban forests provide.

Part 3 of the book looks critically at the various purposes for which urban forest landscapes may be created, such as scenic values, greenbelts and forest remnants, wildlife habitat, and energy conserving, water conserving, and fire-safe landscapes. Discussion includes the purpose of each landscape, what that means with regard to vegetation structure, and how the landscape may change over space and time. Also, factors are examined that increase or decrease one's ability to create effective urban forest landscapes. These include funding, laws and regulations, and ecological issues as well as human preference and understanding.

Part 4 integrates the preceding material by focusing attention on the sustainability of urban forest landscapes. This is done from a conceptual perspective as well as by presenting two practical case studies that address urban forest landscape issues from the city center to the urban fringe. Part 4 closes with some thoughts on integrating the multiple objectives of urban forest landscapes.

ACKNOWLEDGMENTS

Contributions from many individuals and organizations made the symposium and this book possible. Primary financial support came from the Washington State Department of Natural Resources (DNR), Urban and Community Forestry Program, and the United States Forest Service, Northeastern Forest Experiment Station, Urban Forestry Project. Special gratitude is expressed to Jennifer Belcher, Commissioner of Public Lands, and Steve Meacham, Shelley Farber, Philip Rodbell, and Gretchan Garcia. Representatives from the Forest Service were Rowan Rowntree, Urban Forestry Project leader, and Ken Johnson from the Regional Office in Portland. Additional financial support was provided by the Davey Tree Expert Company and Cam West Development Company, and I am indebted to Roger Funk and Eric Campbell.

Individuals from the Center for Urban Horticulture who provided assistance were Clem Hamilton, Fran Trinder, Jean Robins, Rebecca Johnson, Barbara O'Neill, David Stockdale, Darcy McNamara, and Sara Reichard. Individuals from the College of Forest Resources who helped in a variety of ways include Jennifer Powers, David Wortman, Jeff Gorelik, Beverly Gonyea, and Donald Hanley. Invaluable assistance was provided by Beverly Anderson in organizing publication of the book and Margaret Lahde in formatting the final product.

Leila Charbonneau deserves a very special thank you for the excellent work that she has done in the technical editing of this book. Her attention to detail is amazing and her ability to smooth the work of twenty authors into a coherent whole is admirable. Working with her is sufficient cause to consider putting together another book.

Of course none of this would have been possible without the excellent and very thoughtful contributions from each of the authors. They are listed individually at the end of this book under "Contributors," which is an understatement given the fine quality of their work. While developing the logic, content, and flow of material for the symposium and book, I also bounced ideas off several of them, including Rachel and Steve Kaplan, Alan Wagar, Jim Clark, Pat Miller, Robert Perry, and Dorothy Milligan Raedeke.

Finally, special thanks go to Robert Perry for the cover design for the symposium brochure and this book.

Gordon Bradley

PART ONE
Introduction and Historical Perspective

1

Urban Forest Landscapes: Integrating Multidisciplinary Perspectives

GORDON BRADLEY

ABSTRACT In recent years, interest in the urban environment has brought together a new community of people gathered around the idea of urban forestry. To ensure the productivity of urban forests, it is necessary to understand why they are created and the optimal structure necessary to sustain them. By understanding what they furnish to society—scenery, buffers, wildlife, energy and water conservation, to begin with—it is possible to minimize the conflicts between forest types and uses and begin to develop integrated urban forest landscapes that provide multiple benefits. It is also important to recognize that the forest structure may change as one moves along a gradient from the city center to the urban fringe. In addition, the context from which urban forest landscapes emerge must be understood in order to develop successful urban forests. The role that ecological, institutional, and human issues play in enhancing or inhibiting our ability to develop viable urban forest landscapes is significant. Thus combining the concept of the urban forest gradient with an understanding of vegetation structure and the context for analysis contributes to our ability to develop urban forest landscapes of an integrated and sustainable nature.

Landscapes, gardens, and urban vegetation have always played a significant role in the human environment. One need only recall the images of tranquil Asian gardens, scenic English landscapes, the grand boulevards of Paris and Central Park in New York to recognize how urban vegetation has contributed to the livability of cities and towns (Lawrence 1993). Certainly on a personal level, special places give meaning to our lives because of memories connected with a favorite bench in a garden, a view along a riverbank, or a walk in the woods. People value landscapes for many reasons, including both their commodity and amenity benefits.

In recent years, a growing interest in the urban environment has led to the establishment of a new professional and community approach based on the idea of urban forestry. At least two decades ago, the International Union of Forestry Research Organizations (IUFRO) formed a project group on Arboriculture and Urban Forestry and convened a group of interested scientists to discuss trees and forests for human settlements (Andresen 1976). During that period we also saw the emergence of urban forestry programs in colleges and universities of the United States and Canada. In addition, numerous organizations were developed or expanded to address urban forestry issues from community perspectives and through scientific research programs. These included locally based organizations such as the Los Angeles Tree People and the Sacramento Tree Foundation, statewide programs such as Washington State's Urban and Community Forest Council, and national programs such as American Forests' urban forestry program and the U.S. Forest Service's urban forestry research units. Besides community and professional initiatives, interest in urban forestry is found in a variety of university programs, including park administration, landscape architecture, and urban horticulture, as well as urban forestry.

The focus of these programs varies, but there is a growing recognition that individual trees must be considered in the context of the urban forest and that the urban forest must be considered in the context of the urban setting. This includes not only the physical and biological realities of the setting but institutional factors that may influence the development of urban forest landscapes. This comprehensive view is necessary if we are to fully understand what benefits flow from urban forests and how to produce them most effectively. The notion of street tree programs as the central focus of urban forestry has been replaced by a more comprehensive understanding of the concept of urban forest ecosystems.

This book, and this introductory chapter in particular, seek to show what the various disciplinary perspectives bring to the development of viable urban forestry programs and why addressing urban forest problems from a single-tree or narrow disciplinary perspective is no longer sufficient.

BENEFITS OF URBAN FORESTRY

Recent efforts in urban forestry reflect a growing recognition of the many benefits to individuals and society from the availability of vegetation in urban and urbanizing environments. These benefits are discovered to be both global in nature, such as the potential for reducing urban heat island effects, and very personal, insofar as they answer the human need for exposure to green spaces in order to maintain a sense of well-being (EPA 1992). Some benefits are easy to quantify, like the increase in land value because a specimen tree is located on one's property. Others are less tangible, such as the presence of wildlife in one's backyard. While not all benefits are well grounded in science or easy to quantify, it is generally agreed that green spaces contribute substantially to the physical, biological, and psychological well-being of individuals and communities. Benefits of vegetation are provided through the creation of parks, open spaces, corridors, and buffers, which in turn allow direct access to recreation, wildlife, scenery, and a variety of other amenities (Sterns and Montag 1974).

But some recent tree planting promotions would lead one to think that the moment a tree is planted (any tree, in any place), global warming will suddenly decrease and wildlife will appear. This is a kind of "field of dreams" effect: we plant the tree and benefits will come. Unfortunately, this is seldom the case, and all too often the wrong tree is planted in the wrong place.

Urban forest benefits are a function of the vegetative composition of an urban forest. In most cases specific benefits are linked to fairly specific arrangements of vegetation or forest structure. Structure in turn is a function of several factors including the number of plants involved, what types they are (trees, shrubs, herbaceous plants), the mix of species, how the plants are assembled in space, and their age or maturity. This is reminiscent of the "form follows function" adage in the field of design. In other words, purpose is a function of the structure of the forest vegetation. Scenic landscapes may take one structure, while a landscape exclusively for wildlife may take another.

The most simple structure would be a single tree planted in a sidewalk planter for the purpose of providing shade or human scale in a built environment. Assuming that the proper species is selected, problems of sidewalk cracking and messy fruit dropping on the pavement will be minimized. At the other extreme, more complex structures might include a variety of tree species, exhibiting different age characteristics, surrounded by shrubs and ground covers that are spaced purposefully in the landscape. The result is a structure that has both horizontal and vertical diversity, as well as living and dead material standing and lying on the forest floor. While this landscape may not appear orderly, and consequently may score low on a visual preference rating, the opportunities for wildlife may be abundant.

CREATING SUCCESSFUL URBAN FOREST PROGRAMS

Understanding the purpose of an urban forest, and the structure necessary to achieve that purpose, is essential for successful programs. Problems or conflicts may emerge when the structure for one type of landscape is at cross-purposes with another. For example, an energy conserving landscape suggests the placement of trees and shrubs within shadow casting distance of the west- and, to some extent, east-facing walls of a structure. These trees may be deciduous if winters are severe, thus allowing winter sunlight to strike the structure, or they may be evergreen to prevent the winter sun from hitting the structure in warm southern climates. But placing an evergreen tree close to buildings in arid landscapes creates the potential for unsafe fire conditions. Therefore, energy conserving landscapes in certain climates may be in direct conflict with fire-safe landscapes. Conflicting structures are also possible between wildlife and scenic landscapes where considerable diversity and apparent lack of order are essential for one, and some semblance of order and simplicity is necessary for the other.

Problems also exist when we begin to convert a relatively undisturbed forest to urban uses. This is a particular problem in the Northwest, where many new subdivisions are being built in second-growth Douglas-fir forests. Development creates openings in forests, thus weakening their ability to withstand winds and increasing the possibility of trees blowing down on structures. Problems are often exacerbated by trenching, compaction, and other damage to root systems. Further problems exist related to fire, wildlife, and water runoff, but the point is that the vegetation that developed over the years to support a wild, undisturbed Douglas-fir forest is not the same vegetative mix that will safely accommodate a housing development over time. The imposition of housing in a wooded setting requires the careful reconfiguration of the residual forest.

LINKING FOREST PURPOSE TO VEGETATION STRUCTURE

While we have about twenty years of institution building in the field of urban forestry, we are only now beginning to link landscape purpose with vegetation structure in a comprehensive manner. This knowledge must be developed and communicated, given the diversity of emerging programs promoting tree planting and nature conservation. Such programs include urban forest councils which are being established at the national, state, and local levels with an emphasis on the planting of trees in a variety of locations.

Their efforts could be better informed by an increased understanding of the linkage between form and function.

In addition, many states and local jurisdictions have active open space land acquisition programs that could benefit from knowing about the quality of the land being acquired and what management strategies would increase the flow of benefits. Many of these open space programs are being developed—as in the state of Washington—in the context of growth management plans. The challenge here is to develop programs promoting open space lands and greenbelts for recreation, wildlife, development buffers, and scenic backdrops. Of course, each of these landscapes may require a different structure to meet these varied purposes. Other contemporary programs include conservation area management efforts as well as energy and water conservation programs. By linking vegetation structure with an explicit urban forest purpose, urban forest landscapes may be created where the benefits will outweigh potential costs. The rationale for the chapters that follow is to look at urban forests created for specific purposes, such as aesthetics, greenbelts, wildlife, energy and water conservation, and fire-hazard reduction. In examining each purpose, it is possible to understand the vegetative structure necessary to accomplish that purpose, as well as to explore ways to minimize conflicts with other urban forest goals.

In developing comprehensive urban forest landscapes, the challenge is to avoid conflicts while attempting to provide maximum benefits over time. The integration of multidisciplinary perspectives is essential in meeting this challenge. This includes understanding the importance not only of vegetation structure but also the idea of an urban wildland gradient and the contextual factors that may enhance or inhibit one's ability to develop successful urban forest landscape programs.

URBAN FOREST GRADIENT

The notion of an urban forest gradient running from the city center to wildland settings is useful in understanding the opportunities and limitations in developing urban forest landscapes (Figure 1-1). The most obvious differences across the gradient are those

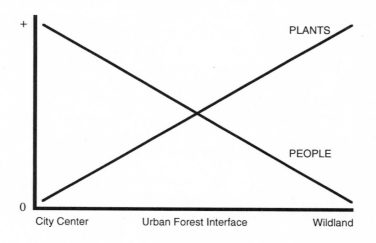

Figure 1-1. Urban forest landscape gradient.

concerning people and plants. At the city center, people are abundant and plants are relatively scarce. At the other end of the gradient the opposite is true.

At the city end of the gradient, there are more of the services that people desire and conveniences such as cars, buildings, and paving. The resultant impacts on urban vegetation include carbon monoxide, sulfur dioxide and ozone gases, road salt, compacted soils, and increased heat from glare. At this end of the gradient, plants are often threatened by their environment. But plants can also be a major salvation to humans in harsh urban environments where they provide shade, buffers, and variation in the cityscape.

Other factors that change across the gradient and that may significantly influence our ability to create different landscapes are building density, parcel size, land value, legal considerations, and natural legacies. All tend to affect the possible form and function that the urban forest may assume.

Building density varies with land parcel size along the urban-wildland gradient. At the urban end, there are more structures per acre, or greater building density, than in wildland settings. And the parcels tend to be much smaller in the city. The implications for the type of forest that may be created are lack of continuous space, greater variation in microclimate due to the influence of buildings, and more disturbed and compacted soils because of the infrastructure necessary to support higher-density development. This infrastructure includes roads, sewers, power and water lines, each of which is often in direct conflict with the roots, limbs, and crowns of urban vegetation.

Land value, or the price per square foot of land, tends to be higher in the city than in the countryside. While this may not directly affect what one can grow, it affects the ability of a jurisdiction to assemble parcels of land for open spaces, parks, greenbelts, and buffers. If land becomes available, it is usually in small parcels or remnants of land left over from other uses. While it is felt that any open space is better than no open space, these remnants may be of little practical utility in the larger scheme of a comprehensive urban forest landscape plan.

Laws regarding land use, until recently, have focused more attention on cityscapes than wildland settings. This is evident when we consider space in a city with regard to the geometric pattern of roads and development, building height and bulk, and ordinances dealing with urban forestry, which seem to focus largely on street tree programs. In recent years we have begun to see a greater emphasis on legal mechanisms to ensure the creation and maintenance of urban forest landscapes from the city center to wildland settings. These include requirements for leaving open space and natural areas in new developments, protecting riparian corridors and wetlands, and requiring the revegetation and regeneration of disturbed landscapes (Bradley 1992).

The notion of natural legacies has to do with the extent to which the landscape bears any resemblance to its original state, including attributes of topography, surface water flow, groundwater levels, and soils and vegetation. Highly modified landscapes, or landscapes that retain little of their original character, are more common in city than in wildland environments. In wildlands the probability is fairly high that native vegetation prevails, soils are generally undisturbed, and water flows over and through the site. All of these suggest that the soils will provide a better growing medium for vegetation than in the city, there will be fewer invasive plants to compete with, and a more complex and diverse forest structure will contribute successfully to both wildlife and amenity values.

Thinking of urban forest landscapes in terms of a gradient begins to suggest the problems facing us and the opportunities available to us in considering the use of vegetation for specific purposes. Some landscapes, such as those providing the optimal structure for wildlife, may be much easier to create at the wildland end of the gradient and highly compromised in city landscapes. This is not to say that we cannot provide for wildlife in the city, but it is reasonable to assume that the space and time necessary to create a diverse landscape with both horizontal and vertical diversity are limited. Other landscapes, such as those where scenic amenities are of concern, may be provided in a variety of ways across the entire gradient without compromising the basic purposes to be achieved. Thus to produce the benefits expected from a particular landscape, one needs to know the optimal structure of the landscape and how the factors along the gradient may influence that structure. Some landscapes may be provided along the entire gradient, with their form changing as one moves from the city center to wildlands, while others may be best situated at some specific point along the gradient. In discussing landscapes for specific purposes, several authors in this book will point to the problems and opportunities of creating landscapes along the urban-wildland gradient.

CONTEXT FOR ANALYSIS

Contextual factors are also important in developing urban forest landscapes. These include ecological, informational, and institutional issues as well as human and historical perspectives. Each may inhibit or enhance our ability to develop successful and sustainable urban forest landscapes. The initial chapters of this book focus on these factors, which are discussed briefly below.

Ecological issues are relevant to developing urban forest landscapes. Landscapes, while appearing to be static or stable, are always undergoing change. This change may be very slow and subtle, such as the changing soil pH resulting from acid precipitation, or it may be rapid and obvious, as when wildfires swept through the Oakland hills in 1991. Landscapes are a function of forces acting over time which help to shape the underlying soil, and the mix, structure, and spatial configuration of vegetation. The forces that influence urban forests vary according to location. Vegetation in the city is subjected to harsh influences that are uncommon in more remote settings. Likewise, a forest in a wildland setting escapes the heat, glare, and confined growing space of an urban street tree, but may be subjected to occasional periods of drought, fire, pests, and disease. Understanding the ecological processes of any particular assemblage of urban vegetation is essential to knowing where the landscape has been in time and where it is in its evolutionary processes (Gilbert 1989).

We are limited in what we know about urban forest landscapes and what we are able to communicate to others about them. Much of the information gathered in years past is anecdotal at best, leaving the profession without a solid base of knowledge on which to build. Only recently have we begun to look critically at the costs and benefits that actually flow from urban forests. This information is important if we are to inform people of the value of urban forests and, more important, if we are to create forests that produce the things we say they will produce. In seeking information about the role of urban forests in society, we need to use the generally accepted conventions of the scientific community as well as recognize and appreciate the wealth of knowledge from local situations where people's perceptions are directly influenced by their experiences with urban vegetation.

In communicating our understanding of urban forests and the benefits they produce for communities, it is important to know how people learn, why they show interest in some but not other information, and the processes that individuals go through before they find something to be important. While we may understand a particular idea and its merits, it may take a while for someone else to understand the concept, why it may be important, how it can be implemented, and its long-term benefits to society. In communicating these ideas, many different methods of "sending" the information should be explored. Much of our time in urban forestry is spent on programs, brochures, slide and video programs, and field trips. These information projects are often developed without an explicit purpose in mind, with little understanding of learning styles, and with minimal attempts to find out if they have any effect at all. If we are in the information age, and if we are to generate and disseminate knowledge about urban forests, then becoming critical scientists, effective transmitters of information, and perceptive listeners is essential to the success of the field (Kaplan and Kaplan 1989).

Institutional issues largely involve four major thrusts: legal, political, administrative, and economic. Concerns about the legal framework within which we operate are important for several reasons. Certainly one of the more obvious is the influence that laws and local ordinances have on the form of the built environment. The city grid, roads, sidewalks, planting strips, and building placement, height, and bulk are all a function of laws. These, in turn, influence the sites on which urban vegetation must exist. In addition, local ordinances provide in many cases the basis for street tree and urban and community forest programs. These ordinances essentially empower governments to develop, fund, and staff programs to acquire, preserve, and maintain urban green space. As urban forestry matures beyond the confines of street tree programs to broader concepts of urban vegetation management, it will be necessary to be more innovative in the use of legal mechanisms to achieve urban forestry goals. These innovations will include regulations; but to be long lasting and gain broader acceptance, they must also include incentive programs and the acquisition of property through a variety of mechanisms that are acceptable to landowners as well as affordable for local and state governments.

Political aspects of urban forestry are the driving force behind many of the more viable programs that exist across the country in both the public and private sectors. The development of supporters, or an enthusiastic constituency, is necessary to garner resources, do the work, and maintain urban forest landscapes. Interestingly enough, while many social issues related to housing and health care are in the forefront, tree planting and fish and wildlife enhancement programs consistently attract large and diverse groups of people for local environmental improvement projects. As a catalyst for community activity, open space programs—programs related to "green" issues—are effective and tend to be enduring, like the environments they create.

Administrative issues relate to the mechanisms established to develop and implement urban forestry programs. Such mechanisms include open space and street tree departments as well as loosely knit neighborhood groups in charge of creating and maintaining a planting area. Urban forestry initiatives are found in a wide variety of places throughout society. Their success is a function of how well they articulate their vision and the extent to which they are effective in bringing their vision to reality. This requires well-developed planning systems. Planning should be a part of securing resources through fundraising, legislative appropriations or bond issues, acquisition programs, program development, management, and maintenance, and long-term monitoring activities. While the benefits of the urban forest are largely consumed out of doors, the foundation for the production of those benefits is the result of well-planned and executed activities in some corner office or living room far removed from the scene (Miller 1988).

Economic issues are only now becoming a significant aspect of the urban forestry vocabulary. This is not to say that we have not been able to "price out" certain parts of the landscape; this, of course, is possible for many landscape components. The price of a tree, the cost per yard of soil, and the annual costs of watering a lawn are fairly straightforward calculations. Values to society that are more difficult to put in dollar terms are the restorative qualities of landscapes, the presence of wildlife, or the existence of a scenic backdrop for a community. The work of estimating these benefits, their flow characteristics, and production costs has become a recent challenge to the field of urban forestry.

Even where we may know the costs of certain landscaped components, we have only begun to look critically at the value of benefits that flow from these costs. As we begin to look at secondary and tertiary costs and benefits, we find that we should cease certain activities and increase others. A case in point is the high cost of maintaining large expanses of turf grass where poor soil fertility and lack of moisture have to be mitigated by massive fertilization and irrigation. We need also to look critically at the efficiency of our energy programs, maintenance schedules, planting schemes, and administrative arrangements. To the extent that economic efficiency is a consideration in our urban forestry efforts, there is much work to do to develop solid evidence regarding the actual benefits of our programs.

Human considerations in urban forestry are becoming a significant part of why we value vegetation in urban settings. While it is fairly obvious to most people from their own experiences that green spaces are important, it is only recently becoming obvious *why* this is so. The restorative and rejuvenative aspects of direct exposure to green spaces, as well as the indirect visual benefits, have been documented through scientific studies in a variety of settings (Kaplan and Kaplan 1989). The soothing and settling psychological and physiological effects that green experiences have on humans provide a renewed sense of well-being. Opportunities for reflection, undistracted thought, and invigorating discovery leave an individual refreshed and renewed for daily activities. The fascinating aspect of this restorative effect is that it occurs whether the green space is a window box or a wilderness. People-plant interactions are only now becoming well understood, but the implications for providing human benefits are substantial.

TOWARD SUCCESSFUL STRATEGIES

The development of integrated urban forest landscapes requires an understanding of vegetation structure, the urban-wildland gradient, and the setting or context in which landscapes are provided. The necessity for incorporating multidisciplinary perspectives becomes obvious when one begins to look at landscapes in this manner. This idea of integrated landscapes also begins to lead toward the development of landscapes that are enduring over time from a biological as well as an institutional perspective. It is this concept of sustainability that begins to emerge from the development of enduring landscapes. Sustainability implies bearing up over time, and this suggests continued support and use that does not degrade the landscape, while the landscape itself continues to provide a stream of benefits. Certainly it is the purpose of the papers that follow to suggest, in greater detail, some of the specifics of how this may be accomplished.

LITERATURE CITED

Andresen, J.W. 1976. Urban forestry research systems. *In* Trees and forests for human settlements. International Union of Forestry Research Organizations. P1.05 Project Group on Arboriculture and Urban Forestry. Centre for Urban Forest Studies, University of Toronto.

Bradley, G.A. 1992. Land use planning on the cutting edge. *In* P.D. Rodbell, ed., Proceedings of the Fifth National Urban Forest Conference, November 15-19, 1991, Los Angeles, California, pp. 33-35. American Forestry Association, Washington, D.C.

Environmental Protection Agency. 1992. Cooling our communities: A guidebook on tree planting and light-colored surfacing. Office of Policy Analysis, Climate Change Division, Washington, D.C.

Gilbert, O.L. 1989. The ecology of urban habitats. Chapman and Hall, London and New York.

Kaplan, R., and S. Kaplan. 1989. The experience of nature: A psychological perspective. Cambridge University Press, Cambridge and New York.

Lawrence, H.W. 1993. The neoclassical origins of modern urban forests. Forest and Conservation History 37(1):26-36.

Miller, R.W. 1988. Urban forestry: Planning and managing urban greenspaces. Prentice Hall, Englewood Cliffs, New Jersey.

Stearns, F.W., and T. Montag, eds. 1974. The urban ecosystem: A holistic approach. Dowden, Hutchinson and Ross, Stroudsburg, Pennsylvania; distributed by Halsted Press, New York.

2

Urban Forestry: A National Initiative

GARY MOLL

ABSTRACT Urban forestry is a significant environmental field that is still in its infancy. As knowledge of the urban ecosystem grows, it is important to mobilize the expertise of a broad spectrum of urban people to address the issues. Knowledge must also be shared between those who know rural forests and those who know urban forestry so that a perspective emerges that encompasses the entire ecosystem, including the people who live in it. One of the greatest challenges to the urban forester is to find ways of reconciling divergent views as well as making the benefits of the urban forest clear to the public and decision makers.

WHAT IS AN URBAN FOREST?

This question has been asked and answered in many different ways over the twenty years I have been working in this business. The definitions range from broad to narrow, and I think the broad view that recognizes urban forests as ecosystems provides the context for building better places for people to live. Simply stated, an urban forest is the area in and around the places we live that has or can have trees. Street trees, park trees, green spaces, residential land, public and private spaces with vegetation collectively make up an urban forest. This includes the urban fringe where subdivisions are under construction as well as the rural land that is being considered for development. It includes the smaller towns and communities as well as those areas considered urban because of the population density.

Two terms are commonly used to describe this resource—urban forests and community forests—and some of the forestry agencies combine the two. I think our vocabulary should have a simple phrase to describe this resource and I prefer to use "urban forest" because it is short and to the point. As technicians, administrators, and researchers, we search for the perfect definition of what we do, and in the process we complicate an important concept that needs clarity. What would serve the profession better is a simple phrase to communicate with people not engaged in the business. The Eskimos have over a hundred words to describe snow, and while that is very useful for building igloos, the simple word "snow" tells most of us what we need to know about the white stuff.

I use the term urban forest exclusively because it brings two very different images together. Combining these extremes into one term seems to express the challenge facing the managers of trees in a city or town. It sets out the context around which this science needs to be developed. It puts city managers and natural resource scientists on notice that there is a large resource between their areas of professional expertise. Our goal is to learn how to apply our knowledge of trees, forests, and people to the development of healthier urban ecosystems.

Urban forests are where people live in a communal social structure with the natural resources dominated by trees. The urban infrastructure is designed to accommodate transportation, utilities, buildings, and other human-engineered structures. Unfortunately, communities don't build urban infrastructure to fit the environment; they build according to standardized engineering and financial plans. The biological requirements of trees are not engineered into city structure. Trees are not allocated the proper space to grow through their successional stages. The natural ecological cycles are fragmented and isolated. Ecological guidelines need to be provided to engineers before they can be included in the engineering plans. Providing these natural resource guidelines is the job of the urban forester.

To meet financial needs, city leaders must decide that the trees have enough value to be saved or added to the infrastructure. Unfortunately, we generally value trees based on what they are worth at sawmills. We know the value of a board better than we know the value of reducing stormwater flow, controlling heat island temperatures, or dealing with poor air quality. But the economics of managing urban forests are not driven by fiber production economics. Although a tree in the city is worth more alive than dead, community leaders have still not bought in on the notion that the value of a living tree can be measured in economic terms.

The values and functions of urban and rural forests are very different, but there is not yet agreement on how to distinguish between the two. The forest planners working for the U.S. Forest Service review aerial photos of the national forests on a regular basis. Forest planners know a lot about rural forests, but not as much about urban forests, or at least they see the urban forest much differently from the way urban foresters or planners do.

The Forest Service has a historic mission to track changes in the size, condition, and value of the rural tree cover and provide information to managers and decision makers. They measure the tree cover in terms of commercial forests. So when the need to inventory a community tree cover arose, forest planners saw their mission as one of separating urban from rural trees: to draw a line that would provide two acreage figures, one for rural and one for urban forests.

Such a simple separation unfortunately does not provide urban planners with the information they need to make important decisions about the ecosystem in which their community is located. For several years I provided technical assistance to the planning boards in three rapidly developing counties in Maryland. The county planning commissions looked upon the rural forests surrounding their cities as vacant land waiting to be developed. It essentially had no value until it was developed. Both urban and rural planners need better information about urban forests and the trees caught between urban and rural land uses. We still do not know how to place a value on the resources removed.

Looking at urban forests from the urban point of view allows developing communities to make better use of the rural forests that surround them. Understanding the land helps to fit the established forest systems into a continuum with the urban infrastructure and deliver the ecological benefits of the natural environment to urban areas. Decision making organizations in the city can be made aware of urban forests and their values, and actions to care for them can be included in the decision making process. Decisions that damage the ecology can be avoided.

When urban forests are viewed as ecosystems, a wide range of values can be connected to the resource. Ecosystems are complex and most suited to a broad definition of urban forests. Urban forests stretch from the downtown of large cities to beyond the suburbs to rural land being considered for development. Urban forests are different from rural forests in that they have high densities of fauna (people) and limited growing space for trees. The quality of our urban forests will improve as community leaders put the values of the urban forest in perspective. Improving the understanding of urban people about forests is important because they are the ones making most of the decisions in this country and worldwide.

What should a forester know when it's time to talk about the costs and benefits of urban forests? Most of the measurable values of urban forests are being expressed by people who have a concern for the environment. Looking at urban forests from the urban point of view is much different from seeing forests from the rural viewpoint. It does not appear that either philosophy has come to grips with the complexity of the challenge. This issue has especially come to roost in the West, where city people carve out a small section of a large forest ecosystem for their homes and assume that their mere presence will tame the wilderness. From time to time they watch their point of view go up in smoke.

Urban forestry has been recognized as a science for only a couple of decades, so the question arises as to the sophistication of the effort. City tree managers have demonstrated their ability to plan, plant, and care for trees on the public right-of-way when they have the financial resources to do so. Obtaining the resources is directly related to their ability to convince the policy makers that what they do is worth the budget needed for management.

American Forests has surveyed the condition of urban forests three times over the last ten years and found them in a state of decline. Our goal has been to help policy makers

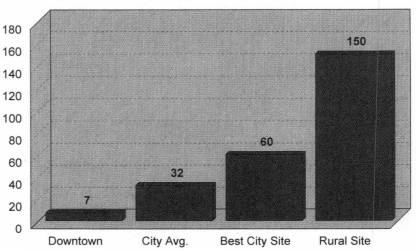

Figure 2-1

Urban Tree Cover Percentages

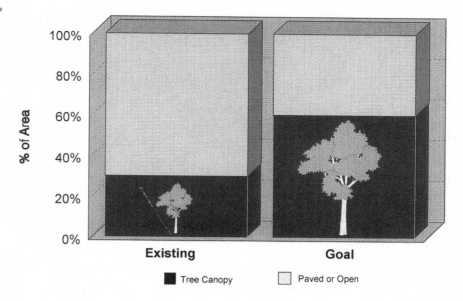

Figure 2-2

Canopy Cover
Average Canopy Cover

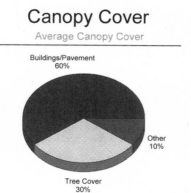

Buildings/Pavement
60%

Other
10%

Tree Cover
30%

Figure 2-3

Street Construction Dollar
Making a Space for Trees

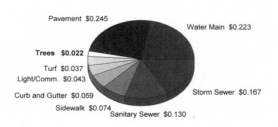

Pavement $0.245

Water Main $0.223

Trees $0.022

Turf $0.037

Light/Comm. $0.043

Curb and Gutter $0.059

Storm Sewer $0.167

Sidewalk $0.074

Sanitary Sewer $0.130

Figure 2-4

see the value of urban forests. Consider the information provided to them using the accompanying graphs.

The physical components of the urban forest can be classified into downtown, city-residential, suburban, and fringe. We can further classify according to street trees, park trees, greenways, yard trees, and open space. But this is only what an urban forester sees. The urban forest is still invisible to others. Our explanation of where urban forests are and why they are important needs to be refined and interpreted for those who see no structure or connection at all.

What Next?

Our understanding of urban ecology is rudimentary. Matching cost and benefit information to the ecology will provide the underpinnings for the next step in the growth of the urban forestry movement. We have developed terminology for the discussion of the structure of the urban forest, but we have only begun to place relevant values on the resource. We have not evaluated the ecological components. We know little about the interactions of urban forest elements and we have only rough estimates of some of the costs and benefits of urban forests. We know very little about the broad range of benefits possible.

New technology like GIS (geographical information systems) will help us see the urban forest in a way we never have before, and to place values on what we see. GIS technology will allow us to combine detailed data about tree values with the structure of urban forests. Currently we do not have the kind of detailed information on the benefits of the urban forest that we do on the costs. We must undertake the job of learning the benefit information through research so that urban policy makers can make better decisions about urban forests in the future.

3

Changing Forms and Persistent Values: Historical Perspectives on the Urban Forest

HENRY W. LAWRENCE

ABSTRACT The use of trees and other plants in urban areas has a long history, as long as urban living itself. This paper reviews the most important landscape forms that have contained the urban forests of European and North American cities before the twentieth century: residential gardens, linear promenades, small squares, and large parks. Plants in the urban landscape also play social roles, and in them we can see the cultural values represented by the urban forest. The three major social roles played by the urban forest before the twentieth century were as a natural element in a humanized landscape, as an aesthetic object in the urban landscape, and as a social object expressing power relations within urban society. The paper concludes with a look at adaptations and reuse today of original urban forest landscape forms and at implications for the present from the lessons of the past.

HISTORICAL OVERVIEW: FOUR MAIN LANDSCAPE FORMS

Plants grow spontaneously when permitted, but since the urban landscape is largely a human creation, most of the vegetation in cities and towns, until quite recently, has been a result of human action. Like buildings, urban vegetation has always been part of a set of landscape forms, developed in the context of particular cultural and ecological conditions. And these conditions have changed over time. Churches, houses, and factories, for example, all have their own forms and locational contexts at any given time, and over the course of time these have changed. In the same way, the landscape forms containing the urban forest have evolved over the years as the forms and activities of urban living have changed. The use of trees in urban environments in the European and North American cultural tradition has taken place largely in the context of four landscape settings: (1) private residential gardens, (2) linear promenades, (3) small squares, and (4) large parks. Each of these has gone through its own historical evolution and each has developed its own repertory of forms in the process. Most of them have developed since the Renaissance and have been strongly influenced by changes in garden and landscape styles (Lawrence 1993b). Urban forests of today continue to use many of these earlier forms, and many of them continue to play the same roles in the urban landscape as in the past.

Private Residential Gardens

Individual houses with their gardens have always been important sites for urban vegetation. In medieval Europe, backyard gardens growing fruits, vegetables, and herbs were the predominant landscape form of the urban forest. However, most towns had defensive walls which limited the areas available for gardens and for urban growth. In the sixteenth and seventeenth centuries new weapons and siege tactics required that walls be made much larger than in the Middle Ages and it became increasingly expensive to build new walls farther out to accommodate urban growth (Figure 3-1). As growth was constrained, population density increased and the space available for private gardens decreased. A few large private gardens remained in most cities and some new ones were built on the urban periphery, but for most of the larger cities of Europe the years from 1600 to 1800 saw decreases in small private gardens. It was not until cities finally outgrew the confines of old walls that the small private garden returned in importance as a site for urban forests. Since most of the other landscape forms rose to prominence during these two centuries, I will discuss them first and then return to the house and garden as a site for the urban forest.

Linear Promenades

Rows of trees used alongside walls, streets, and waterways have been important elements of the urban forest since the time of the Renaissance. From various early forms have evolved modern types of promenades, boulevards, and tree-lined streets (Lawrence 1988). The walls and accompanying earthworks that constrained urban growth were themselves often used as recreational sites (Figure 3-1). At the edge of the city, facing the countryside, they provided views and fresh air unavailable elsewhere in town. By the late sixteenth century some European towns were planting rows of trees on top of their city walls as promenades for public use. Those at Antwerp in Belgium and at Lucca in Italy in the 1570s were apparently the first (Girouard 1985:143).

Various sports and recreational pastimes also used rows of trees. The game known in English as pall mall, originally of Italian origin, somewhat like croquet, was played under rows of trees; so was lawn bowling. Two malls were laid out alongside the walls of Paris in the 1590s. By 1650 they were joined by Pall Mall in London and Unter den Linden in Berlin. The latter was used as a tree-lined street in later years and became one of the most important in Berlin as the city grew out around it. In other places, especially France, trees were planted along a city's major approach roads, as with the Avenue des Champs Elysées. Others were planted for use as promenades for carriage riding, a new recreational pastime in the early seventeenth century. The Cours la Reine laid out along the right bank of the Seine in Paris in 1616 is the oldest surviving example (Lavedan 1975:299).

In the Netherlands, rows of trees were planted alongside canals within towns, beginning in the early seventeenth century (Burke 1960). This brought trees within the built-up parts of towns, quite unlike the peripheral promenades elsewhere in Europe. Those of Amsterdam, laid out in the 1610s, are the best known, but many other Dutch towns also had them. Very few towns outside the Netherlands followed the Dutch example, however.

These rows of trees used by themselves at the urban edge or along canals were all variants on the allées of trees that figured so prominently in gardens of the Renaissance and Baroque eras. Garden allées were parts of larger garden compositions, but when

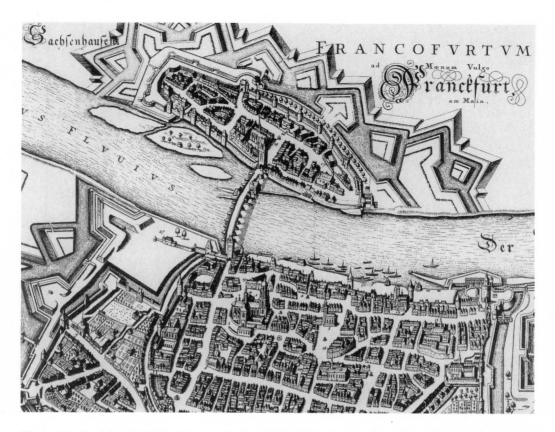

Figure 3-1. Frankfurt am Main, Germany, in the middle of the seventeenth century. This view by Matthew Merian shows the medieval town constrained by the new fortifications and a tree-lined promenade on the walls of suburban Sachsenhausen across the river. (Courtesy of Library of Congress)

used in isolation along walls and waterways they became new urban landscape elements and carried a different social value. Gardens have traditionally been enclosed, private places, but these new urban tree rows were largely used in more public settings. They affirmed a new role for the urban landscape as an amenity in itself, requiring only the planting of trees to create places for enjoyment along formerly utilitarian walls, roadways, and canals (Figure 3-2).

Their use increased in the eighteenth century, and by the early nineteenth century almost every western European city of any considerable size had at least one such promenade, and in France most towns had several of them. They came to have an association with French culture, and the names by which they are known today are mostly French: allées, avenues, boulevards, promenades. The most influential examples were the tree-lined boulevards of Paris in the middle of the nineteenth century, laid out during the rule of Napoleon III, many of which were cut into the preexisting urban fabric (Alphand 1868-73). They served as a model for many other cities in Europe, the Americas, and other areas influenced by European culture.

In North America there was another tradition of using trees along streets in cities and towns that seems to have begun early in colonial times: individual trees were planted in front of homes and businesses for shade and ornament, but in a less regimented way

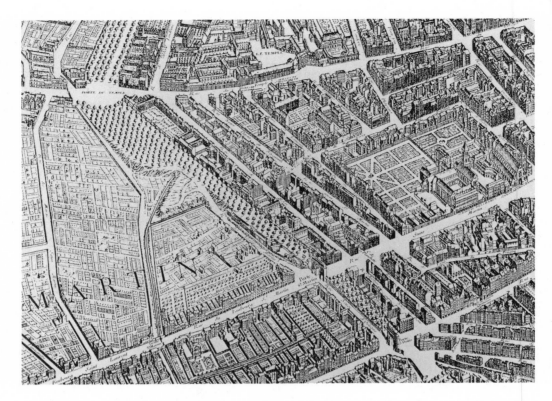

Figure 3-2. The boulevards of Paris, seen in a view from 1739 by Turgot, were laid out atop the remains of the city's walls on orders of Louis XIV in the 1670s. (Courtesy of Historic Urban Plans)

than the European promenades. Broadway in New York and Market Street in Philadelphia are examples. Less formal and less regular than European urban allées, colonial American street trees reflected in their irregular spacing and use of diverse species the individualism that characterized American society in comparison to Europe. By the late nineteenth century, though, most large cities were making organized efforts to formalize their street tree plantings (Solotaroff 1912).

Small Squares

Within the dense urban areas of medieval towns, there were few open spaces and even fewer of these contained plantings. Most market squares were paved, though some that were adjacent to churches contained a tree or two, usually with religious symbolism. And some churchyards, whether used as cemeteries or as gardens, functioned as quasi-public garden squares. But most medieval urban open spaces were devoid of vegetation (Zucker 1959).

In the Renaissance, urban open space became more important, first in Italy, then Spain and France, but Renaissance plazas had trees only in rare circumstances, at least in the beginning. By the eighteenth century, some of these were given little groups of shrubs or trees as an added ornament (Hautecoeur 1975) (Figure 3-3). The plantings were sparse and stiffly formal, often in container boxes, and the ground surface was usually gravel or stone, so they can hardly be seen as urban parks. But the eighteenth-century public squares were important, because they were often the first places where trees were used in the midst of the built-up area in the public urban landscape.

In Britain a specialized landscape form was developed using squares as centerpieces for new upper-class residential areas as the city expanded beyond its old walls. The British residential squares were initially patterned after French and Italian squares, but by the eighteenth century they had been transformed into a distinctively British urban landscape form (Lawrence 1993a). Most significantly they included gardens in the open space of the square, planted with anything from open turf to neat rows of trees or shrubs. By the end of the eighteenth century they had become little landscape parks, reflecting with their trees and grass an urban variant of the large pastoral landscape parks being designed on rural estates (Figure 3-4). Unlike the continental public squares, however, the British residential squares were almost always private places and were usually fenced off from public access, kept as exclusive amenities reserved for the private use of the surrounding residents. The British green squares brought even more vegetation within the built-up area than their counterparts on the Continent, and by the nineteenth century they were influencing the design of urban squares there. Most prominent were the small squares laid out in the renovations of Paris in the 1850s and 1860s. When Napoleon III returned from his exile in London to the throne of the French Empire in Paris, he brought with him the idea of green squares in residential areas, but insisted they be public places rather than private as in London (Pinkney 1958).

162. - NANCY. - Place de la Carrière
Carrière's Place

Figure 3-3. The Place de la Carrière in Nancy, France, was built in the middle of the eighteenth century and was one of the first French urban squares to have a garden in it. This postcard view is from about 1910. (Collection of the author)

Figure 3-4. Berkeley Square in London, laid out in the eighteenth century, was originally a private garden reserved for surrounding estate tenants but is now open to the public. Its plane trees are reputed to be the oldest in the city. (Photo by the author)

Figure 3-5. Peoria, Illinois, contains a typical American county courthouse square, seen in a postcard view ca. 1915. (Collection of the author)

In North America there was a mixture of both the public (Continental) type of square and the private (British) residential square (Lawrence 1993a). Private residential squares along British lines were relatively few in number; Boston and New York each had a handful, for example. But by the middle of the nineteenth century almost no new private residential squares were built. The public squares of New England towns owed something to the common land tradition of village greens, but most colonial American public squares were used as civic plazas, sometimes also as market squares rather than as parks (Jackson 1984). The courthouse square became a later variant that combined the form of a civic plaza with that of a small park (Figure 3-5). It was used widely from the Appalachians to the Pacific in the founding of new towns in the nineteenth century (Price 1968).

Large City Parks

The largest areas that contain vegetation in the built-up areas of most cities today are large parks. Some of them appear very natural, with their lakes, rolling lawns, and groves of trees. Almost without exception these are creations of the nineteenth century, their trees planted carefully to imitate nature on land that was previously in very different condition. The tradition of large naturalistic urban parks can be traced back to the royal hunting parks just outside London (Sexby 1898). Over the years, since the seventeenth century, these were progressively opened to increasingly larger segments of the public, repeatedly renovated and redesigned until by the early nineteenth century they had arrived at a form that was imitated by urban landscape designers in other large cities, from Paris and Berlin to New York and Buenos Aires (Chadwick 1966).

The transformation of royal hunting parks into city parks in England was part of a larger tradition of quasi-public use of large private gardens that had been widespread in Europe since medieval times (Figure 3-6). These included gardens not only of the royalty but of other aristocrats, as well as religious houses, colleges, and other quasi-public corporate groups. Most of these were large, walled gardens and the public could be selectively excluded or admitted as the owners saw fit. By the late seventeenth century most of them were admitting any well-dressed people, but few were open to the poorly dressed lower classes until the nineteenth century. The Tuileries and Luxembourg Gardens in Paris, the Tiergarten in Berlin, and the Retiro in Madrid are prominent examples.

Compared to the formal gardens on the Continent, the British parks had a more rural character (Figure 3-13). When the British style of naturalistic landscape design rose to prominence in the eighteenth century, some of the large royal parks near London were redesigned in the new mode and came to resemble pastoral landscapes at the same time that they were becoming the city's most popular recreation grounds. By the early nineteenth century they were imitated in the creation of wholly new parks such as Regent's Park in London and Birkenhead Park near Liverpool. By the middle of the century the pastoral British city parks were being imitated elsewhere: in the redesigned Bois de Boulogne at Paris, the Tiergarten in Berlin, and in New York City's Central Park. The latter inspired a movement in the United States that led most major cities to lay out large new parks in the second half of the century (Schuyler 1986). A further American contribution was the development of tree-lined carriage parkways connecting separate city parks. These carried an element of the pastoral park into the larger urban landscape,

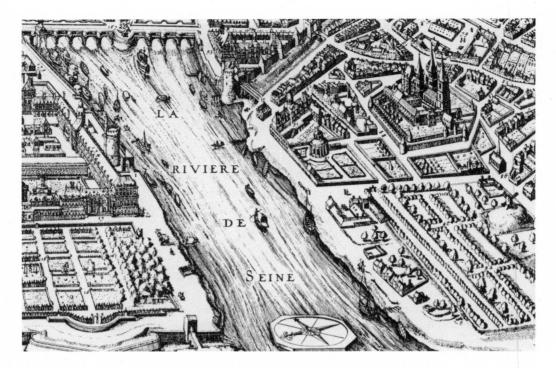

Figure 3-6. The western edge of Paris, from a view in 1618 by Visscher, shows the royal garden of the Tuileries on the left and the private garden of ex-queen Marguerite on the right. Both gardens were open to a wide section of the upper-class public in the seventeenth century. (Courtesy of Historic Urban Plans)

much the same way that tree-lined boulevards in European cities brought an element of formal gardens into the urban landscape.

When first laid out, the large city parks were peripheral to their cities. Some were even well beyond the built-up area, such as New York's Central Park, which in the 1850s was some twenty blocks north of the major residential areas of Manhattan. It was continued urban expansion that allowed the cities to envelop them, and it was only in the twentieth century that they became central to their urban areas. It was also in the twentieth century that most of their trees reached full size, achieving the effect that their nineteenth-century designers intended. Others have simply been enclosed rural fields, with or without later improvements. The large open areas of Blackheath and Hampstead Heath near London are examples. In the twentieth century many large natural areas on the urban fringe have been preserved as parts of urban open space systems, even including large areas of natural forest, thus bringing the urban area to the forest rather than the reverse, as had been the case earlier.

Private Residential Gardens (Continued)

By the late eighteenth century a few cities, mostly in France and Britain, were developing extensive suburban areas beyond their walls (Fishman 1987). These suburban developments were still densely built, consisting of connected houses or blocks of apartment buildings. But in the 1820s houses were built on the northwest edge of London that were detached from each other, set in their own private gardens. While most of the housing built in Britain in the nineteenth century continued to be attached town houses, the number of detached single houses or semidetached duplexes increased steadily. Given their greater use of space, they came to occupy an ever increasing area of low-density development that contained more garden space than building space and more trees than people (Edwards 1981). They were concentrated along newly built commuter rail lines often adjacent to existing villages. The new low-density urban zone extended into the countryside and broke the formerly sharp distinction between the landscapes of city and country.

Elsewhere in Europe, detached and semidetached housing was only slowly adopted in the nineteenth century, mostly in Germany, northern France, the Low Countries, and Scandinavia. Industrialization and the use of mechanized transportation aided the process, as distance from the city became associated with prestige, the reverse of the previous pattern that associated centrally located residence with access to power and amenities. In southern Europe and Latin America, enclosed gardens close to the urban center remained the norm for the upper classes and detached housing for the middle classes was the exception. Wherever they developed, low-density residential suburbs were characterized by their gardens, and that meant more trees, both behind the house and in front of it; and thus the suburbs became leafy enclaves of middle class prosperity.

In North America there had been a tradition of detached housing dating back to the earliest colonial times. Private gardens around detached houses were common in most towns from Montreal to Mobile. The plantings were rarely coordinated, even the street trees having a random appearance in most places, but the residential landscape had a large number and variety of trees and gardens. The rise of planned commuter suburbs of the larger cities in the late nineteenth century was thus a smaller break with existing forms, but it did extend the residential landscape considerably farther from the city

Figure 3-7. East Colorado Street in Pasadena, California, in a postcard view ca. 1910, shows the composite residential landscape of an American streetcar suburb. (Collection of the author)

center and blurred the division between city and country (Jackson 1985) (Figure 3-7). At the same time, the older inner residential areas of the larger cities were replaced by dense blocks of apartments and town houses, so that trees were disappearing near the centers of cities at the same time new ones were being planted in the suburbs. The rise of the automobile in the twentieth century accelerated the process of suburban expansion. As suburbs spread even farther into the countryside, they extended the urban periphery over a large area, encompassing rural and natural areas that would later be considered part of the urban forest.

These four landscape forms came to shape the urban forests of Europe and North America in the years between the Renaissance and the Automobile Age: linear promenades, small squares, large city parks, and private residential gardens. Each of them developed in a distinct setting and had its own uses. The linear promenades and the small squares were located closer to the center of the city, were more formal in character, and carried close associations with the forms of the garden, adapted for urban use. The large city park and the suburban garden were less formal in character and carried associations with rural landscapes and natural areas.

THREE MAIN SOCIAL ROLES PLAYED BY THE URBAN FOREST

In their various uses and locations, trees in the urban environment express some basic sets of social values, representative of the human motives that led to their planting. The most common element among the values expressed by urban trees is that they are environmental amenities: they improve the urban environment. Yet they do this in very different ways, and they take on different roles in the process. There are three main social roles played by the urban forest: as a natural element in a humanized landscape, as an aesthetic object in design compositions, and as a social object expressing power relations.

Trees as a Natural Element in a Humanized Landscape

As a natural element in an artificial environment, trees play two related roles: they are ecological organisms, subject to and influencing environmental conditions around them, and they are symbols of nature in the abstract, representing a wide range of real and imagined natural forces.

As ecological organisms they respond to opportunities and limitations of soil, water, sun and shade, pests, and so forth. This has influenced the choice of species used in urban plantings from the earliest days. Elms were commonly the first trees used in cities of northwestern Europe in the seventeenth century, from the boulevards of Paris to the canals of Amsterdam and Pall Mall in London. Elms were selected for their ease of transplanting, rapid growth, large size at maturity, and ability to tolerate poorly drained urban soils. In return, trees influence their surrounding environments, and their ecological benefits have been appreciated from early times. To use an example from the mid-nineteenth century, shade provided by trees was seen as a major benefit to the health of a city. Frederick Law Olmsted, the designer of New York's Central Park, felt that "the lives of women and children too poor to be sent to the country can now be saved in the thousands of instances, by making them go to the Park" (Olmsted and Kimball 1970:172). Later in the nineteenth century, trees were appreciated for their ability to clean urban air of some of the pollutants produced by industrialization based on burning coal; and in the late twentieth century, they are appreciated for their ability to contribute to energy savings by cooling the urban environment in summer. And the urban forest provides the majority of the habitat for urban wildlife. In the past this was concentrated in large parks and consisted mostly of birds and small mammals. But as cities have spread farther into the countryside, with low-density suburbs, many other types of species have become urbanized, including deer, bears, and coyotes, not all of which are welcome in the urban environment.

As symbols of nature in the abstract, urban plants play an important role, one that is increasing in our own times. Cities have traditionally been seen as nonnatural places, and plants of any kind have been seen as elements of nature, highly symbolic when planted prominently in the urban landscape of stone and brick. Some of this can be attributed to their aesthetic role, discussed below, but much of it is a more general sense that urban vegetation represents a connection with the wider world of nature beyond the city. In this, trees play a special role. In many cities they are the most prominent nonhuman life forms visible in the landscape. They provide a psychological link with life beyond the purely social environment of the city. They provide an important connection for city dwellers to the living forces of nature. And since their lifetimes are similar to those of people, their growth and changes over the years provide temporal markers to human lives that are growing and changing at the same time.

An urban landscape that includes vegetation seems a more natural place. In the seventeenth century when towns in the Netherlands began planting trees alongside their canals, foreign visitors were struck by the unexpected juxtaposition of trees and buildings. René Le Pays, a Frenchman who visited Holland in the 1660s, remarked somewhat facetiously that one could not tell if there were cities within forests or forests within the cities (Murris 1925:37). Some of the green residential squares of London a century later sought to imitate rural landscape parks, even having their grass cut by small flocks of sheep. There were those who found the idea absurd, such as the anonymous critic who wrote in 1771 of the sheep in Cavendish Square, "to see the poor things starting at every coach, and hurrying round and round their narrow bounds, requires a warm imagination indeed, to convert the scene into that of flocks ranging the fields, with all the concomitant ideas of innocence and a pastoral life" (1771:10). But for others the green squares were an important link with the surrounding countryside. Queen Square in the Bloomsbury section of London was, for many years in the late eighteenth and early nineteenth centuries, at the northern edge of the built-up area. There were buildings on only three sides of the grassy square, and it was open to the north to bring in a view of the rural countryside, including the nearby hills of Hampstead and Highgate.

As long as cities were only a mile or two in diameter, the surrounding countryside provided some access to rural nature and outdoor recreation. But with the growth of large industrial cities in the nineteenth century, the built-up area spread farther than a person could easily walk. It was then that large city parks came to play such an important role. With block upon block of grim tenement housing for the working classes, the large parks were seen as a way for town dwellers to find some solace and psychological relief by contact with nature (Figure 3-8). Frederick Law Olmsted felt that the main purpose of Central Park was to provide "natural, verdant and sylvan scenery for the refreshment of town-strained men, women and children" (Olmsted and Kimball 1970:523; see also Stephen Kaplan's essay in this volume).

Suburban residential areas have also been seen as closer to nature. When Regent's Park was laid out in 1812 on the northwestern fringe of London, it included several

Figure 3-8. Central Park in New York City, seen from Fifth Avenue. (Photo by the author)

detached villas inside the park as well as terraces of town houses surrounding it. As one commentator described it: "all the elegancies of the town and all the beauties of the country are co-mingled with happy and blissful union" (Elmes 1827: 21). When Olmsted designed the suburban settlement of Riverside outside Chicago in the 1860s, he laid it out with curving tree-shaded streets, generous private lawns, and large communal parks, "the idea being to suggest and imply leisure, contemplativeness and happy tranquility," much the same psychological effect intended for Central Park (Fein 1972:35). More directly, one of the main values of private gardens is the very act of gardening itself. Whether one is growing vegetables, flowers, or merely lawn, one has more direct contact, in an active relationship, with nature than is possible with the passive activities of appreciating street trees and parks (Kaplan and Kaplan 1989).

Urban trees as symbols of nature could also take on religious and political overtones. In Revolutionary France in the 1790s, the established Church was temporarily replaced by outdoor pantheistic celebrations to the Supreme Being, which was represented by a single tree atop an abstract monument (Biver 1979). Something of the same value is seen in the planting of trees in cemeteries or in civic plazas to commemorate fallen war heroes. Religious meanings for nature in the abstract have been important as a value for urban forests in their more naturalistic settings at least since the nineteenth century, and they are becoming increasingly important in the second half of this century. Many people have encouraged urban tree planting as a way to help counteract the effects of global warming. While much of this is based on nothing more religious than atmospheric chemistry, some of it is motivated by the Gaia hypothesis that postulates that the earth itself is a living organism, superior to all individual species, including humans (Lovelock 1991).

Trees as an Aesthetic Object in Design Compositions

Whether as single specimens, continuous lines, small groups, or large masses, trees can be seen as objects in the overall visual landscape of the city. They play an important aesthetic role. Some of this involves their use as symbols of nature, but much of it also comes from their forms, textures, colors, and fragrances, even their ways of moving in a breeze. They can enliven the view of otherwise monotonous urban landscapes, and they gain from their juxtaposition with buildings. Most of the beauty of the boulevards of Paris and other French cities comes not from the architecture of the buildings, much of which is of mediocre quality, nor from the trees themselves, which are often bedraggled. Rather it comes from the interplay between the buildings, their geometry, their ornament, and their surface materials, with the repetitive trunks of the trees, the space created beneath the canopy, the arching lines of the branches, and the delicate patterns of the leaves (Figure 3-9). More prosaically, trees can sometimes act as screens that shield us from poorly designed buildings.

Most planted urban vegetation contains some of the aesthetic quality of the garden, and this gives the city some of the qualities of a garden, as a pleasant place to be enjoyed in a relaxing way (Figure 3-3). It changes the mood of the urban landscape and makes it a place where beauty and grace become public values. Promenades and parks can be seen as large ornaments in the overall composition of the urban landscape. Sometimes they are its greatest beauties. When the British writer Arthur Young traveled through France in 1787, he found little to admire in Poitiers, "which is one of the worst built towns I have seen in France; very large and irregular, containing scarcely anything worthy of notice, except the cathedral which is well built and very well kept. The finest thing by far in the town is the promenade, which is the most extensive I have seen" (Young 1915: 61). In the late nineteenth century, linear promenades were one of the most important landscape elements in the Beaux Arts school of urban design in Europe. In the City Beautiful movement in the United States, tree-lined boulevards, city parks, and connecting parkways became important in urban design and planning (Wilson 1989).

Of course, tastes change over time and the development of various landscape forms incorporating urban vegetation has been affected by this (Clifford 1966). The linear geometry of the baroque and neoclassical aesthetic found expression in the tree-lined boulevards and promenades which adapted the garden allée to the geometry of city streets and walls. But rigid geometry was later felt to be out of place in large city parks. Most of the older city parks have had many of their linear allées replaced by curving pathways, oval lawns, and irregular groupings of trees. This has been the case with Hyde Park in London and the Bois de Boulogne in Paris. By the late nineteenth century, naturalism had become the predominant element in the design of some large parks, and regional ecological patterns were used as the basis of an aesthetic for landscape design. The work of Jens Jensen and others in Chicago's parks system is a prominent example (Chicago Historical Society 1991).

In residential neighborhoods, the private gardens consist of a wide variety of plants, from lawn and annual flowers to woody trees and shrubs, in a wide variety of forms,

Figure 3-9. The Avenue de St. Cloud was one of three radiating avenues laid out in the 1660s to form the town of Versailles, adjacent to the palace of Louis XIV. (Photo by the author)

from flat expanses to hedges and single specimen trees. It is the complexity of the vegetative landscape that provides much of its aesthetic appeal. While individual residential gardens are attractive in themselves, most of the aesthetic quality of the suburban environment comes from the composite effect of the entire neighborhood landscape. This was recognized in 1870 by the American garden writer Frank J. Scott, author of *The Art of Beautifying Suburban Home Grounds of Small Extent*, who felt that the composite landscape was worth more than individual landscapes. He particularly disliked screening hedges and fences, saying: "It is unchristian to hedge from the sight of others the beauties of nature which it has been our good fortune to create or secure" (Scott 1870:61). This is the same viewpoint necessary to see beyond the individual trees in individual gardens and consider them collectively as an urban forest.

In the second half of the twentieth century, tree planting has been used as one of the central elements of "urban beautification," from tall hedges screening junkyards to street trees on declining downtown commercial streets. Some of these have been carefully thought out as part of an overall urban design scheme, but others have been little more than a band-aid approach to deeper urban changes, and many cities are now removing trees from ill-planned downtown pedestrian malls laid out in the 1960s and 1970s.

Trees as a Social Object Expressing Power Relations

Like other urban amenities, the urban forest and the places where it is present are social creations and they respond to social patterns of power and influence. These are most often seen in the ownership of and rights of access to the places that contain the urban forest. As public amenities these places are often unequally available to different social groups, and as private amenities they are usually unequally distributed within the urban landscape. It is important to keep two questions in mind when looking at urban amenities: who caused them to be created, and who has access to them. Sometimes the answers are clearly evident and sometimes one has to dig a little deeper to reveal the social forces behind the plants that compose the urban forest.

Up until the rise of large-scale residential suburbs in the nineteenth century most vegetation visible within the urban landscape was planted and maintained by a few people with social power: kings and queens, other aristocrats, religious houses, guilds, and in more democratic towns, the town councils. In the age of absolutism it was considered an obligation of the ruler to endow his subjects with amenities, including public promenades, parks, and squares. Thus Pope Alexander VII planted a promenade in the ruins of the Roman Forum in 1656 and Louis XIV planted a promenade atop the walls of Paris in 1670.

There were other power relations expressed by these baroque plantings as well. The bold geometry of broad avenues in a city expressed a control over the urban landscape that could only come from a paramount ruler. Tree-lined promenades often had a strong association with military power (Figure 3-10). They were usually planted only on the most important streets in town and served as routes for military parades. Lewis Mumford has found this association so strong that he calls the baroque avenue "essentially a parade ground" (Mumford 1961:370). Louis XIV planted promenades on the remains of the city walls of Paris in 1670 only after having them dismantled as fortifications (Figure 3-2). The removal of the city's defensive walls eliminated any threat of a popular uprising seizing the city from his hands, as had happened during the civil war of the Fronde in 1652. The promenade of elms served in a way as window dressing on the destruction of the independence of the city. There is also a linguistic association: the first section of the walls planted was atop the great eastern bastion known as the Grand Boulevart, adjacent to the Bastille. The word *boulevart* was related to the English word *bulwark* and meant a fortified part of a wall. The promenade atop it was known as the *promenade du boulevart* and over time the latter word has become synonymous with the former. A further association between tree-lined boulevards and military power came in the 1850s when Napoleon III had new tree-lined streets cut through some of the most congested neighborhoods in Paris. They were partly to improve circulation within the city but they were also meant to provide police access into areas that might rebel against the central authorities, a threat that did materialize in the Commune of 1870.

Access to places where trees are planted has not always been freely open to the general public. Many of the early European urban allées and promenades were privately owned. Of the first two malls at Paris, one was the property of the king and the other was a private profit-making venture. The Cours la Reine was enclosed by a wall and open only by invitation of the Queen, Marie de Medici. Even royal parks that were later to become public parks were initially open only to the upper classes: as late as 1830 in London, St. James's Park, Kensington Gardens, and Regent's Park were officially closed to ill-dressed

Figure 3-10. A military procession in Paris on Bastille Day, July 14, 1990, on the Boulevard de l'Hôpital, echoes the baroque parades that used early tree-lined boulevards for displays of power. (Photo by the author)

people of the lower classes. In places that were open to the general public, such as the Champs Elysées in Paris, one had to pay a rental fee to use the park benches.

In London the owners of some private property even forced the public from previously open areas. Many of the residential squares were built on fields that had been commons lands, and landowners were required to allow access to the open space in the garden squares. Beginning in 1725, surrounding residents went to Parliament to obtain acts that gave them exclusive control of the gardens in the squares, and they put up iron fences with gates to which only residents were given keys (Lawrence 1993a) (Figure 3-11). In eighteenth-century London the lack of available public open space spurred a business in commercial garden amusement parks, known as pleasure gardens, which charged an entrance fee (Wroth 1896). In 1833 the Parliamentary Select Committee on Public Walks found: "During the last fifty years . . . many open spaces have been inclosed, and every day the increasing multitude become more and more restricted in their means of reaching any open and healthy place to walk in" (1833:5).

The opening of large parks and other semipublic open spaces to the general public gained momentum in the nineteenth century. In Britain it was tied to the reform movement of the 1830s and 1840s that sought to extend the electoral franchise and improve the health and economic condition of the working class (Chadwick 1966). In the United States it gained strength in the 1840s and 1850s and was tied to efforts to strengthen democratic cultural institutions in general, including public schools, libraries, and art galleries (Schuyler 1986). When large parks were opened to the general public in the middle of the nineteenth century, it was seen as a way to improve the moral condition of the lower classes, to educate them in social behavior by observing their social betters, and to provide a peaceful outlet for the tensions of working class life that could have potentially unstable political consequences. The British Select Committee on Public Walks of 1833 felt: "A man walking out with his family among his neighbours of different ranks, will naturally be desirous to be properly clothed, and that his Wife and Children should be so also; but this desire duly directed and controlled, is found by experience to be of the most powerful effect in promoting Civilization, and exciting Industry" (1833:9). Special park wardens were appointed to monitor behavior to ensure that the wholesome passive recreation not become an occasion for gambling and rough sports. Americans, too, believed in the idea of moral improvement through contact with beauty and nature. Olmsted, for example, felt that Central Park exerted a "distinctly harmonizing and refining influence over the most unfortunate and lawless classes of the city—an influence favorable to courtesy, self-control, and temperance" (Olmsted and Kimball 1970:171). Much the same moral concern lay behind the creation of San Francisco's Golden Gate Park (Young 1993).

Most private residential gardens almost never allowed public access, so the spread of detached suburban housing in the nineteenth century gave large numbers of people in

Figure 3-11. Bedford Square in London, laid out in the 1770s. Its garden was fenced and reserved for the private use of surrounding residents. It remains private today. (Photo by the author)

the middle classes direct personal control of part of the urban forest. But the rights of property owners have been somewhat limited in the twentieth century by zoning and environmental regulations. And there is often an unstated but powerful social pressure of conformity in residential neighborhoods that is based on the public character of the visual landscape. What one neighbor does with his property, including his garden and yard, affects the larger landscape setting of other neighbors. In the past, the main concern with neighbors' trees has been aesthetic, but in recent years concerns have been raised also over views, solar access, and wildlife habitat (considered both as amenity and nuisance, depending on the species).

ADAPTATION AND REUSE OF URBAN FOREST LANDSCAPE FORMS

Many of the specific places that first brought trees into the urban landscape in the past are still there today (Figure 3-12). Others are gone or changed beyond recognition. Most of those that have disappeared have been victims of larger urban landscape changes. Antwerp's walls were completely dismantled in the nineteenth century, destroying its promenades. One of the seventeenth-century malls alongside the walls of Paris was replaced by new blocks of streets and houses in the eighteenth century, the other by a roadway along the Seine in the nineteenth century. The promenade in the Roman Forum was removed as part of archaeological restoration in the nineteenth century. Street

Figure 3-12. The Allée Buffon in the Jardin des Plantes in Paris was first planted in the eighteenth century. It continues as a public amenity in the urban landscape. (Photo by the author)

Figure 3-13. Regent's Park, London, designed by John Nash in the early nineteenth century, included several isolated villas, such as the Holme, in its pastoral landscape. (Photo by the author)

widening in the twentieth century has been particularly destructive to old boulevards and malls, though many of them have been replanted.

More important have been changes in use and landscape context. Most promenades, malls, parks, and residential areas were peripheral to the urban area when first laid out; now most of them are in the historic cores of large metropolitan areas. Their new inner city context puts new demands on them and has made them much more "urban" than they were originally. They have almost all become completely public places, in contrast to the private origins of many of them. A few remain private, however, most notably some of the squares of London, such as Bedford, Manchester, and Belgrave squares. Early urban green spaces have also acquired a large measure of historic value in the process of aging; and for some, that will ensure their preservation far into the future (Figure 3-13).

But some require more than simple protection. Many of the landscape forms of the past were planned in an age when labor costs were much lower and the destructive pressures much less than those today. Conservation of legacy landscapes becomes increasingly costly. Large parks and public street trees in particular need a kind of regular care and maintenance that has become more and more difficult for some cities to finance in recent years. They suffer from diseases and insect pests, invasion by exotic species, soil compaction and erosion, vandalism, arson, trash dumping, and air pollution. And they need to be replanted on a continuing basis, since old trees die prematurely in the urban environment. For many city governments, low maintenance cost has become the primary operational criterion, rather than ecological, aesthetic, or social values as in the past.

In the residential landscape the leading changes have come from urban growth, which has left older areas within new inner city contexts, and from changes in garden styles, which has led to a steady change in types of species and spaces in the residential landscape. One recent trend is the preservation of as much of the natural landscape as possible in new developments on the urban fringe, both on individual lots and in the open space systems of clustered developments. Much of this takes place, however, in urban fringe woodlands and wetlands that had been used in a quasi-public way, by nearby residents, for passive recreation and even for hunting. Development turns them into more purely private areas even as it preserves them. Overall, urban expansion has destroyed many more natural areas than it has preserved.

IMPLICATIONS FROM THE LESSONS OF THE PAST

The three main social roles of the urban forest have remained important as their different landscape settings have changed over the years. The landscape forms that incorporate the urban forest are themselves expressions of human needs and social settings in physical form. In the future, as social situations change, new forms will develop that will provide new opportunities for vegetation in the urban landscape. We can look at some of the physical changes in urban form that have taken place in the recent past to see how today's urban forest represents the values it represented in the past.

One of the most persistent trends in urban form in the past few decades has been decentralization, not just of building density but also of land use functions of all types. Cities of today are no longer organized into a series of areally limited functional zones as they were in the past. Now urban uses, from manufacturing to services and from residences to government offices, are dispersed throughout the metropolitan area, including the rural regions in which the city is situated. Linking these together is a transportation and communications network that is also tied to regional, national, and international locations.

One of the most characteristic features of the new urban form is the development of relatively dense clusters of commercial and service activities in the suburbs. This has dispersed much of the former central business district with its mix of functions, but in a new suburban setting. The older downtowns are themselves being transformed, with green pedestrian malls, "festival marketplaces," and mixed use megastructures that combine office, entertainment, retail, and residential functions (Attoe and Logan 1989). Urban decentralization has been accompanied by a continued spread of residential areas, much of it in a leapfrog manner that has left undeveloped rural areas within the expanding metropolitan perimeter. But not all the suburban residential development has followed the even pattern of low-density single-family housing that characterized the middle of the twentieth century. Much of it now consists of clusters of town houses and apartment blocks amid small, private open space systems.

For the urban forest, this creates a variety of new landscape forms. The satellite "downtowns" generally are liberally ornamented with plantings, much more so than the old central business districts. Revitalized downtowns are also being planted much more heavily than before, though some of this runs counter to efforts at historic restoration in areas that were previously devoid of plants. In all of this a new semiformal style of design is most common, incorporating combinations of linear promenades with small lawns, shrub borders, and shade trees. Most characteristic of the new landscape forms is the integration of buildings and landscape plantings: planter boxes in stairways and walls, roof gardens that function as outdoor terraces, enclosed entrance courtyards built as interior atriums with tropical plants. All are used to create new landscape forms that incorporate plants within the physical structures of the city.

As the metropolitan area spreads over the countryside, the character of open space is changing also. Farmland on the suburban fringe is seen as a metropolitan landscape amenity, and great efforts are made to conserve it for the public good. Large natural areas, mostly on forested hillsides or in wetlands, are left within or adjacent to the metropolitan perimeter. When funding permits, these have been preserved as metropolitan parks and some of them have been connected to each other by corridors of natural areas. For most cities the various parks, squares, and undeveloped areas are now seen as components of open space systems, all playing a vital part in the life of the city (Hecksher 1977).

In these new landscape forms the plants play a role much the same as before. They represent nature in the humanized landscape: literally so in wetlands where they may include habitat for endangered species, symbolically so in downtown atriums where they provide a tropical tree canopy for business power lunches. They bring the aesthetics of the garden into the city in new ways, pioneering urban aesthetic frontiers in entirely new landscape forms, such as Seattle's Freeway Park, built above a downtown interstate highway, and its Gas Works Park, built amid the ruins of an abandoned industrial site. The variety of new urban forest landscape forms has made some cities into aesthetic objects in themselves in a way that rivals the elaborate system of boulevards, squares, and parks of nineteenth-century Paris. Portland, Oregon, is a good example, with its old and new downtown squares and Park Blocks, pedestrian malls, atriums, roof gardens, riverfront promenades, leafy residential neighborhoods, mountainous Forest Park, and its watershed reserve in nearby Mount Hood National Forest. The urban forest in its many forms plays the key role integrating the city with its surrounding landscape in a way that incorporates old and new aesthetic forms (Hecksher 1977; Price 1987).

At the same time, the urban forest plays a role in the acting out of social forces. In this we can see some of the same tensions as before, as questions of public and private control remain an issue. Much of the new urban landscape includes public participation in the decision making process, but it also involves different types of public-private partnership that sometimes subordinate the public landscape to private interests, in the name of creating jobs and building the local tax base. And not all groups in society are equally able to use the urban forest, whether for contact with nature or to ornament their landscape. Most of the urban forest in suburban areas—whether in shopping malls, satellite downtowns, or the open spaces within clustered residential development—is in private ownership, and public rights of access are subject to private controls. Inner city residential areas, and their street trees and small parks, suffer from overuse and lack of maintenance, and many older large urban parks on restricted budgets are losing more trees than can be replaced. Many local governments have seen their park budgets cut drastically in recent years as suburban voters, content with their own private landscapes and their ability to travel to distant natural areas, refuse to pay for needed work on the public urban landscape. This is due to the fact that throughout history access to the urban forest has been treated as an amenity and a privilege rather than as a necessity and a right.

The lack of access is not helped by the recent inclusion of urban fringe natural areas in urban open space systems, for these are most accessible to suburban residents who already have their own private residential landscape and least accessible to those in the inner city who need them most. But there are some exceptional cases. Washington's Tiger Mountain State Forest fifteen miles east of Seattle in the foothills of the Cascade Mountains is connected to the city's public transportation system by a bus route that can bring people from all parts of the metropolitan area to trailheads in a large natural recreation area (see McClelland, this volume). Access to Tiger Mountain continues to serve the public of Seattle in ways that large central parks did in the nineteenth century by providing, in the words of Frederick Law Olmsted, "a poetic and tranquilizing influence on its people as comes though a pleasant contemplation of natural scenery, especially sequestered and limitless natural scenery" (Schuyler 1986:93).

LITERATURE CITED

Critical observations on the buildings and improvements of London. 1771. London.

Report from the Select Committee on Public Walks. 1833. House of Commons, London.

Alphand, A. 1868-73. Les promenades de Paris. J. Rothschild, Paris.

Attoe, W., and D. Logan. 1989. American urban architecture: Catalysts in the design of cities. University of California Press, Berkeley.

Biver, M.-L. 1979. Fêtes révolutionnaires à Paris. Presses Universitaires de France, Paris.

Burke, G.L. 1960. The making of Dutch towns: A study in urban development from the tenth to the seventeenth centuries. Simmons-Boardman, New York.

Chadwick, G. 1966. The park and the town: Public landscapes in the nineteenth and twentieth centuries. Praeger, New York.

Chicago Historical Society. 1991. Prairie in the city: Naturalism in Chicago's parks, 1870-1940. Chicago Historical Society, Chicago.

Clifford, D. 1966. A history of garden design. Rev. ed. Praeger, New York.

Edwards, A.M. 1981. The design of suburbia. Pembridge Press, London.

Elmes, J. 1827. Metropolitan improvements, or London in the nineteenth century. Jones and Co., London.

Fein, A. 1972. Frederick Law Olmsted and the American environmental tradition. George Braziller, New York.

Fishman, R. 1987. Bourgeois utopias: The rise and fall of suburbia. Basic Books, New York.

Girouard, M. 1985. Cities and people: A social and architectural history. Yale University Press, New Haven.

Hautecouer, L. 1975. Les places en France au XVIIIe siècle. Gazette des Beaux Arts 85:89-116.

Hecksher, A. 1977. Open spaces: The life of American cities. Harper & Row, New York.

Jackson, J.B. 1984. The American public square. The Public Interest 74:52-65.

Jackson, K.T. 1985. Crabgrass frontier: The suburbanization of the United States. Oxford University Press, New York.

Kaplan, R., and S. Kaplan. 1989. The experience of nature. Cambridge University Press, New York.

Lavedan, P. 1975. Histoire de l'urbanisme à Paris. Hachette, Paris.

Lawrence, H.W. 1988. Origins of the tree-lined boulevard. Geographical Review 78:355-374.

——. 1993a. The greening of the squares of London: Transformation of urban landscapes and ideals. Annals of the Association of American Geographers 83:90-118.

——. 1993b. The neoclassical origins of modern urban forests. Forest and Conservation History 37:26-36.

Lovelock, J. 1991. Healing Gaia. Random House, New York.

Mumford, L. 1961. The city in history, its origins, its transformations, and its prospects. Harcourt, Brace and World, New York.

Murris, R. 1925. La Hollande et les Hollandais au XVIIe et au XVIIIe siècles vus par les Français. Librairie Ancienne Honoré Champion, Paris.

Olmsted, F.L., Jr., and T. Kimball, eds. 1970. Frederick Law Olmsted, landscape architect, 1822-1903. Benjamin Blom, New York.

Pinkney, D.H. 1958. Napoleon III and the rebuilding of Paris. Princeton University Press, Princeton.

Price, E.T. 1968. The central courthouse square in the American county seat. Geographical Review 58:29-60.

Price, L.W., ed. 1987. Portland's changing landscape. Department of Geography, Portland State University and the Association of American Geographers, Portland, Oregon.

Schuyler, D. 1986. The new urban landscape: The redefinition of city form in nineteenth-century America. Johns Hopkins University Press, Baltimore.

Scott, F.J. 1870. The art of beautifying suburban home grounds of small extent. John Alden, New York.

Sexby, J.J. 1898. The municipal parks, gardens, and open spaces of London: Their history and associations. Elliott Stock, London.

Solotaroff, W. 1912. Shade-trees in towns and cities. John Wiley and Sons, New York.

Wilson, W.H. 1989. The City Beautiful movement. Johns Hopkins University Press, Baltimore.

Wroth, W. 1896. The London pleasure gardens of the eighteenth century. Macmillan, London.

Young, A. 1915. Travels in France and Italy. J. M. Dent and Sons, London.

Young, T. 1993. San Francisco's Golden Gate Park and the search for a good society, 1865-80. Forest and Conservation History 37:4-13.

Zucker, P. 1959. Town and square: From the agora to the village green. Columbia University Press, New York.

PART TWO
The Environmental Setting

4

Toward Ecosystem Management: Shifts in the Core and the Context of Urban Forest Ecology

ROWAN A. ROWNTREE

ABSTRACT The core of urban forest ecology is the body of scientific knowledge found in the literature. The formation of this core began in the 1950s and 1960s and took shape in the 1970s and 1980s with formal studies of structure and function. During the following ten years, the idea of the urban forest ecosystem was introduced, and is now the basis for further development of the scientific core. The context for this core is provided by statements of public policy and perceptions of land management needs. An important shift is occurring in context as land management organizations, ranging from urban-based alliances to state and federal agencies, embrace the ecosystem concept as an approach to understanding and governing complex mixtures of biophysical and human phenomena using a hierarchy of time and space scales. This rapid shift in context places a burden on the scientific core to articulate and test models of urban forest ecosystems. To accomplish this, an approach to research is needed that will help us understand how urban, periurban, and exurban lands interact functionally with other components of the larger landscape. Part of this approach requires scientists and managers to develop a common vocabulary and set of realistic expectations to confront problems of systems complexity and uncertainty.

Both the core and the context of urban forest ecology are changing. The core is evolving slowly from a body of studies focused on structure and function to one including the ecosystem concept. The public and political context is shifting more rapidly to embrace the ecosystem approach to land management in both urban and wildland regions. The ecosystem approach is explicitly "science based." The question is whether resource science in general and urban forest ecology in particular are equipped to provide the support necessary to implement ecosystem management. The fact that ecosystem science and the antecedents of ecosystem management have historically dealt with nonurban areas exacerbates the problem for urban forest ecology.

A preliminary definition of terms will serve as a point of departure. The *urban forest* is all the vegetation in an urbanized area. The *periurban* area immediately surrounds the urban forest, and the *exurban* area is the larger hinterland into which people are migrating from urban and periurban zones and from which resources for the city are taken. Rather than defining three separate areas, it is more realistic in many regions to think in terms of a gradient of "urbanness" (e.g., population or building/road density) from a high in the city to a low in the exurban hinterland. The *core* of urban forest ecology is the body of scientific literature that develops concepts and methods, explicates principles, and interprets empirical results. It focuses on relations among vegetation, soils, wildlife, water, energy, the atmosphere—and, of course, humans.

The *urban forest ecosystem* is a concept that enlarges the scope of the urban forest to include humans. People are not part of the urban forest, but they are part of the urban forest ecosystem. The ecosystem concept also enlarges our temporal and spatial scales of concern. As such, it is an accounting system that requires us to examine how our actions produce costs and benefits not only within our ecosystem but in ecosystems linked to ours across large units of space and time. The urban forest ecosystem is a concept that requires us to understand ecosystem processes that produce changes over time. These changes occur gradually (the aging of trees) and episodically (a large urban fire in the Oakland-Berkeley hills of California).

The *context* of urban forest ecology comprises the public policy and implementation strategies that inform scientists about the needs of land managers to have useful concepts, methods, and management approaches. This context also provides scientists with data about how forest ecosystems are operating and the constraints and opportunities of management. Thus core and context must interact functionally: science informs policy, and the implementation of policy informs science. The scientific core does not operate in isolation of public perceptions about such concerns as the value of science, what is good in nature, and the complexity and uncertainty in this world.

In the sections following, I first restate the problem of urbanization and forests, then describe how urban forest ecology has addressed that problem. Questions and conceptual dilemmas emerge from the gap between the problem and where the core of science stands today. The gap can be closed, and the science can become more capable of answering fundamental questions, if a more systems-oriented approach is taken in the research. This approach can better nurture the development of both the scientific core and the public policy context of urban forest ecology. The theme of this book is integration, and this chapter examines the potential for integrating core and context so that the combined human effort invested in science and management achieves a higher degree of efficiency.

PHENOMENON AND PROBLEM: DEFORESTATION AND AFFORESTATION DURING THE COURSE OF URBANIZATION

As people migrate, settle, and establish economic and social organizations, these activities change the soil and vegetation with consequences that we do not fully understand, even though we have been asking questions about the human impact for more than a century. These consequences distribute themselves at various scales of time and space, among different types of people as benefits and costs expressed in both monetary and nonmonetary terms. We are changing landscapes daily without knowing the magnitude and distribution of these costs and benefits. It is not just *deforestation* for roads, cities, and industry that is of interest to us, but also the processes of *afforestation* of urban lands, and of derelict and discarded lands. By a combination of both removing and planting trees, our society is changing the functioning of whole ecosystems and the course of global ecological evolution.

During the last fifty years, scientists have addressed the dynamics of vegetation and soil changes in natural ecosystems. But now it is difficult to find an ecosystem that has not been influenced by humans. This knowledge about natural ecosystems is slowly being augmented with research on how human land uses related to urbanization change vegetation and soil attributes that in turn modify ecosystem structure, function, and future trajectory. The problem can be stated in a more prescriptive way: How do we mitigate the costly environmental effects of human settlement, land use, and urban development? Much of the demand for research information comes from individuals and organizations already acting to ameliorate these negative effects. Ecological restoration, urban forestry, and greenspace management are but a few of the international efforts begging not just for more technical knowledge but for a comprehensive and integrated approach that fully accounts for the spatial and temporal distribution of benefits and costs of different actions. The rationale for developing an ecological science and management policy for urban forestry is simple. Nature and society operate as systems. Any action will affect the operation of the whole system; and various system states, or modes of operation, generate various spatial-temporal distributions of benefits and costs.

During the last two decades, urban forestry took its first steps in employing ecological concepts and methods, thus putting the discipline on sound, but preliminary, scientific footing. Scientists, teachers, and managers in urban forestry are being asked to take the next step and formulate their future in terms of ecosystem management by incorporating expanded time and space horizons, accounting for externalities, and monitoring fluxes of energy, water, and matter within and between adjacent and proximate ecosystems. Is urban forestry ready for ecosystem management? To answer this we need to examine how the core and context are informing each other. From this examination, we can determine if the scientific core is evolving in conjunction and synchrony with its management context.

THE CORE OF URBAN FOREST ECOLOGY

As a new field of study and practice emerges, concepts and methods are either borrowed or invented. Those who have participated in the construction of the core of knowledge in urban forest ecology wisely have avoided making up new concepts that would create a narrow and somewhat exclusive vocabulary. The task has been to import and test concepts from forest ecology to see if they are useful in establishing a scientific foundation for urban forest ecology. The fundamental concepts of structure and function are traditionally used in examining any system, from cell to landscape, and have served forest ecology well. Thus there was little difficulty in importing and successfully using them in urban forest ecology. More difficult is the search for means to describe how the parts make up the whole.

Structure and Function

Structure is the array of static attributes of the urban forest, the concept that asks the question "What is where?" *Function* is the dynamic operation of the forest: how the vegetation interacts with other components of the urban forest ecosystem, including humans, and how internal and external forces change urban forest structure over time. Examples of structure are the spatial distribution of species, biomass, size, age, and condition classes—the attributes one would record in an inventory of all the trees in a city. A slightly expanded definition of structure—one that would move our thinking toward the concept of the urban forest ecosystem—would include other attributes determining the condition of trees, plants, and soils. For example, just as the size and spatial distribution of rock outcrops are part of what determines the structure and function of mountain forests, the spatial patterns of buildings and other artificial surfaces define the geography of growing space for urban trees and plants and determine many of the conditions under which they will live.

Examples of function are the physiological operations sustaining life in the vegetation and soil and how these operations affect other components of the urban forest ecosystem, including people. Trees transpire and create a moist microenvironment for insects while cooling the air for humans. Roots break sidewalks in their search for nutrients, water, and gas exchange. Shade allows people to turn down their air-conditioners. When a tree affects something else in the system, or vice versa, that is ecological function. The functions of disease and aging change forest composition over time. The functional interactions with weather and humans provide for episodic changes like fires and ice storms. Inherent in the ecological approach, and the foundation for ecosystem management, is the capacity to understand structure and function at different spatial and temporal scales and to incorporate both gradual and episodic (often termed "catastrophic") changes.

At the smallest scale, the ecological functioning of the urban forest begins with the interactions between individual trees and with other components of the ecosystem. When thinking about structure and function at different scales, one asks how activities at one scale influence those at another. How, for example, does the operation of a single tree fit into the functioning of the forest ecosystem? Answering this question incorporates the study of arboriculture into urban forest ecology. Therefore, sound ecological thinking integrates the operations of individual trees with the functioning of groups of trees, or stands, at the scale of the yard, block, neighborhood, planning district, census tract, city forest, urbanized area forest (including built-up areas outside the city limits), and the region. It's axiomatic that activities at each spatial and temporal scale influence the scales above and below them. Fitting the urban forest ecosystem into this scheme requires, first, a brief discussion of entities and boundaries.

Boundaries, Gradients, and Linkages

We use boundaries to define entities. An attribute of urban forest structure is its spatial extent. Thus a basic question is "Where is the urban forest's boundary with nonurban vegetation?" This raises allied questions about integrating our understanding of the structure and function of urban, periurban, and exurban forests. Urban forest boundaries can be defined in several ways, such as the political boundaries of the city, the "urbanized area," and the Standard Metropolitan Statistical Area (SMSA). These political, jurisdictional, or morphological criteria can be part of a definition of the urban forest if we augment them with biological or ecological considerations. For example, one attribute of structure distinguishing the urban forest from the wildland forest is the absence of a fully articulated understory. A functional difference is found in the truncated nutrient cycles of the urban forest where people import fertilizers and export fallen leaves.

Undeveloped areas within the city limits or the urbanized areas or the SMSAs may appear, in both structure and function, to be nonurban forests or stands. These woods may have fully articulated vertical stratification, unbroken biochemical cycles, and other structural and functional attributes similar to nonurban forest stands. However, one perspective is that while there is little visible evidence of human influence in these stands, their current and future status is governed entirely by invisible but powerful human processes of land speculation, regulation, taxation, and development. Therefore, their existence is wholly determined by socioeconomic processes based in the general and local urban culture.

Following this line of reasoning raises the question "Aren't all forests whose structure and/or function are predominantly governed by urban-based processes—visible or invisible—to be considered urban forests?" Forests whose current and future structure and function are determined principally by urban forces are certainly different from forests evolving under nonurban conditions. Further development of this line of reasoning leads to (1) a semantic discussion that could easily become preoccupied with what is and what is not urban; (2) the notion that forest science and policy of the future, at least in urbanizing states, will draw more and more upon the accumulated knowledge and wisdom of what is now called urban forestry; or (3) the need for an overarching concept that does not rely on distinctions between urban and nonurban for its efficacy. I will pursue the third alternative in the next section.

As preparation for an elaboration of that concept, visualize the urban forest as part of a mosaic of functionally connected vegetation systems laid out across the landscape like a patchwork quilt. The borders of quilt patches are discrete. On nonurban landscapes, the edges of the pieces in the mosaic are often "fuzzy," more like gradients than discrete boundaries. Urban activities commonly impose discrete boundaries, but there are increasingly cases where the edge of the urban forest is hard to distinguish from that of the surrounding wildland landscape. An example is found along a transect from a city to the dispersed settlement of exurban areas. The gradient of urbanization may occur sharply in some places and more gradually in others. The form, or morphology, of the gradient determines the behavior of functional processes linking urban, periurban, and exurban zones along the gradient. For example, Zembal (1993) found that the endangered lightfooted clapper rail, a bird found in periurban coastal marshes, decreased in numbers when certain patterns of land use intervened to prevent coyotes from preying on introduced foxes and cats, predators of the rail. In addition to wildlife connections, we are beginning to understand energy, water, and nutrient fluxes among urban, periurban, and exurban segments of the landscape gradient.

The innovative work of Pouyat, McDonnell, and Pickett (in press) and others at the Institute for Ecosystem Studies (Millbrook, New York) has helped scientists free themselves of the constraints of viewing the urban forest in jurisdictional or Census Bureau terms by suggesting that we use an "urban-to-rural gradient" of land use intensity to explain the continuum of vegetation change from city to country. Bradley has recently updated a model for understanding the sequence of land uses along this gradient in a way that illuminates the relationship between the hierarchy of urban-influenced uses and vegetation structures that will occur along the gradient (Bradley 1984; Bradley and Bare 1993).

Needed: A Systems Approach Embracing Multiple Scales of Space and Time

There is a need for a systems-oriented approach to guide the core and context of urban forest ecology into the future. This need is nurtured by modern changes in the urbanization process and resulting settlement patterns. It is nurtured also by changes in the kinds of questions being asked of scientists and managers. The ease of telecommunicating with modems and faxes encourages more dispersed settlement in high-amenity exurban wildlands. A portion of the western slope of the Sierra Nevada lies just to the east of Sacramento, California. This area is being populated by people with urban values, urban-generated equity, and urban histories. They have socioeconomic links with the Sacramento urban area. There are biophysical links as well. The structure of the Sacramento urban forest determines how much automobile-emitted air pollution will migrate on the easterly flow of air to the forests surrounding these homes on the west slope of the Sierra. This air pollution can make a critical difference to Sierra forest health. Conversely, the health of the Sierra forests directly affects the people in the Sacramento urban forest. A recent forest fire in the Sierra forests disrupted the water supply and damaged electric-generating capabilities. All of this has an impact on what is done in the Sacramento urban forest. Reduced hydroelectric-generating capacity in the Sierra increases the need for planting energy-saving trees in Sacramento.

Another example points up the need to have a systems approach that can link biophysical and socioeconomic relationships across long distances in a meaningful way. McPherson (1991) calculated that 17 percent of the water requirements of a yard tree planted to reduce a householder's air-conditioning energy use was saved by reducing the power plant's cooling water use. If we can account for changes in the flux of energy, pollution, and water across ecosystem boundaries, as in these examples, we will have a truer accounting of the spatial distribution of benefits and costs resulting from changes in urban forest structures and functions.

Because of the way urban forests are linked by a large number of biophysical and human processes to periurban and exurban forests, we need a concept that can take urban forestry forward in both science and management. The ecosystem concept allows the urban forester to see structural and functional characteristics inside the urban forest in relation to characteristics in adjacent vegetation systems. This helps, for example, in understanding the ecological consequences of a city's expansion into undeveloped wildlands, or of urban exotics escaping into native forest stands. We now look at how the ecosystem concept is beginning to dominate the policy-management context for urban forest ecology, today, and what attributes of the concept may govern the future evolution of both core and context of urban forest ecology.

RENAISSANCE FOR THE ECOSYSTEM CONCEPT

The year 1995 will mark the sixtieth anniversary of the publication of A.G. Tansley's classic paper advancing the notion that "it is the [eco]systems so formed which . . . are the basic units of nature on the face of the earth" (Tansley 1935:299). (Readers interested in the development of the ecosystem concept are referred primarily to Golley 1993, with examples of important papers available in Real and Brown 1991.) It took more than thirty years before a full articulation of the ecosystem concept in natural resource management was published by leading ecologists and resource scientists (Van Dyne 1969). Another quarter century had to pass before federal and state land management agencies adopted ecosystem management as policy. This was as bold and challenging a step as the introduction of Pinchot's "multiple use" concept of the early 1900s. (For a concise review of the early history of forest ecosystem policy, see Caldwell 1970.) The new philosophy requires that the public and private sectors join to plan and manage ecosystems that cross jurisdictional boundaries and comprise multiple ownerships, thus it is particularly important as context for urban forestry. The policy emphasizes that the ecological behavior and condition of these lands will be determined by the coordinated effort of private and public land planners and managers.

State land agencies together with other federal agencies also are adopting ecosystem management as their guiding policy. This is a major shift for land planning and urban forestry over a relatively short time. Because of the rapidity of contextual change, the new approach has its detractors, especially concerning the potential for constraints on private property. Nevertheless, federal and state agencies are adopting the policy, and professional organizations like the Society of American Foresters and the Ecological Society of America are forging their own interpretations of what ecosystem management means. In several cases, urban-based organizations are one to two years into an examination of how they can use and implement this policy for urban forestry. Because the U.S. Forest Service provides most of the funds for urban forestry research and application, we shall examine more closely this organization's articulation of ecosystem management inasmuch as it has become the context in which we do our science and think about urban forest planning and management.

Ecosystem Management as Context for Urban Forest Science and Practice
In February 1994, the Chief of the U.S. Forest Service described the main orientation of ecosystem management as a land policy (USDA Forest Service 1994a): "Ecosystem management is a holistic approach to natural resource management, moving beyond a compartmentalized approach focusing on individual parts of the forest. It's an approach that steps back from the forest stand and focuses on the forest landscape and its position in the larger environment in order to integrate the human, biological, and physical dimensions of natural resource management. The purpose is to achieve sustainability of all resources." Applied to urban forest ecology, this would suggest that we stop viewing urban, periurban, and exurban forests as separate compartments and focus on what connects these systems and how actions in one system affect the operation of the systems linked to it.

In most statements about ecosystem management, Forest Service policy makers have stressed that it is a science-based approach to land management. Thus it is pertinent to our discussion to read how the research branch of this agency has responded to the new policy. This research policy statement sharpens the focus of the evolution and development of urban forest ecology's core and context. The Forest Service Research (FSR) Strategic Plan for the 1990s (USDA Forest Service 1992) defines three high priority research problems that are closely related to the work urban forest scientists do. The headings are taken from the FSR Strategic Plan. I have added comments relating the Plan to urban forest ecology's core and context.

1. *Understanding Ecosystems.* The FSR plan seeks to understand the basic structure and function of ecosystems. Urban forest ecology examines the human-induced attributes of ecosystems, specifically the results of human land use changes, especially those occurring when land is developed and used for residential, commercial, and industrial purposes.

2. *Understanding People and Natural Resource Relationships.* If we are to grasp the ecological changes resulting from shifts in land use, and inform land managers how to anticipate and mitigate them, our research should understand those forces motivating spatial and temporal migrations of land uses. This type of demographic, cultural, and sociological information is required if we are to predict where future uses will occur and

what they will do to the land. In order to assign values (benefits or costs) to alternative ecosystem and/or landscape vegetation structures, we will have to understand what drives those values and how they are best expressed, quantitatively and qualitatively, for different groups of people.

3. *Understanding and Expanding Resource Options.* The ecosystem management policy implies very strongly that resource options should be preserved for future generations. To do that requires scientists and managers to employ an ecological accounting system that describes who will benefit and who will pay, when and where, for a given resource decision. Ecosystem management is an accounting system that links resource systems in space and in time.

How Does Urban Forest Science Respond?

For the scientific core and policy context to be efficiently integrated, they must inform one another. Articulation of the general ecosystem management policy followed by the specific ecosystem management research policy is context informing core. How can science respond in order to inform land management? First, it has to identify the central question that will drive the research and advice to management.

That central question can be stated as "How do, and how should, vegetation-soil complexes (and associated biophysical attributes of the ecosystem) change as people settle and urbanize the land?" Or, "How do various land uses, manifested in various spatial-temporal patterns, change forest vegetation and soils at different scales of inquiry?" And "How do these patterns translate into benefits and costs?" Part of the problem is we do not fully understand how to develop information about these altered ecosystems, or parts of them, that can be utilized up and down the interscalar ladder. For example, we can examine how effective a tree's shade is in reducing the need for air-conditioning in a house. Up the spatial scale, we can model a neighborhood or town tree-planting program to increase the magnitude of these savings. Further up the spatial scale, we can design a tree-planting plan for an electric utility's service area that comprises hundreds of such towns. But, this proposed increase in tree density will have unknown effects on micro, meso, and macro climates, as it will on regional water, carbon, and hydrocarbon budgets and on regional air quality. There will be some good effects, some bad effects. So, just as we inquired up the ladder of spatial scales we must inquire up the ladder of temporal scales to see who will bear the costs and who will reap the benefits over time. Perhaps, in this example, the current generation of householders will bear the cost of planting, a second generation will reap the benefits of lower energy bills, and their children's generation will bear the cost of removing a large population of aging trees.

Research must begin by designing studies along three dimensions: (1) from small to large spatial scales, (2) from small to large temporal scales, and (3) from low to high levels of ecosystem disturbance from land uses. The third can be described by experimental sites or domains along a gradient from low to high modification of presettlement ecosystem structure. This can be called the "urban-to-rural land use gradient," though it does not always occur in space as a smooth continuum from city to country. The experimental domains are defined by their land use attributes, such as dense commercial, sparse residential, or transportation corridor. It is at this point that the types of land use have to be limited to focus the research. For example, urban forest ecology should not include wildland recreational use of a nonresidential character (e.g., hiking, camping). Yet the study of how a second-home residential, commercial, and recreational community set in a mountain forest ecosystem is changing the functional role of vegetation and soils takes advantage of the core skills of urban forest ecologists.

If research is conducted at different spatial and temporal scales, it will illuminate the linkages between knowledge at one scale and knowledge at another. This will also reveal the links between the various experimental domains along the gradient of ecosystem modification. For example, learning that increasing the density of tree cover in an urban center loads ozone precursors (volatile hydrocarbons) on downwind forests (near the rural or unmodified end of the gradient) helps us understand the elusive relations that impart a benefit to one domain (in this case the urban center) and a cost to another.

This approach can result in a nested set of studies from smaller to larger spatial and temporal scales. "Nested" means that the studies are designed, often concurrently, so that results generated at one scale can be evaluated for use at smaller and larger scales. This interscalar approach is also helpful in building decision support models that will address the scale of, for example, the homeowner who wants to steward his or her trees through a season of drought (a small spatial-temporal scale) to an interagency council wanting to know what the cumulative effects of private land development in eleven counties will be twenty-five years from now. In evaluating how interscalar information is used, scientists will pay particular attention to two inherent problems: (1) the expansion of error as small-scale information is "blown up" to larger scales; (2) different variables becoming important at different scales, making it difficult to assume that processes operating at one scale operate similarly at another.

What follows is an example of how the questions discussed above can be restated so as to organize studies into two groups. In practice, however, a single study can address both of the following questions:

1. *How has presettlement forest structure and function changed as a result of different settlement patterns?* This work can be conducted at three spatial scales of inquiry—the community, the county, and the multicounty region. There are various temporal scales, but the intent is to speak to the problem of long-term, cumulative effects of settlement, tree removal, soil disturbance, and revegetation, including tree planting. Presettlement, and preurban, forest structure is a baseline condition against which changes can be measured and value judgments made. The scales are described below in terms of political units, but the ecosystem approach precludes drawing discrete boundaries around political or jurisdictional areas. In the measurement of both structure and function, the researcher can include adjacent and surrounding areas by looking one level up the scale.

Community Scale. Presettlement forest structure can be documented from historical sources for communities in different forest types (McBride and Jacobs 1975, 1986). Contemporary forest structure and function are specified and compared to presettlement structure to learn how community land uses have changed the ecosystem. For example, research in the upper montane Sierra forest type at the community of Bear Valley, California, uses an undeveloped forest nearby as the presettlement "control" forest. The road network and water supply reservoir in Bear Valley have modified the natural distribution of water for meadow and tree growth. A prohibition against tree removal works together with these changes in water distribution to change the trajectory of forest succession from that occurring on the control plot (McBride and Rowntree, in preparation). This study is developing a benefit-cost array that will support a forest management plan for Bear Valley that utilizes knowledge about these changes. (The community wishes to arrest succession and manage for early- to middle-seral plant associations.) It is being determined how representative Bear Valley is of all upper montane Sierra communities and to what degree these results can be extrapolated throughout that forest type. In other regions of the country, community scale studies can, for example, examine how exotic tree species (such as Norway maple) compete with, and replace, natives (such as sugar maple), and how imported natives might change the genetic architecture of a local native population of trees.

County Scale. County general plans specify where residential and commercial land uses can occur and at what densities. An example of research at this scale is to take a county plan and determine what changes will occur to forest and ecosystem structure and function as the general plan is implemented. This determination considers both tree removals and tree plantings that, among other things, bear on natural regeneration, or lack of it, and the mixing of native and exotic species and genetic material. Future projections are augmented by an analysis documenting historically the cumulative effects of land use change to the present. Work at this scale feeds immediately into regional scale research (Zipperer 1993). Once these structural scenarios are complete, studies under question 2, below, can examine changes to function, such as modified countywide water, carbon, and pollutant fluxes.

Regional Scale. Here, information from community and county scales is aggregated upward in spatial scale to a region of about three to eleven counties attempting to discern large-scale patterns in land use induced changes. Often, the region under study contains both developed and undeveloped land, and there is a range of land use/vegetation mixtures. At the regional spatial scale, results are often expressed at large temporal scales. For example, a seven-county study of future impacts of residential and commercial land use change employs county general plans as the data base for constructing a twenty-five year "build-out scenario" that is superimposed on the existing vegetation map for the seven-county area. This describes what vegetation changes would occur if building proceeds according to the counties' general plans (Rowntree et al. 1993). The results form the basis for calculating loss of wildlife habitat, changes in visual and recreational quality, and (see question 2 below) changes in regional water, energy, and pollutant patterns.

2. *How have fluxes or flows of energy, water, and pollutants changed with land use induced changes in forest structure and function?* These studies also should be conducted at several spatial scales and seek to understand modified fluxes into, through, and out of the ecosystem or landscape when land use modifies vegetation and soil structure.

Site Scale. Research in urban forest ecology has, for a number of years, measured changes in energy flux resulting from changes in vegetation, particularly as these relate to human benefits and costs, such as studies measuring energy savings to a homeowner from the reconfiguration of trees and landscape plants around the residence to form windbreaks and shade trees (Heisler 1986, 1990). Associated changes in water utilization can be calculated for any changes in vegetation configuration that may save energy, and the two are combined to estimate a net savings or cost. Basic research at the site scale seeks to understand the flux of incoming solar radiation as it bears on winter solar heating potential (e.g., amounts of winter sun transmission through the crowns of different species), human thermal comfort or stress, and human exposure to the ultraviolet (UV) portion of the light spectrum (Yang et al., in press).

Other flux studies at the site scale link the interaction of energy and water, such as ambient air cooling potential of trees and ground cover in various configurations. Together with the shading potential of trees, evapotranspiration (ET) cooling has the potential for reducing air-conditioning energy use. However, to engage in ET a tree must have access to soil water, and in urban areas soils are often dry due to rainfall runoff from impervious surfaces or too compacted to hold and deliver sufficient water for effective ET cooling. Thus our research must understand the interaction of these factors (Simpson 1993). In addition, there is potentially a wide range of "pumping rates" among the species used for residential and commercial planting. Rates at which different natives and cultivars use water, intercept and transmit solar radiation, produce volatile hydrocarbons, absorb noxious gases, and collect airborne particulates should be examined at the site scale to establish basic flux relations, then extrapolated to larger spatial scales.

Parking lots are important site-scale research locales. Without trees they become urban heat islands, produce high amounts of polluted runoff, and are places where people bear high heat and UV loads. Trees modify the energy and water fluxes so that there is less heat and UV stress on people, less heat is advected (horizontally) to adjacent sites, and less energy and gas (and less air pollution) are used to cool automobile interiors. Research at the site scale can refine these facts, establish relationships, quantify benefits and costs, and form the basis for aggregation to larger spatial scales.

Community Scale. Because towns and cities are political jurisdictions, this scale is useful in providing certain types of planning and management information dealing with energy, water, and pollutant flux. Other kinds of information are better passed to managers at the county or regional scale. Some scientific questions are more effectively addressed by adding a scale between site and community, such as "neighborhood." For example, Simpson (1993) seeks to answer the question "What is the minimum area of trees, at high urban densities, required to achieve measurable ET cooling?" This requires testing at several scales ranging from site to community. Similarly, Nowak (1994a, b) employs measurements of urban forest leaf area at different scales to estimate the quantity of pollutants removed from the atmosphere.

Scientists can develop a typology of experimental sites along the urban-to-rural gradient, such as high density urban commercial areas, parking lots, quarter acre single-family residential communities, and freeway interchanges. For each type, the range of fluxes for water, energy, and pollutants can be established from empirical measurements and simulation studies that rely on inherent site attributes as well as on the way the site is linked to adjacent sites.

County and Regional Scales. Models of water, energy, and pollutant flux can be constructed at the county and regional scales based on relations established at the site and community scales. At the regional scale, we can begin to see interactions between large urbanizing areas and adjacent forested areas. For example, three of the major urbanizing regions in the West—the Colorado Front, the Salt Lake Valley, and the Sacramento-San Joaquin Valley—are adjacent to major forested mountain ranges, and the urban air pollution affects vegetation, soils, and runoff quality in the mountains. Because these cities rely on mountain runoff for water, air pollutants can theoretically be returned to the cities in the water. This is an example of how accounting for fluxes between two ecosystems can illuminate the role of the urban forest. Research can now begin to model the fraction of gaseous and particulate air pollution removed from the airstream by various densities and configurations of urban vegetation in both present and future urbanized areas. This will estimate reductions in future air pollution loads on adjacent mountain forest lands. The model can also estimate the production of ozone precursors (volatile hydrocarbons) by the urban vegetation, water use and the effects of runoff, energy use, and carbon sequestering and storage.

DIFFICULTIES WITH THE ECOSYSTEM CONCEPT

Whether it is used in core scientific studies or in the policy and management context, the ecosystem concept is not without its problems. For natural systems, some of these difficulties are minimized. For modified systems where humans are rearranging structure and function, some of these difficulties are exacerbated. The following discussion includes, but is not limited to, problems that confront urban forest ecologists.

Where Do Humans Fit In?

There are few ecosystems today that haven't been modified, directly or indirectly, by humans. However, a question that comes up early in any discussion about applying the ecosystem concept to human-modified landscapes is "How does one accommodate the activity of humans in a model of structure, function, and flux?" A corollary is "Are humans internal or external to the ecosystem?" (USDA Forest Service 1994b). They can be viewed usefully as both internal and external components. That is, humans are tool-using "megafauna" operating within an ecosystem, albeit with more consequence than other fauna. They rearrange the flux of energy, water, and matter. (In smaller amounts, so does a hummingbird.) In the Sierra Nevada Ecosystem Project (SNEP), analysis proceeds on the assumption that ecosystems are being modified by humans internal to Sierran ecosystems, but also as forces producing fluxes into those systems from outside (SNEP 1994).

The point is that ecosystem theory and ecosystem science easily accommodate human activity. In fact, the usefulness of the ecosystem concept to human society may be largely in the area of understanding and guiding interactions between humans and nature. Ecosystem theory incorporates feedback loops, and these can be used to clarify human-ecosystem interaction. For example, humans perceive a given ecosystem state. They evaluate it in relation to their needs and usually make changes. They watch how these changes affect system properties and processes and evaluate the new system state. Further changes are made, and so on. The feedback of human evaluation and modifications into the sequence of ecosystem states either amplifies or dampens the degree to which an ecosystem's trajectory will vary from what would have occurred naturally.

Complexity

Reality is complex, and the ecosystem concept is a mental construct that attempts to model the real world. When it does fairly well at that, it approaches a complexity that may frustrate its use in science and/or management. The ecosystem concept requires a high level of scientific participation if it is to reach its potential. Can the core of urban forest ecology participate at the required level? As a science, urban forest ecology is just beginning to deal with complex systems.

For example, scientists and practitioners have long believed that adding trees will make a city cooler. Tree-planting programs and demonstration projects have been based on this idea. Evapotranspiration (ET) cooling is one of the oldest hypotheses in urban climatology, yet the scientific information is inadequate to indicate how many degrees reduction in average air temperature will occur with an addition of a number of trees in any given pattern (Simpson 1993). The physics of evapotranspiration and heat transfer suggest that the relationship is based on sound theory. If so, why don't we have a more precise understanding of the relationship?

First, the relationship, like so many aspects of urban forest ecology, is more complex than it seems. There is great variation in the rate that different species transpire water. Many urban trees have too little water and too much radiation, and consequently close up their stomata and don't transpire for much of the day. An excessive density of trees restricts airflow, and heat and moisture build up in and below the canopy. Years ago, it was sufficient to assume there was roughly a linear relationship: more trees equals a cooler city. This assumption adequately supported tree-planting programs. Today, however, cities and electric utilities demand a more precise relationship. How many trees in what configuration will bring down temperatures by how much over how large an area? The more precise relationship is required for benefit-cost analyses, yet it will be years before scientists can produce these numbers for planners and managers.

A similar problem may develop in the context of ecosystem management. At first, the idea is attractive, but we don't appreciate the information and knowledge requirements of implementing it. As time passes, urban forest management becomes committed to it, but scientists cannot participate at the level required to make ecosystem analysis and management work. At the outset of this chapter, it was stated that we have to understand how the core and context of urban forest ecology inform and support one another. For ecosystem management to work—given its inherent complexity—there has to be (1) improved communication between scientists and managers (i.e., core and context need to efficiently inform one another), and (2) a realistic ratio between program and science funding.

Program funds nurture the activities of urban forestry which in turn create the demand level for scientific information. Over the last fifteen years, the ratio between Forest Service program funds (administered to the states by the State and Private Forestry branch of the agency) and funds dedicated to urban forest research has been in a range between 10:1 and 20:1 (program to research). As urban forest ecology shifts to a higher plane of scientific expectation in the context of ecosystem management, the ratio will have to change in order to reduce the disparity between demand for knowledge and the scientific core's ability to provide it.

Uncertainty

Uncertainty in ecosystem management might be described as the disparity between what we know and what we believe we should know about how these systems work. Because the ecosystem concept is a more complete representation of reality than previous mental constructs, one feels closer to the truth. But, because it is difficult to meet the information demands of this more complex view of the world, there will be more uncertainty. Thus scientists and managers move from one kind of uncertainty—where our models were imperfect representations of reality—to another, where our models are more complete, but we haven't the information power to document and run them with confidence.

According to Frank Golley, ecologist and historian of the ecosystem concept, some scientists have charged that the concept is too deterministic, giving the false impression that we can control these systems (Golley 1993:190). These critics say that deterministic cause-and-effect models do not take into consideration the inherent chaos in nature, particularly in disturbed systems. This charge is important to our discussion because urban forest ecosystems are disturbed ecosystems. Golley agrees with these critics that disturbed ecosystems tend to be more chaotic, but he makes the error of lumping natural and human disturbances together (p. 197). There is an important distinction that is particularly relevant to urban forest ecology.

Human-disturbed ecosystems, including urban forest ecosystems, may be less chaotic than many natural-disturbed systems because of the relatively predictable behavior of human institutions compared to natural disturbances. Of course, natural systems into which humans have just begun to intervene can become quite unpredictable and chaotic because of the many yet unknown interactions between human and natural processes. In established urban forest ecosystems, however, the human hand is much more dominant, and thus control over fluctuations is greater. Internally, chaos and uncertainty are less of an issue than in natural systems. It is externally, where urban forest ecosystems are linked with natural ecosystems (particularly those functioning under one or more disturbance regimes), that there is a high potential for chaos and uncertainty.

Multiple Ownerships

Because ecosystems include more than one landowner or manager, a challenge for ecosystem management is having all landowners understand and accept the concept. This issue is of particular interest to urban forestry professionals. Lynton Caldwell, a senior scholar of land and forest policy, advocated an ecosystem approach to land management twenty-five years ago, stating: "the natural processes of physical and biological systems that comprise the land do not necessarily accommodate themselves to the artificial boundaries and restrictions that law and political economy impose upon them" (Caldwell 1970:203). There seems to be no disagreement that parts of a system must be coordinated in order for that system to run efficiently and accomplish its objective.

Federal and state plans to implement ecosystem management respect private property rights. Yet the trend over the last century has been to gradually curtail private property rights as society has learned how the environment works and about the importance of property owners' cooperating for the common good. We are still on the steep part of the learning curve regarding how our individual activities affect the ecosystem in which we live and the ecosystems to which ours is coupled. Thus the challenge is in education rather than regulation. This places even more responsibility on scientists to explain what ecosystems are, how they work, and how landownership and land management affect their structure, function, and long-term trajectory.

Members of the urban forestry community will be interested in how this effort proceeds, because they have been involved for years in educating homeowners and commercial property owners toward a better understanding of how their individual properties contribute to the urban forest ecosystem. Without a doubt, this is another critical topic on which the core and context of urban forest ecology need to inform one another.

CONCLUSION: SCIENCE AND CONTEXT

The core and context of urban forest ecology can take the first steps toward ecosystem management by boiling the concept down to a fundamental principle on which scientists and managers can focus. It will not be new, for it has been part of conventional wisdom in land management, indeed in our view of the world, for years. It is that everything is related, and nothing changes without having consequences throughout the system and adjoining systems. The task is to understand and account for these changes. Theoretically, ecosystem management must account for all changes, with each change given a human value—a magnitude of benefit or cost expressed quantitatively or qualitatively. While this may be difficult if not impossible for a while, ecosystem management makes explicit the responsibility for scientist and manager to make as full an accounting as possible. Thus the ecosystem concept infuses into both the core and context of our field not only a better representation of reality but a higher level of responsibility.

During this paradigm shift, I am optimistic about the core and context of urban forest ecology advancing in a mutually beneficial manner. The basis for this optimism is exemplified by a course developed in 1993 by a group of urban forest ecologists—planners, managers, and scientists. Entitled "An Ecosystem Approach to Urban and Community Forestry" (USDA Forest Service 1993), this week-long workshop was tested in several cities in the Midwest and East, where the students ranged across the spectrum of urban forestry professionals. The Urban Forestry Center of the University of Pennsylvania's Morris Arboretum conducted an evaluation of the course and concluded that it successfully conveyed ecosystem principles and management strategies for urban forestry (R.L. Neville, USDA Forest Service, Syracuse, New York, pers. comm., 1994). The course is being fine-tuned for a second round of offerings in 1994-95.

Kai Lee begins the preface of his recent book, *Compass and Gyroscope*, with the observation that "civilized life cannot continue in its present form" (Lee 1993). The sheer number of people, combined with our powerful technologies, guarantees that we will alter the planet on which we must continue to evolve. *Homo sapiens* is trying to adjust quickly to changing ecosystems we don't understand. The peril lies in our fear of complexity and our desire to have science tell us what to do. Kai argues that the response to that fear is in an approach called "adaptive management" where the best science, albeit incomplete, is brought to bear on an ecosystem, management is implemented under rigorously monitored conditions, and adaptations in management are made as the feedback from monitoring teaches us more about the way the ecosystem behaves. Adaptive management is being tested in rural ecosystems, such as the Hayfork Adaptive Management Area in northern California, which is part of the implementation of the Forest Ecosystem Management Assessment Team's study of the northern spotted owl region.

Adaptive management areas for urban forest ecosystems must be established soon, for it is this approach that will test the ability of scientists and managers to cooperate in apprehending these complex systems. (See McPherson 1993 for a discussion of urban forest ecosystem monitoring.) This cooperation can be enhanced if there is a conjunction of meaning and purpose founded on common vocabulary and concepts. And this conjunction will occur if the two domains of urban forest ecology—scientific core and policy context—can continue to inform one another as they shift and evolve.

ACKNOWLEDGMENTS

The author thanks Joe McBride and Gordon Bradley for helpful reviews of earlier drafts.

LITERATURE CITED

Bradley, G.A., ed. 1984. Land use and forest resources in a changing environment: The urban/forest interface. University of Washington Press, Seattle.

Bradley, G.A., and B.B. Bare. 1993. Issues and opportunities on the urban forest interface. *In* A.W. Ewert, D.J. Chavez, and A.W. Magill, eds., Culture, conflict, and communication in the wildland-urban interface, pp. 17-32. Westview Press, Boulder, Colorado.

Caldwell, L.K. 1970. The ecosystem as a criterion for public land policy. Natural Resources Journal 10:203-221.

Golley, F.B. 1993. A history of the ecosystem concept in ecology. Yale University Press, New Haven.

Heisler, G.M. 1986. Effects of individual trees on the solar radiation climate of small buildings. Urban Ecology 9:337-359.

——. 1990. Mean wind speed below building height in residential neighborhoods with different tree densities. ASHRAE Transactions 96 (1):1389-1396.

Lee, K.N. 1993. Compass and gyroscope: Integrating science and politics for the environment. Island Press, Washington, D.C. 243 p.

McBride, J., and D. Jacobs. 1975. Urban forest development: A case study, Menlo Park, California. Urban Ecology 2:1-14.

——. 1986. Presettlement forest structure as a factor in urban forest development. Urban Ecology 9:245-266.

McBride, J., and R.A. Rowntree. In preparation. Changes to the structure of a high-elevation mixed-conifer forest in the Sierra Nevada, California, resulting from urbanization.

McPherson, E.G. 1991. Economic modeling for large-scale urban tree plantings. *In* E. Vine, D. Crawley, and P. Centolella, eds., Energy efficiency and the environment: Forging the link, pp. 349-369. American Council for an Energy-Efficient Economy, Washington, D.C.

——. 1993. Monitoring urban forest health. Environmental Monitoring and Assessment 26:165-174.

McPherson, E.G., D.J. Nowak, and R.A. Rowntree, eds. 1994. Chicago's urban forest ecosystem: Results of the Chicago Urban Forest Climate Project. General Technical Report NE-186. USDA Forest Service Northeastern Forest Experiment Station, Radnor, Pennsylvania.

Nowak, D.J. 1994a. Urban forest structure: The state of Chicago's urban forest. *In* E.G. McPherson, D.J. Nowak, and R.A. Rowntree, eds., Chicago's urban forest ecosystem: Results of the Chicago Urban Forest Climate Project. General Technical Report NE-186. USDA Forest Service Northeastern Forest Experiment Station, Radnor, Pennsylvania.

——. 1994b. Air pollution removal by Chicago's urban forest. *In* E.G. McPherson, D.J. Nowak, and R.A. Rowntree, eds., Chicago's urban forest ecosystem: Results of the Chicago Urban Forest Climate Project. General Technical Report NE-186. USDA Forest Service Northeastern Forest Experiment Station, Radnor, Pennsylvania.

Pouyat, R.V., M.J. McDonnell, and S.T.A. Pickett. In press. The effect of urban environments on soil characteristics in oak stands along an urban-rural land use gradient. Journal of Environmental Quality.

Real, L.A., and J.H. Brown, eds. 1991. Foundations of ecology: Classic papers with commentaries. University of Chicago Press, Chicago. 905 p.

Rowntree, R.A., G. Greenwood, and R. Marose. 1993. Land use development and forest ecosystems: Linking research and management in the Central Sierra. *In* A.W. Ewert, D.J. Chavez, and A.W. Magill, eds., Culture, conflict, and communication in the wildland-urban interface, pp. 389-398. Westview Press, Boulder, Colorado.

Sierra Nevada Ecosystem Project (SNEP). 1994. Progress report. University of California, Davis (Hart Hall). 70 p.

Simpson. J.R. 1993. Testing the relationship between urban forest structure and air temperatures. Study Plan PSW-4952 (unpubl.), California. USDA Forest Service, Pacific Southwest Research Station, Albany, California.

Tansley, A.G. 1935. The use and abuse of vegetational concepts and terms. Ecology 16:284-307.

USDA Forest Service. 1992. Forest Service Research Strategic Plan for the 1990s. Washington, D.C.

——. 1993. An ecosystem approach to urban and community forestry: A resource guide. Northeastern Area, State and Private Forestry, Radnor, Pennsylvania. 723 p.

——. 1994a. Briefing by the Chief of the USDA Forest Service of the Congressional Committee on Natural Resources. February.

——. 1994b. Draft Region 5 ecosystem management guidebook. Vol. 1. Pacific Southwest Region, San Francisco.

Van Dyne, G.M., ed. 1969. The ecosystem concept in natural resource management. Academic Press, New York. 383 p.

Yang, X., G.M. Heisler, M.E. Montgomery, J.H. Sullivan, E.B. Whereat, and D.R. Miller. In press. Radiative properties of hardwood leaves to ultraviolet radiation. International Journal of Biometeorology.

Zembal, R. 1993. The need for corridors between coastal wetlands and uplands in southern California. *In* J.E. Keeley, ed., Interface between ecology and land development in California, pp. 205-208. Southern California Academy of Sciences, Los Angeles.

Zipperer, W.C. 1993. Deforestation patterns and their effects on forest patches. Landscape Ecology 8(3):177-184.

5

Informational Issues: A Perspective on Human Needs and Inclinations

RACHEL KAPLAN

ABSTRACT Humans crave information, horde it, exchange it, fabricate it, and ignore it, depending on the circumstances. Humans who have vast information about some domain—known as experts—are particularly useful for certain situations, yet they can also be harmful to the very cause they intend to nurture. Finding ways to share information effectively plays an important part in making the efforts of experts more likely to succeed. This chapter examines broadly the human need for information and the circumstances when information exchange works well.

There is a pervasive misunderstanding of people, at least us western people, that assumes that money is what drives our world. Far more basic than money, however, is information. Information is the source of good and evil, we love it and hate it, we collect it and trade it, we hide it and leak it, we are overwhelmed by it and addicted to it. Information is central to our functioning, to our personal sense of esteem, to our interdependencies, to the basis for distinguishing ourselves from others—for better and for worse. By the same token, information is also central to our wars, distrust, and dismay. The solution to many of our battles—personal, interpersonal, international, and global—is dependent on information and the exchange of information.

In the sense I am using it here, information is inescapable. All our senses are receiving information virtually all of the time. We carry with us an awesome system of information storage and retrieval, and we have invented many additional devices for accessing information. We speak information. We think information. Thus this sense of "information" is not restricted to the stuff of formal education, the wisdom of the elders, or alphanumeric material. The environment is rich in information, whether or not we have tried to put it into words.

Given the reliance on information for our existence, one could naively assume that we humans understand its management and exchange. But this is not the case. Unfortunately, it is also not the only naive assumption that leads to substantial difficulties. For example, we readily equate the provision of information with its comprehension. "Show and tell" is not the same as "see and hear." We often take for granted that the information that is "out there" is received similarly by all who have access to it. A corollary of that assumption is that those who lack information, or perhaps have contradictory information, are stupid or incompetent. Further difficulties arise because we lose track of the human costs of informational excesses and readily ignore the human dependence on the informational richness of the unspoken world around us.

This chapter focuses on two major themes related to the implicit costs of mishandling information. The first deals with a brief analysis of the environment in informational terms. Given the many environmental contexts addressed in this volume, it is useful to recognize that each entails information and that such contexts can be handled in ways that are responsive to the human dependence on information. The second theme explores a variety of manifestations of information exchange. Some involve explicit efforts to provide information, such as through educational materials, or to obtain information from the public. Others entail implicit information exchange, such as well-intended efforts by experts (those assumed to have more information) to design, plan, and manage the environment and policies related to it. Central to both themes is a view of humans as information-based creatures; that is the subject of the initial section.

WHAT MAKES PEOPLE FEEL GOOD: AN INFORMATIONAL ANALYSIS

The desire to win the lottery and acquire all the things that money can buy drives many people to play this compelling game. Nonetheless, monetary wealth provides no assurance of personal well-being. Even if one were surrounded by all the material things one wishes, benefiting from all the services that can be bought, and secure in the knowledge that one's financial resources will cover future contingencies—even these unrealistic dreams will not guarantee satisfaction and fulfillment. In fact, the headlong, mindless accumulation of consumer goods may be a reflection of unmet human needs rather than a useful index of satisfaction. As Durning (1991:162) points out, "when alternative measures of success are not available, the deep human need to be valued and respected by others is acted out through consumption."

The feeling of being connected to others, to the environment, and to larger issues, the sense of personal dignity and of competence, the knowledge that one is needed—these are at the heart of human well-being (R. Kaplan 1993). They are also needs that are information-based. Unfortunately, they are also desires that readily go unfulfilled.

The human need for information can be usefully divided into two basic components: understanding and exploration (Kaplan and Kaplan 1978, 1982). People want to be able to make sense of their world, to comprehend what goes on around them. Understanding provides a sense of security. The failure to understand, by contrast, can readily bring out some of the worst qualities in what otherwise appears to be a reasonable person.

Important as it is, understanding is not enough. Humans have a need to expand their horizons, to enrich, enlarge, explore. They need new challenges, they seek more information. A world devoid of opportunities to explore is a grim prospect. Yet, the opportunities for "legitimate adventure" (Ladd 1977) are not equally distributed even in our rich nation.

The combination of these two vectors—understanding and exploration—provides a useful handle for examining many of the situations that contribute to human welfare. Competence is clearly based on understanding and the consequence of a great deal of exploration. Being needed and respected similarly have a basis in understanding. The sense of being connected to and rooted in a social and spiritual world can come only from comprehension and exploration.

Why then are people ignoring information? Why are so many opportunities for exploration not sought? Some of the answers to these questions will become evident in the next two sections when we look at barriers to effective information exchange.

UNDERSTANDING AND EXPLORING THE ENVIRONMENT

The perspective that the environment itself is a source of information may not be self-evident. It requires no elaboration to say that verbal or visual signs, such as stop signs, traffic lights, duck crossings, or a fuel pump icon, are sources of information. People in the environment also provide information. So do buildings—school, church, industry, residence. But even without words or icons, without buildings or people, the environment conveys information. Think about each of the special purpose landscapes discussed in the chapters of this volume: greenbelts, habitats that foster wildlife, landscapes that look parched as opposed to those that conserve water, parkland, agricultural lands. What about a single tree? Consider the diverse ways such a tree might be described—in terms of species, size, type of leaves, season, use. Such descriptions exemplify that the content of the environment, the things in it, are capable of communicating enormous amounts of information.

No one is born knowing a Douglas-fir. In other words, the information one extracts from the environment is strongly influenced by prior experience. Familiarity involves the accumulation of information and it shapes the way one "reads" the environment. Understanding and exploration are thus closely related to the information one can bring to bear in each environmental context.

The environment also provides information beyond the objects or categories—what I have called "contents"—that we rely upon in descriptions. The juxtapositions of elements in the environment, the way the environment conveys a space, are also essential sources of information. Consider what leads one to interpret an environment as safe. Rarely is this based on verbal signals, though perhaps a "no hunting" posting could contribute to a sense of security. Perhaps the presence of law enforcement (e.g., security guard) provides pertinent information. More often, however, the interpretation is based not only on particular contents but on their relationship to each other. Two settings that contain the same elements or contents might be perceived very differentially in terms of safety, depending on these juxtapositions. In other words, the overall organization of the space helps in the understanding of the setting and has direct consequences in one's willingness to explore.

The "understanding and exploration" framework provides insight into the design and management of spatial configurations. As a matter of fact, this conceptual framework evolved from our research on environmental preference (R. Kaplan and Kaplan 1989). Briefly, understanding of an environment is enhanced by its *coherence* and *legibility*. A coherent setting is one that is orderly and organized into clear areas; legibility involves the ability to be oriented. Exploration, by contrast, calls for *complexity* (the richness or variety available) and *mystery*. This involves various ways in which one senses that there is the promise or opportunity to learn more—a particularly effective factor in environmental preference. We have called these four qualities *informational predictors* because they point to ways in which the information in the environment can be organized to enhance human functioning.

The informational predictors function in concert. For example, the combination of a setting that is high in complexity but low in coherence is likely to be overwhelming. The same diversity of "elements" could be a satisfying and supportive environment if arranged more coherently, with some of the richness used to provide distinctive landmarks (thus enhancing legibility).

We are rarely aware of the pervasive influence of these environmental cues. When one stands at the entryway to a setting, for example, one rapidly evaluates substantial amounts of information about what lies ahead. Decisions about which way to go, how to find one's way back, where will the next opportunities for such assessments occur, what conditions might one encounter if one were to proceed, are all based on subtle information that the environmental context itself provides.

The information we constantly derive from the way an environment is organized, from the configuration of the "space," is a vital source of human well-being. Perhaps because this information is generally not the subject of our verbal exchanges, people are largely unaware of the powerful impact of spatial organization. Similarly we often fail to be sufficiently sensitive to the dire consequences of spatial configurations that impair human functioning. Environments that lack complexity, are deprived of coherence, and offer no aids for way-finding are all too common. The compounded psychological cost of environments that bombard one with information that is not relevant to what one is trying to do, and that we cannot do anything about, is by no means trivial.

THE CHALLENGE OF INFORMATION EXCHANGE

Humans are social animals that depend on information. Why then do our efforts to exchange information so often fail? How can it be so difficult? Even if we limit the discussion to efforts that are well intended, to contexts that involve people with a great deal of experience, to exchanges among people who live within the same culture, the outcomes frequently leave much to be desired. The cumulative consequences of such negative results translate to a pervasive sense of malaise and low sense of well-being for many people.

Exchange of information requires the seemingly simple task of transferring something from one head to another. Heads, alas, function very differently from many other receptacles used for transferring information. They are not like file drawers or boxes. One cannot pour or shovel or dump information in. Nor is it safe to assume that the provision of information ensures that it was received. Despite our lifelong experience with this task, none of us are particularly astute when it comes to understanding the circumstances for effective exchange of information.

The reasons lie in the many contingencies. For example, the nature of the information can make a big difference in how easily one communicates it. How vital is the information? Is it contrary to or in line with the recipient's prior knowledge? Related to this is the amount of information that one can assume is already available. In addition, there are the many issues related to the emotional aspects of the content of the information (e.g., bad news versus good news). And easily forgotten are considerations of the current state of mind of the intended recipient. Receptivity to information is often affected by contextual circumstances.

The effective exchange of information requires information about the recipient. All of us know a great deal more about ourselves than about these nondescript recipients. Two approaches, deriving from opposite positions, often guide efforts to exchange information. On the one hand, there is the implicit assumption that these generic "others" are not particularly different from us, that to a large extent people share the same perceptions. The other approach assumes that the unknown others are quite incompetent, since they seem to be basically ignorant about the matter at hand. Each perspective fails to lead to the desired result. Both perspectives are related to an overly innocent view of the role of experience in human perception.

The Assumptions of Shared Perceptions

The exchange of information is certainly more difficult among people who do not speak the same language. Such exchange relies on a vocabulary, and the shared vocabulary presumes shared experience and knowledge. Communication is thus easier, more efficient, and more likely to lead to desired effects when linguistic barriers are minimal. But as all of us have discovered on numerous occasions, the apparent existence of shared vocabulary does not ensure successful information exchange.

The deceptive truth of the matter is that even though we use the same terms, the experiences that they draw upon are often different. We all live in very different worlds. What we see, hear, and remember about the same place or event can differ substantially. To complicate matters, one is rarely aware of one's perceptions and generally assumes that others who have shared the same experience, experienced it in a similar fashion. In fact, our perception of any new situation is necessarily strongly influenced by previous experiences, and these, in a sense, provide us with a personal language for witnessing what goes on around us.

The circumstances that provide evidence for these assertions are common enough, though often dramatic. For example, situations involving experts and those who do not share that particular expertise bring these differences to light. Thus, the "facts" in a specific situation as portrayed by a long-term resident, a developer, a lawyer, and a municipal clerk may draw on a common vocabulary but in other respects have little in common. In many other instances even the vocabulary may be unshared as each party accuses the other of resorting to jargon—terminology that is a convenient shorthand for one group but may seem like a smoke screen to others. Such failures in exchanging information often happen with no ill intent, no desire to deceive or withhold, to mystify or impress. They are the consequences of the natural expression of the way each party perceives the situation, necessarily colored by prior experiences, training, and knowledge.

The Assumption of Lack of Competence

Failures in efforts to communicate too readily lead the expert to conclude that the intended recipient is not very bright. After all, if the person were competent, the explanation should have been sufficient. From the expert's perspective, the elegance and sophistication of the explanation were totally wasted and even the basic, simple idea was not grasped. Such a conclusion clearly fails to appreciate that part of the difficulty may lie in the way the information was presented. The very elegance and sophistication may depend on shared perceptions. The seemingly basic ideas may require words and images that draw on what the recipient already knows.

The assumption of incompetence is distressing for yet another reason. Even if the observation of failed communication is accurate, the interpretation that it is due to ignorance may not be. It is quite likely, in fact, that the intended recipient has a great deal of knowledge and information that is also pertinent to the situation at hand. The failure to appreciate such "local knowledge" is at the heart of much human anguish. The assumed utility of different kinds of information is at stake here.

Fischoff's (1993) discussion of research on the public's understanding of risk provides vivid examples of the differences between lay and expert perceptions. Extensive research suggested that the public failed to understand the magnitude of major risks and had an exaggerated sense of risk from events that receive substantial media coverage. These findings readily supported the notion of public incompetence. It took quite some time, however, before researchers appreciated that the evaluations of potential risk made by experts could not be viewed as statements of fact by the public. The differences between estimates made by laypeople and those of the experts involved differences in priorities. For example, the experts weighted fatality heavily in their judgments. The public's estimates of fatalities were no different from those of the experts, but their risk estimates were based on other criteria as well. Such matters as potential effects on community, on society, and on future generations played a more central role to the public (Allman 1985). Fischoff remarks that the research "has made it apparent that . . . there are reasons for mutual respect (and suspicion) among various laypersons and experts" (p. 9).

Information provided for the public often neglects the role of information already held by the public. At the same time, the public's wisdom or knowledge is not readily transmitted to those who need to know it. As Parker (1992:85) remarks, "professionals in the United States have a lot to offer, but also a lot to learn." The difficulties of information exchange are no less when the direction is reversed. Here, too, the same words may have different meanings when the underlying perceptions are unshared. While neither experts nor citizens can readily convey the pertinent information to the other, it is vital to recognize that all parties are endowed with important information to share.

TOWARD EFFECTIVE INFORMATION EXCHANGE

Most of our waking hours are devoted to the exchange of information: what we say or write, read or watch on a screen all involve efforts to provide information. Many exchanges are between individuals who do not know each other and have no direct contact with one another. Information exchanges often take place between parties that are considered unequal with respect to their available information: doctor/patient; police/citizen; teacher/student; expert/novice. Many others are between parties that have different information without presumption of inequality, such as individuals who are considered experts in different fields. Fortunately, there are also exchanges between individuals who know each other well and have had many experiences in common.

Some of these efforts work very well: both the transmitter and receiver of the information consider the exchange to be effective. The intent of the exchange is accomplished. The individuals involved feel understood and respected. They feel that they are heard and that their information is given due attention.

It is difficult to derive principles that will reliably lead to such successful results, as the circumstances will necessarily differ. Despite the differing contexts, however, there are some issues that can make information exchange more likely to succeed. The discussion here is oriented toward situations where the exchange occurs among people who do not know each other well and may not even have personal contact with each other. Such situations include the ubiquitous public meetings as well as most communication efforts that rely on the written word (for example, fact sheets, promotional material, newspapers).

Limited Capacity

A major difference between one who knows and one who is learning manifests itself in the quantity of information each can handle. In both instances there are limitations of capacity. But in areas where one has greater familiarity, the knowledge base is more organized, providing a greater capacity for dealing with new information.

This discrepancy in capacity leads to one of the most detrimental mismatches in efforts to exchange information. With all good intentions, the one who knows is very likely to offer far too much information. The one who is learning is likely to be overwhelmed. Unfortunately, the net result is often richer in emotion than substantive content. In other words, little if any of the intended information might have reached its destination. The recipient may remember only the discomfort and other negative manifestations of the situation.

This is a difficult lesson to learn. While all of us have been overwhelmed by too much information or too many choices and thus have firsthand experience with the distress this can cause, we do not recognize that information that seems straightforward to us may be mystifying to someone lacking the needed background. The temptations to add one more fascinating aspect, to include yet another line of support, or to show one more amazing ramification are difficult to resist. Yet the cost of these seemingly small embellishments can be colossal in terms of the intended information exchange.

The solution involves holding back. This is often a case where less is more, since the consequence of too much information is likely to be that none is remembered. In addition, however, the way the information is structured can also make a big difference in how much can be offered. The commonly cited "magic number 7 ± 2" is more magical than useful as a guideline in this context. In many oral presentations the *appropriate* number may be three; in written material, perhaps five (Mandler 1975; Posner 1973). How often does one remember even three main points from a presentation? How rarely are presentations delivered mindful of such a goal!

But it is not simply a matter of numbers. A list of nine major points (i.e., 7+2) has little chance of successful information transmittal. Three major points, each having two subthemes, also amounts to nine items, but can work quite effectively. In other words, attention to hierarchical organization of the issues speaks to the dilemma that limited capacity poses.

The "Where They're At" Principle

How often have we ignored information because it struck us as being "the same old stuff"? And how often has information we offered and knew to be of vital importance been greeted in the same fashion? People are not eager for information they *think* they already know. Nor do people welcome information contradictory to what they hold dear. This is even true when the information might be of great personal consequence.

These difficulties suggest the importance of relating information to "where they're at." By trying to connect information to the mental models and perceptions already in the heads of the intended recipients, their resistance to what seems irrelevant or boring or threatening has a greater chance of being overcome. In other words, the effort here is to turn familiarity to advantage, rather than permit it to get in the way.

How to achieve this will vary. To take a typical but problematic situation, it is hard to ascertain "where they're at" in producing an informational booklet. Nonetheless, one can orient educational materials so as to build from existing information, and existing concerns. One can make clear that the news to be offered may be unwanted; one can acknowledge information that is likely to be shared and then describe how what is to be offered differs; one can ask the recipients to consider their own perceptions of the situation before proceeding. In that way, there might be greater recognition of discrepancies between what is offered and what might have been considered obvious. In other words, rather than assuming that readers are dying to read whatever is offered, attention to their knowledge, worries, and circumstances can lead to more effective information exchange.

Telling a Story

Many books intended for younger audiences are markedly different from books written for adults. They may frequently use shorter words and sentences, more pictures, and wider margins. They also tend to be written with more concreteness and vivid examples. Books for younger people seem to take seriously that maintaining the attention of the reader or listener is not to be taken for granted. As a result, they are often more interesting, easier to grasp, and more likely to engage the imagination. "Understanding and exploration" seem to be implicitly incorporated in such materials.

For some inexplicable reason, much of what adults read (excluding fiction) is less fun. Attention span and motivation to process the material are presumed to be abundant. Layout (e.g., white space on the page, illustrations) may be recognized as salient for material that is intended to impress, but less so if the purpose is merely to communicate. Grayness of page, abstractness of content, minimal thought about what the reader is to gain from the material—these are all familiar characteristics of much that we read, assign to others to read, and, alas, are responsible for generating. In some cases these characteristics may lead to nothing more harmful than boredom; but at other times failure to consider the way information is transmitted can have far more dire consequences, such as product labels displaying major precautions in a way that consumers are unlikely to read (Magat and Viscusi 1992).

The earlier discussion of understanding and exploration was by no means intended to be age specific. It is possible that the urgency for understanding takes some time to develop, making younger people more oriented toward exploration. Conceivably, in some domains, older adults have a stronger need for understanding—for seeing the connections between what they already know—than for seeking new directions and domains. In any event the exchange of information, even for adults, is facilitated by attention to this framework.

It may be interesting to revisit the factors that foster understanding and exploration to see how they apply to the exchange of information. Think about someone who can hold an audience as a complicated tale unfolds. Or consider some technical material that seems more readable than most. Such stories or material can incorporate a great deal of information (in other words, complexity) if the organization is coherent.

Coherence is pivotal. It is enhanced by efforts that make clearer what the "pieces" are. In other words, ways to make the organization and the substance more concrete and vivid help with understanding. From this perspective, it is useful to examine the frequently offered advice to begin by clearly defining one's terms. While definitions may appear to encourage understanding, they more often confuse than edify. Definitions are not the way people come to know meanings (Kaplan and Kaplan 1982). People learn concepts through examples and experience. Further, the precision of a definition is at odds with how concepts are actually used (Rosch 1978). Coming early on, definitions provide information that is often difficult to assimilate. They thus tend to clutter rather than clarify.

Particularly useful for increasing understanding is the *structure* of the piece. Structure is communicated visually with headings and "white space." Orally, indications of structure are provided by signaling transitions, by orienting the listener to where one has been and where the story is going. These features are close analogues to ways in which a physical environment is made more coherent and more legible. Structure helps one see that there are a manageable number of parts to the whole, and to keep track of where one is along the story's path.

Exploration is closely related to interest. Enticing the reader or listener to get deeper into the story, to wonder, to seek the resolution to uncertainties that have been created— these are all devices that operate much as mystery does in the environment. Starting with a few questions or a paradox can increase curiosity and the desire to find out. While such devices can be misused and overused, their total absence in technical materials is an unfortunate omission.

Asking For Information

Most of the issues raised so far have focused on ways to provide information so that the transfer effort is more effective for the recipient. It is also important to consider what makes the exchange successful when one seeks information from others. In our daily conversations with friends and colleagues we frequently ask for information and it hardly seems to be a major event. In more formal contexts, or when asking for information from a stranger, seeking such information can become more challenging. Certainly many such efforts have been known to go badly. Not only are such questions frequently ambiguous or poorly worded, the tone of the transaction can generate negative reactions from the start. There are plenty of examples: medical histories, police interrogations, court appearances, anything called a "test." These all require information from someone, whether written or oral.

The many situations that involve polling, surveys, market research, or other contexts for questionnaires are other familiar examples of asking for information. Given that the respondent or informant may have substantial information to offer, many efforts to seek such information err on the side of limiting or constraining the options, such as questions that permit no more than a "yes" or "no" response. Allowing more reasonable choices can go a long way toward making the respondent feel comfortable and ensuring that the reply can be used responsibly.

The other extreme can also create difficulties. Offering too many choices or leaving the question totally unstructured can make the respondent feel uncomfortable and concerned that any answer will be misconstrued. "What are the major issues facing X today?" "How would you recommend that our government do Y?" Such questions can leave people feeling incompetent or annoyed. And furnishing written answers is certainly a demanding task for most people. But even if asked on the phone or at the door, such questions may be intimidating.

These dilemmas cannot be resolved by some rule that applies to every circumstance. The context is crucial. This includes who is asking, who is answering, for what reasons, about what kind of situation, and with what expectations about how the information will be used. While no simple principles can guide such efforts, some broad understanding of the nature of the animal is likely to be helpful. It is the same creature, after all, that is more likely to feel competent and satisfied when it can make sense of a situation, when it feels useful, when it feels respected. All of these human qualities are often undermined in the way we seek information.

The discussion here is necessarily brief and cursory. The chapter on "Research as Intermediate Technology" in Kaplan and Kaplan (1982), the discussion of "assessing human concerns" (Kaplan 1984), and the examples in S. Kaplan and Kaplan (1989) provide more extensive treatment of this topic.

Summary

There are many reasons for information exchanges to fare badly. Fortunately, there are ways to improve the process as well. The focus here has been on some issues related to providing information as well as concerns that pertain to obtaining information. The issue of familiarity is central to effective information exchange. Our own understanding of information and inclinations to explore are closely related to what is familiar to us. The process has a greater chance of succeeding to the extent that one can draw on what is familiar to the intended recipient or help reduce the unfamiliarity of a new situation. That means that finding common ground, building on what the listener or reader is likely to find familiar, facilitates the process.

At the same time, however, the recipient's perception that the information involves nothing new can lead to undesired outcomes. There is also the fear that one's existing mental models will be undermined, leaving one in a state of ineffectual confusion. While these tendencies are useful and adaptive in many situations, they can also become major roadblocks in efforts to exchange information. Such responses to what appears familiar need also be taken into account if the exchange of information is to be productive.

ACTION MANDATES

So humans are information-seeking, information-sharing, information-hungry organisms. Many of the joys and disappointments in our lives are directly tied to these addictions. We want to be asked about the information we have, but are readily disgruntled about the way we are asked. We want to know more, but we ignore much of the information that is available. We like to create information, but are paralyzed by the choices thus generated (Waldman 1992). We are surprisingly uninformed about how to manage this resource that is so central to our sustenance.

The various contexts for analysis that the next several chapters address all concern different ways of packaging information to meet human requirements. The chapters concerned with special purpose landscapes, in turn, deal both with information in the landscape and information about making such settings more viable. In all these contexts and settings, successful outcomes—for the land, humans, and other species—depend on efforts to share information.

Sharing information is more likely to be useful if we take the following four issues seriously.

- *Valuable information is not the exclusive property of those with expertise or status.* The information held by "locals" is no less pertinent than the information held by those who wield power, money, or scientific "truths."

- *Humans are sensitive to signs of making a difference.* Asking for information and promptly ignoring it is worse than not asking at all! The cumulative effect of ill-fated participation is a demoralized citizenry.

- *People need to know what their choices are.* They do better in providing information if they understand the context, the situation, the constraints. Being told or shown some alternative solutions, for example, is a way to facilitate understanding while at the same time seeking information.

- *Information in the hand is not information in the mind.* The delivery of educational material is no assurance that it will be read, understood, or heeded. It is essential to invest considerably greater effort in determining the circumstances for the effective transmission of information. This is at the heart of affecting change. Good intentions have never been enough. The differences between what experts know and take for granted and what the public knows and holds dear are too often unexamined.

The list could easily be extended. We know all too well, however, that adding to it comes at great cost. If only these four points in their full richness and vast implications were heeded this could be considered a useful effort to share information. But even if such a hope is overly optimistic, at least this analysis should increase one's appreciation of information exchange that works well, given how difficult it is.

ACKNOWLEDGMENTS

Portions of the work discussed here were funded by the U.S. Forest Service, North Central Forest Experiment Station, Urban Forestry Project, through cooperative agreements. Dr. John F. Dwyer's support and encouragement are greatly appreciated.

LITERATURE CITED

Allman, W.F. 1985. Staying alive in the 20th century. Science 85:31-37.

Durning, A.T. 1991. Asking how much is enough. *In* L.R. Brown, ed., State of the world 1991, pp. 153-169. Norton, New York.

Fischoff, B. 1993. Controversies over risk: Psychological perspective on competence. American Psychological Association's Psychological Science Agenda 6(2):8-9.

Kaplan, R. 1984. Assessing human concerns for environmental decision making. *In* S.L. Hart, G.A. Enk, and W.F. Hornick, eds., Improving impact assessment: Increasing the relevance and utilization of scientific and technical information, pp. 37-56. Westview, Boulder, Colorado.

———. 1993. Environmental appraisal, human needs, and a sustainable future. *In* T. Gärling and R. G. Golledge, eds., Behavior and environment: Psychological and geographical approaches, pp. 117-140. Elsevier, Amsterdam.

Kaplan, R., and S. Kaplan. 1989. The experience of nature: A psychological perspective. Cambridge University Press, Cambridge and New York.

Kaplan, S., and R. Kaplan. 1978. Humanscape: Environments for people. Duxbury, Belmont, California. (Republished 1982 by Ulrich's, Ann Arbor, Michigan.)

———. 1982. Cognition and environment: Functioning in an uncertain world. Praeger, New York. (Republished 1989 by Ulrich's, Ann Arbor, Michigan.)

———. 1989. The visual environment: Public participation in design and planning. Journal of Social Issues 45:59-86.

Ladd, F.C. 1977. City kids in the absence of ... *In* Children, Nature, and the Urban Environment Symposium Proceedings, pp. 77-81. Northeastern Forest Experiment Station, USDA Forest Service, Upper Darby, Pennsylvania.

Magat, W.A., and W.K. Viscusi. 1992. Informational approaches to regulation. MIT Press, Cambridge, Massachusetts.

Mandler, G. 1975. Consciousness: Respectable, useful and probably necessary. *In* R.L. Solso, ed., Information processing and cognition, pp. 229-254. Erlbaum, Hillsdale, New Jersey.

Parker, J.K. 1992. Hanging question marks on our professionals. Journal of Forestry 93:21-24.

Posner, M.I. 1973. Cognition: An introduction. Scott, Foresman, Glenview, Illinois.

Rosch, E.H. 1978. Principles of categorization. *In* E. Rosch and B.B. Lloyd, eds., Cognition and categorization, pp. 28-48. Erlbaum, Hillsdale, New Jersey.

Waldman, S. 1992. The tyranny of choice. New Republic, January 27, pp. 22-25.

6

Land Use Control as a Strategy for Retaining and Integrating Urban Forest Landscapes

KONRAD LIEGEL

ABSTRACT Land use controls for retaining and integrating urban landscapes, from city center to the rural fringe, are described and evaluated in this paper. Traditional mechanisms, such as the grid street plan, Euclidean zoning, and subdivision regulations, have produced monotonous landscape patterns, broken only occasionally by city parks and forested or shrub-covered hillsides and ravines, and have contributed to the destruction and fragmentation of natural landscapes along the rural fringe. To retain diversity in urban landscapes, and integrate existing remnants of natural landscapes along the rural fringe into the urban landscape, it is necessary to look beyond the standard street tree ordinance for additional land use controls: regulations (e.g., critical areas ordinances), landowner incentives (e.g., preferential taxation), public education (e.g., forest landowner assistance programs), and public acquisition (e.g., purchase of development rights). Used individually, these methods are limited in their ability to retain special purpose landscapes. But used together in a coordinated action plan, they offer local governments the best strategy for retaining and integrating the diversity of landscapes from the center of the city to the rural fringe.

Laws influence the pattern and morphology of our urban landscapes (Platt 1991). The "impress" that a law makes on the landscape depends on the land use controls we have in place and choose to utilize. Historically, such controls have substantially influenced the development, character, and sustainability of our urban landscapes along the gradient from city center to the rural fringe. Traditional land use mechanisms, such as the grid street plan and Euclidean zoning, have produced a monotonous landscape pattern of regularly spaced trees along the margin of rectangular city blocks, broken only occasionally by city parks and forested or shrub-covered hillsides and ravines. More recent land use mechanisms, such as subdivision regulations, have allowed for curving streets, irregular lots, and abundant landscaping and greenery; but they have also contributed to the destruction and fragmentation of natural landscapes along the rural fringe.

If we are to retain the diversity of urban landscapes resulting from haphazard human settlement and development, and integrate remnants of natural landscapes along the rural fringe into the urban landscape, we must utilize a land use control strategy that helps, and does not hinder, us in meeting our goal. The purpose of this chapter is to describe and evaluate the general effectiveness of the following regulatory and nonregulatory land use controls for retaining and integrating urban landscapes: **(1) requiring** private landowners to use or not use their land in certain ways (*regulation*); (2) paying private landowners not to change the use of the land, mostly in the form of negative income such as reduced taxes or being allowed to build at higher densities (*landowner incentives*); (3) encouraging private landowners to choose not to use the land in certain ways (*public education*); and (4) paying private landowners for their land or for certain rights in their land, such as the right to develop (*public acquisition*).

LAND USE CONTROLS AND THEIR EFFECTIVENESS

Regulations

Regulations are laws enacted by local jurisdictions to restrict certain uses of private property in order to protect the health, safety, and general welfare of the community. They have traditionally been the principal means of land use control because they are easy to develop and implement at low cost to the local jurisdiction.

Land use regulations are generally permissible under the federal and state constitutions. Where a regulation goes "too far" in restricting private uses of land, however, the regulation may constitute a "taking" of private property for public purposes. If a court determines that a taking has occurred, then just compensation to the landowner is required.

The question of what constitutes a taking has proved to be a problem of considerable difficulty. The U.S. Supreme Court's recent pronouncement on the subject, *Lucas v. South Carolina Coastal Council*, 112 S. Ct. 2886, 120 L.Ed.2d 789 (1992), held that the application of a land use regulation to a particular property constitutes a taking if the regulation denies an owner *all* economically viable uses of his or her property and the government cannot show that the restriction is one that background principles of the state's law of property and nuisance already place upon ownership. The *Lucas* case involved a South Carolina regulation that barred landowners from erecting permanent habitable structures on ecologically fragile barrier islands.

In the more common case where some economic use is left to a property owner by the regulation, the court will determine whether or not the regulation advances a legitimate public purpose, such as health, safety, and general welfare of the community, and then balance the governmental need for the restriction with its economic impact on the private landowner. Generally, if the regulation advances a legitimate public purpose and allows the landowner some economic use of the property, it will not be held to constitute a taking. But in some cases, even if the court finds that the regulation advances a legitimate public purpose (such as limiting development of environmentally sensitive areas unsuitable for building, maintaining habitat for wildlife, or relieving the monotony of continuous urban development), it may still conclude that the regulation constitutes a taking where the economic impact of the ordinance deprives a landowner of profitable uses on a substantial portion of his or her property. For example, in a state court case, *Allingham v. City of Seattle*, 749 P.2d 160, 190 Wn.2d 947 (1988), overruled on other grounds in *Presbytery of Seattle*, 114 Wn.2d 320, 327, 787 P.2d 907 (1990), the Washington Supreme Court held that a City of Seattle greenbelt ordinance constituted a taking where the ordinance required that 50 to 70 percent of certain lots be preserved or returned to a natural state. Thus local governments must be careful in enacting regulations that are intended to prevent the development of natural landscapes, no matter how ecologically unsuitable development might be.

Landscape regulations can be an effective tool for establishing and maintaining an urban landscape appropriate to local environmental conditions. The street tree ordinance, for example, has been critical to the establishment of municipal urban and community forestry programs (Bradley 1992; Miller 1988). It often provides the legal basis, prescribes the administrative framework, and contains provisions for the planting, protection, maintenance, and removal of trees for urban forestry programs. More recent landscape ordinances mandate or encourage the establishment and maintenance of certain special purpose landscapes, such as water conserving landscapes, fire-safe landscapes, or energy-efficient landscapes. A landscape ordinance that requires the use of water conserving vegetation, for example, can conserve water, improve environmental quality, and strengthen sense of place by creating a direct link between the urban environment and the natural desert context (McPherson 1990). These landscape regulations typically can avoid a "taking" problem because they advance traditionally accepted public purposes, such as health and safety, and do not deprive landowners of profitable uses of their property.

Subdivision regulations also can be an effective tool for retaining some land, especially along the rural fringe, for open space purposes as a condition of development. For example, many subdivision ordinances exact the transfer of property (or cash payments) from private to public ownership as a condition of subdivision approval, or impose impact fees on developers to pay for the costs to the community of providing services to a new development. Planned unit development ordinances allow the grouping or "clustering" of uses through a density transfer rather than spreading such uses throughout a parcel as in a conventional lot-by-lot development. The area equal to the total reduction in the normally required lot remains in open space (Schiffman 1989). To avoid a "taking" problem, these subdivision exactions must reasonably relate to the activities of the developer and must be limited to meeting needs attributable to the subdivision and not the larger community.

Subdivision regulations are more effective for large subdivisions because of the problems involved in coordinating small-scale developments (Patterson 1988). Because most subdivisions are small, the use of subdivision regulations as a tool for retaining natural landscapes within urban areas is limited.

Land protection regulations, such as critical areas and greenbelt ordinances, are a less effective tool for retaining natural landscapes within urban areas and along the rural fringe. Critical areas ordinances control development in environmentally critical locations, such as aquifer recharge areas, frequently flooded areas, wetlands, steep slopes, liquefaction and landslide prone areas, and fish and wildlife conservation areas. Greenbelt ordinances control development in urban forests, typically on steep hillsides and ravines. Unless narrowly focused and carefully drafted, both forms of land protection regulations can result in a taking, either because they are not recognized by the state courts as advancing a traditionally acceptable public purpose or because they must restrict virtually all profitable uses of property to protect the land resource. Of the two, critical areas ordinances are more effective in retaining natural landscapes. They typically have specific state enabling legislation justifying their environmental need and public purpose, and the potential for public harm resulting from certain uses of the property outweighs the economic costs to landowners and developers in the form of lowered land values.

Landowner Incentives

Landowner incentives offer preferential taxation or other benefits to landowners who voluntarily agree to protect and maintain special purpose landscapes on their property. Such incentives encourage certain kinds of development, discourage premature development, or compensate for regulations preventing change of use.

Preferential taxation, the more common landowner incentive, provides that land actively farmed or predominantly open will be assessed only for the value of its agricultural or open space use, not for any alternative development values. Preferential taxation has been applied as well to other than open space, forest, or agricultural land uses by dividing uses into classes, each of which is assessed at a different percentage of market value according to current use or according to uses permitted in the zoning district in which the land falls (Patterson 1988).

Transferable development rights (TDR) programs allow the development rights from one parcel of property (the "sending" parcel) to be transferred to another parcel (the "receiving" parcel). The development rights represent the unused development potential of the property. These rights can be used on additional properties of the owner or sold for use elsewhere. Still in their infancy, the TDR programs have been used to compensate landowners affected by restrictive regulation, to preserve historic buildings, to save agricultural and environmentally sensitive lands, and as part of a community's general growth management program (Schiffman 1989).

Zoning bonuses are another landowner incentive by which a builder or developer agrees to provide certain amenities or other community benefits, such as public plazas or low income housing, in exchange for a bonus. The bonus is usually permission to build at a higher density (Schiffman 1989).

Landowner incentives, such as preferential taxation and TDR programs, can be effective tools for preserving open space and keeping land in forest, agricultural, or horticultural uses, especially in urban fringe areas where development pressures are most severe. By themselves, however, such voluntary programs provide only temporary protection. Landowners will use their property for other purposes when the incentive to retain land for an open space use is considerably less than to develop it for other uses.

Public Education

Public education programs encourage landowners to maintain special purpose landscapes on their property, and they also provide landowners with the technical information to manage their lands appropriately. In registry programs, for example, landowners voluntarily agree to do, or not to do, certain things on their property and to notify the government of plans for any changes on their property. In forest landowner assistance programs, a governmental agency provides technical assistance to landowners on forestry management of their land.

Public education programs, such as volunteer registry and landowner assistance programs, can be an effective tool for educating landowners about the special landscape values of their property and how to maintain those values, and in alerting local governments before sensitive natural areas or open space lands are developed. But like landowner incentive programs, they provide only temporary protection. Landowners will use their properties for other purposes when they have an economic need to do so.

Public Acquisition

Local governments can acquire land for public ownership, administration, and maintenance through purchases or donations. Donors of land, or interests in land, may receive income, estate, and property tax benefits for such donations. Fee simple acquisition involves acquiring complete interest in the land. This allows the responsible agency full control over the management of the land for a special purpose. Acquisition of less than fee simple interests, such as development rights or conservation easements, involves acquisition of something less than the complete interest in the land. Less than fee simple acquisition allows landowners to continue to own the land and use it for purposes consistent with the conservation values of the land.

Public acquisition can be a useful means of protecting "open space" landscapes, such as greenbelts and other forest remnants, and wildlife habitat. It is the only way of ensuring that natural landscapes will remain a part of the urban landscape. But public acquisition is expensive. Governments must have the financial resources to acquire the land and protect and manage it for special purposes. In recent times, states and local governments have issued bonds to create revenue with which to purchase land for special purposes (see Chapter 7, which addresses the political and administrative issues associated with a public preservation program).

Public acquisition has other limitations as well. Landowners may attempt to raise the market value of their property artificially once they know their land is targeted for acquisition. Delays between the time the land is available and the time money is appropriated to buy the land can result in the property being lost to development. In such circumstances, nonprofit land trusts can be useful partners to government by temporarily acquiring the land until public funds become available to complete the transfer to public ownership (Endicott 1993).

CONCLUSION

Our strategy for retaining and integrating urban landscapes must make the best use of a combination of regulatory and nonregulatory land use controls. All of the methods currently available to local government have limitations. Regulations are effective in mandating the use in urban areas of special purpose landscapes that serve basic life support purposes and in retaining small parcels of "open space" along the rural fringe, but are less effective in protecting sensitive natural areas and open space lands from development. Public acquisition, on the other hand, is effective in protecting sensitive natural areas and open space lands from development, but is too expensive for general application. Both landowner incentive and public education programs help to defer the conversion of sensitive natural areas and open space lands. Used individually, therefore, none of these controls will be effective in retaining natural landscapes within urban areas. Used together in a coordinated governmental action plan, they offer local governments the best strategy available today for retaining and integrating the diversity of landscapes from the center of the city to the rural fringe.

ACKNOWLEDGMENTS

I wish to acknowledge the University of Washington's Growth Management Planning and Research Clearinghouse, whose report "Local Government Planning Tools" was very useful in preparing my paper. This 1992 report analyzes the use, purpose, and effectiveness of local ordinances and planning mechanisms used to manage growth, including many of the land use control strategies discussed and evaluated here. The report is based on survey responses from local officials in 190 towns, cities, and counties across the United States, ranging in population from eleven hundred to nearly three million. It provides some of the most current and specific information on effective growth management programs. I also wish to thank my colleague Charles Hensler for commenting on the manuscript before its submission for publication.

LITERATURE CITED

Bradley, G.A. 1992. Land use planning on the cutting edge. *In* P.D. Rodbell, ed., Proceedings of the Fifth National Urban Forest Conference, November 15-19, 1991, pp. 33-35. American Forestry Association, Washington, D.C.

Endicott, E., ed. 1993. Land conservation through public-private partnerships. Island Press, Washington, D.C. 361 p.

Growth Management Planning and Research Clearinghouse. 1992. Local government planning tools: Executive summary. Department of Urban Planning and Design, University of Washington, Seattle. 11 p.

McPherson, E.G. 1990. Creating an ecological landscape. *In* P.D. Rodbell, ed., Proceedings of the Fourth Urban Forestry Conference, October 15-19, 1989, pp. 63-67. American Forestry Association, Washington, D.C.

Miller, R.W. 1988. Urban forestry: Planning and managing urban greenspaces. Prentice Hall, Englewood Cliffs, New Jersey. 404 p.

Patterson, T.W. 1988. Land use planning. R.E. Krieger Pub. Co., Malabar, Florida. 352 p.

Platt, R.H. 1991. Land use control: Geography, law, and public policy. Prentice Hall, Englewood Cliffs, New Jersey. 390 p.

Schiffman, I. 1989. Alternative techniques for managing growth. Institute for Governmental Studies, University of California at Berkeley. 117 p.

7

Keeping It Green: Political and Administrative Issues in the Preservation of the Urban Forest

GENE DUVERNOY

ABSTRACT Discussion focuses on preserving large-scale elements of urban forests, particularly tracts of open space being considered for conversion. Administering an urban forest land preservation program requires financial and administrative skills, political dexterity, and an intimate knowledge of the city's land base. Programs are most successful when they are a collaborative effort of local government, preservation organizations, and the citizens of the community. Step-by-step guidelines for planning and implementing such a program are presented.

Urban forest lands civilize and make livable otherwise inhospitable communities of asphalt and cement. They are a fundamental element necessary to create and maintain communities and neighborhoods as desirable places to live and raise families. These lands define home to a resident and speak of community to the attentive visitor. They merit our preservation, careful stewardship, and respectful enjoyment.

Preservation of the urban forest can take many forms, from the care and protection of the individual specimen at the street tree level all the way to the preservation of significant acreages of mature forest. This discussion will focus on developing and implementing programs to preserve the larger-scale elements of an urban forest—particularly the major tracts of open space in cities and towns that are increasingly threatened by conversion. While such urban land preservation programs are complicated to administer, the payoffs are extraordinary. In just one city alone, an urban land preservation program can generate millions of dollars and preserve thousands of acres.

The threshold question for a potential program, urban or otherwise, is whether existing regulations will adequately protect the conservation values of the lands targeted for protection. Regulation categorically is less expensive than the urban land preservation options explored in this discussion. States require or authorize local adoption of land use regulations which can be used to protect important urban forest lands, such as lot clearing limitations. Implementing and enforcing these regulations may be adequate protection for all but the most critical urban forest lands.

Urban land preservation programs should move forward only where there is reasonable certainty that investment of the capital funding, staff, and other resources will ensure a significant gain in the conservation of the forest base. Typically, the specific sites included in an urban land preservation program should be selected because: (1) public access is proposed, (2) intensive stewardship or management is required to ensure the long-term viability of the urban forest, or (3) the habitat, open space, or resource values to be protected extend beyond the protection afforded by existing or probable regulations.

The benefits of an urban land preservation program are numerous. First and most important, the protection is permanent. The acquired system of properties is placed beyond the political winds and storms that bring change to regulatory protection programs. Second, public ownership of lands critical to our urban forest can provide exceptional opportunities for interpretative and educational programs that encourage better public understanding and treatment of this precious resource. Third, a pleasant site for an afternoon family picnic or solitary evening stroll can no longer be taken for granted in our towns and cities, but must be formally provided. The public ownership of city forest lands makes such recreation possible, strengthening the public constituency for preservation of the urban forest. Finally, public ownership of these lands enables cities and towns to conduct the stewardship and research necessary to ensure the vitality of the urban forest over the long term.

ADMINISTERING AN URBAN LAND PRESERVATION PROGRAM

Successfully administering an urban forest land preservation program requires financial and administrative skills, political dexterity, and an intimate knowledge of the city's land base. The programs are intricate, and tradeoffs abound. The first consideration is that such programs require significant sums of money. Property costs are high, opportunities for below market sales are limited, and there are many competing demands for limited pubic revenues. Consequently, on this point alone, urban land preservation programs generate great public, media, and political interest.

Land is a defining element of our society. It literally provides food, water, clothing, and shelter. It confers prestige and status and frequently guarantees wealth. Moreover, many of our most basic social and cultural beliefs revolve around the use of our lands. As a result, a variety of conflicting expectations and competing potential uses exist for the remaining undeveloped wooded lands in our cities and towns that are the target acquisitions for an urban land preservation program.

Our public institutions often fail to recognize that the preservation of ecologically significant open space, such as urban forest lands, is fundamental to the quality of life of our communities. By saving those specific lands or features which are important to our citizens—those "special places" we all have in our neighborhoods—we help to protect the sense of place of our communities. Instead of including preservation of forest land among its other infrastructure activities, however, government typically views protecting the urban land base as far removed from its primary mission.

These various factors converge to create a challenging climate for the administration of an urban land preservation program. Success requires attention to politics and public relations as well as substance in each of the four stages to an urban land preservation program: (1) design of the proposed conservation program, (2) the adoption campaign of the proposed program, (3) implementation of the program, and (4) the stewardship of the preserved properties after the program is completed. Different administrative and political issues prevail at each stage. This discussion will emphasize considerations related to the design of a program, because it is the stage at which the foundation is developed. Many problems that may not become apparent until later can be either created or avoided during a program's design.

Designing a Public Preservation Program

Because urban forest land preservation programs still are not seen as a basic function of state or local government, legislatures typically resist devoting anything but modest sums unless the program is ratified by the public. Consequently, most programs must be designed to pass two thresholds. First, a jurisdiction's legislative authority must be sufficiently convinced of a program's merit to place it on the ballot. Second, the public must be convinced to approve the ballot measure. Depending on the jurisdiction, the required voter approval rate may range from 50 percent all the way to a near watershed level of 66 percent. Following is a review of the two major design phases for developing a program that can pass muster with a legislative authority and the electorate.

Phase 1. Defining the Initial Concept for the Program

In the initial phase of developing a land preservation program, leadership is identified, goals are established, a statement of purpose is drafted, funding sources are examined, and the size of the program is proposed. These elements will be discussed sequentially below. In practice, however, decisions made for one of the elements interact with the others. The elements of phase 1 must be pursued iteratively until all the initial issues and decisions are settled.

1. *Identify Program Leadership.* Urban land preservation programs may be the spark of an individual, but they must be developed by a coalition of interests with high credibility among participating jurisdictions, the press, and critical constituencies. The leadership for the urban land preservation program should be established at the outset and expanded as the program is developed and moves into the campaign stage. The initial leadership should be broad based and credible to all necessary constituencies. The leadership can include professionals with the scientific expertise to identify lands critical to a city's urban forest, parties who can build the coalitions necessary to pass a ballot measure, and people who can reach out to important neighborhoods and communicate the need for this program. Urban preservation programs that are developed and led solely by environmental interests generally have failed at a city's ballot box, even in our "green" oriented communities of the northwestern United States. Programs led by a consortium of individuals with environmental, civic, business, and community ties have succeeded, even in purportedly conservative towns.

2. *Draft Reasonable Program Preservation Goals.* Realistic, measurable goals should be established early in the design of the program. The preservation goals should be drafted so that they do not promise more than can be delivered. They must account for the size of the tax base which will generate the revenues, the rate at which the revenues will be collected, and the cost of the urban land resources to be preserved. Simply put, a larger tax base and a greater tax rate will allow for a greater preservation effort, while a more expensive resource base will reduce the scale of the effort.

Promising only what can be delivered goes beyond mother's basic rule of never telling a "fib." The ability to develop future, follow-on programs is also at stake. The preservation of resource lands in many jurisdictions is not completed with just one program.

Instead, a sequence of efforts can take several decades. Invariably, interest groups and citizens rightly want to know how the last effort went before committing additional dollars. As this day of reckoning comes around, you want to be able to demonstrate how a prior program met its preservation goals rather than spend time explaining why a current land preservation proposal will not repeat the mistakes of its predecessor.

In 1979, King County—the urban county which includes Seattle, Washington—passed a $50 million farmland preservation program following two unsuccessful ballot attempts. After two campaign failures, the pressures on program sponsors were intense to promise whatever might be necessary for passage. But the major proponents held firm to the well-researched claim that the program could preserve between ten thousand and fifteen thousand acres of farmland. After passage, five years intervened before implementation, because of lawsuits and financial market difficulties. The program ultimately was implemented and about thirteen thousand acres were preserved a short distance from the city of Seattle. King County was in a position to promote the program as a solid success because the original sponsors never created unrealistic expectations. Consequently, the program was used extensively as justification for the later $116 million County Open Space Program that received overwhelming voter approval.

3. *Draft a Concise Statement of Purpose.* A statement of purpose encapsulating the preservation goals established for a program should be drafted at the outset. The statement of purpose should be clear, easily understood, and measurable. It will provide focus and help to set the tenor for discussions with legislative bodies, interest groups, the general public, and the media.

The statement of purpose communicates the vision for an urban land preservation program: its vitality and vibrancy will help to rally the support needed for the program's adoption and success. It can help or hinder the program from its earliest stages of development to the end of its implementation. For example, early polling conducted for an urban lands preservation program in Los Angeles County indicated that crime was a major issue for the region's voters. From the outset of the design stage, a statement of purpose was developed that emphasized that the program would provide safe open spaces for the enjoyment of families and seniors. This statement was included in virtually all the public information documents and campaign literature of this successful program.

4. *Identify the Funding Source.* While the majority of urban land preservation efforts depend on voter-approved financing, the precise legislative authority for the proposed funding can vary and may profoundly influence the character of the program. It can determine the potential level of funding available, the majority vote percentage needed for adoption, the kinds and location of the land acquired, and the use and stewardship of the preserved sites. In addition to voter-approved local bonds based on a local property tax, funding sources for urban land preservation programs across the United States have included revenues from a local sales tax, real estate excise tax, and business and occupation tax. Special taxing districts also have been considered, from the standard park and recreation districts available in many states to an imaginative use of diking districts that has been explored in Texas. The advantages and disadvantages of each potential funding source depend on state and local law and are beyond the scope of this general discussion. It is imperative, however, that a detailed review and insightful analyses of all potential revenue sources are conducted at the outset of the development of an urban land preservation program.

5. *Determine the Size of the Urban Land Preservation Program.* The size of the program will depend on the tax rate and base supporting it. Urban land preservation programs are critical and timely and can be presented to the public in a compelling adoption campaign. But they also must compete with many other important needs for limited tax revenues. As an admittedly unscientific but understandable rule of thumb, regardless of the source of the tax, the public generally is willing to support preservation programs that cost about a couple of pizzas a year for the average taxpayer. Looking at land preservation programs from around the nation, they range in cost to the average homeowner or taxpayer from less than $10 a year for a regionwide preservation program to more than $50 for a program proposed for an affluent urban center.

A frequent practice for preservation programs that are going to be submitted to voters is to set the proposed funding level based on the results of an early opinion poll. Polls can be powerful tools assisting in the formation of a successful preservation measure, but their results must be interpreted with care. Polling can enhance the process, but does not replace personal knowledge and judgment of the local electorate and experience with campaigning for land preservation programs. Poll results should be scrutinized and the proposed program funding level determined with advice from experts who have conducted ballot campaigns and know the local electorate.

The only poll that really counts is the election day vote. Generally, at least a 10 percent margin should exist between the voter support evidenced in an early poll (for a particular dollar amount) and the majority percentage needed for passage. To allow less is to invite a second trip to the ballot box. It is easy for poll respondents to agree to a proposal months before the actual vote, but as election day approaches and voters seriously confront the possibility of a new tax, invariably some of the early support will melt away. A recent ballot measure in Kitsap County, Washington, was set for $75 million, costing the average taxpayer about $48 yearly, an amount which an early poll indicated would just receive the necessary 60 percent supermajority. After a nearly flawless citizen bond development effort and a strong election campaign, the issue lost by several points. Many observers attributed the loss to a failure to discount early poll returns sufficiently to account for the election day approval slump.

Phase 2. *Developing the Contents of the Preservation Program*

After the initial concept for the urban land preservation program has been established and determined to be politically viable, the very crucial work should be undertaken to detail its design and operating mechanisms. This second phase of developing a program should be deliberate, thorough, and rational, with a broad and diverse public invited to participate.

1. *Establish a Citizen Urban Preservation Program Drafting Committee.* The building of broad consensus for an urban land preservation ballot measure which began at the conceptual phase should be significantly expanded in the actual design phase. Passage not only requires building a better mousetrap, but also making everyone feel they had a say in its design. A straightforward means of developing the required broad-based support for an urban land preservation program is to create a citizen-led ballot drafting committee.

The membership of the ballot drafting committee should be carefully considered and well balanced. The committee should include corporate, environmental, parks, neighborhood, civic, and university representation. Its membership should strike a good regional balance across the urban area to be included in the ballot measure. This group can effectively either co-opt or disarm otherwise potential credible opposition and can be used to make the case for the ballot measure to virtually all interest groups and constituencies necessary for ultimate ratification.

2. *Draft the Selection Criteria and Procedure.* This step is a make-or-break element in the development of an urban lands preservation program. The selection criteria and procedure may be employed to identify the properties prior to the campaign for adoption of the program; on the other hand, some programs present the goals of the program and the proposed selection criteria and procedure but wait to apply them until after funding has been obtained. Either system can work, and there are tradeoffs for each.

For instance, identifying properties prior to the ballot stage increases the confidence of voters or legislative decision makers that the program will acquire the kinds of properties intended. However, early identification can make price negotiations difficult and limit the ability of the program to respond to later preservation opportunities. Identifying properties after funding is achieved maximizes a program's ability to respond to changing conditions. But it is far more difficult to promote a program to a constituency that is not sure of the exact properties that will be acquired. A potentially successful marriage of these two approaches is a program that identifies the "anchor" parcels prior to the campaign for adoption while reserving a sizable share of the proposed funding for an opportunity fund, to be administered according to strict selection criteria and process that are also part of the ballot measure presented to the voters.

Whether properties are identified before or after the program has been approved by the voters, it is of paramount importance that the selection criteria crisply define the types of properties eligible, and that the selection procedure is broad based, fair, and includes citizen input. The selection of the specific properties invariably is scrutinized by the media and public. Proponents of properties that were not chosen should be satisfied that their property was fairly considered.

The selection criteria should not be overly complicated. They should be useful, balanced, and reflect the priorities of the community. They should also advance important programmatic considerations, such as balancing geographical distribution of the preserved property, acquiring property offered below fair market value, and, most important, creating a true system of urban lands where preserved parcels make up an "ecological whole" greater than the sum of its parts.

Well-drafted materials help a program weather the hard decisions and resulting media and political storms. For instance, a private racetrack was proposed for preservation during King County's early stages of implementing its farmland preservation program. The proposal was not as farfetched as it may sound now, over a decade later. The property was attractive open space in a rapidly urbanizing area of the county. Because of the clearly written selection criteria and evaluation procedure, the program was able to reject the property and explain the action to the supporting elected officials, media, and public. Without the criteria, the program could have become mired in a controversial property acquisition that would have interfered with its efforts to preserve the best and most threatened farmland in the county.

3. *Provide an Extensive Public Involvement Process.* An urban land preservation program must reflect the values of the electorate. The best way to achieve that goal is to subject the program's development to an extensive public review.

A citizen drafting committee is critical to the design of a program and to the development of the required support. By itself, however, it is not a substitute for an extensive, well-managed, public process which underscores citizen interest in the ballot measure, achieves community consensus on its contents, and identifies and activates important constituencies. The drafting committee must conduct a dialogue with a much broader public. A variety of legitimate methods can be used to accomplish this outreach. Citizen drafting committees in King County relied on rather formal hearings, and in Kitsap County successfully sponsored dozens of small community meetings where people covered maps with sticky dots placed over their favorite sites.

Whatever public involvement process is selected must clearly present the goals of the measure and effectively solicit citizen input. All facets of a program's design should be reviewed with the public, including its goals, potential level of funding, selection criteria and process, and the planned stewardship and recreational uses for the preserved properties. The ultimate design of the urban land preservation program must demonstrate on its face that the input of the affected citizens was seriously considered by the ballot drafters and has been amply reflected in the measure.

While polling can provide important information about the interests and views of a community, it can never replace a well-managed public involvement process. The 1988 attempt by King County to develop an open space preservation program did not include extensive public involvement. It relied on opinion polling which indicated strong citizen interest in preserving major regional parcels. After the program failed at the ballot box, a second attempt in 1989 was led by a citizen drafting committee that held extensive hearings reaching virtually all the communities in the county. The number of high quality neighborhood open space properties that were identified by local residents overwhelmed the drafting committee. In the 1989 ballot measure many of these neighborhood properties were included along with the major regional sites that had been included in the 1988 proposal. The proponents of the neighborhood properties were among the most ardent and energetic campaign volunteers in 1989, and the measure won handily. An important lesson was learned: like politics, open space is local. A poll respondent may urge the preservation of those regional open space "gems." But, when it comes to actually voting on a program, citizens want to know what will be protected close to home. This lesson may never have been learned if King County had relied on polling instead of greatly benefiting from a public involvement process.

4. *Development of a Land Preservation Measure Must Avoid Controversy.* Whether the program will be approved by voters or a legislative body, consensus is paramount. Voters typically refuse to invest in a measure surrounded by debate. Controversy may be the mother lode of candidate campaigns, but it should be stringently avoided during the development and campaign for an urban land preservation program. Any dissent from a credible source may prompt even a previous supporter to vote no and avoid risking his or her limited tax dollars on a program that is being questioned. Good measures have failed when there was credible opposition, even though the proponents otherwise did everything correctly. Measures also have weathered opposition in those instances where a broad citizen coalition has been used to develop the urban land preservation program and the controversy has been demonstrated to be from a narrow, self-interested, or irresponsible opposition.

5. *The Program Must Ensure Credibility.* The old adage still counts: "It's not what's said but who says it." As an urban land preservation measure is developed, the consensus

and support of a broad array of opinion leaders should be obtained, including: civic groups (League of Women Voters, City Club, chambers of commerce, etc.); mainstream interest groups (realtor associations, Audubon Society, Volksmarchers, garden clubs, etc.); elected officials; neighborhood and community councils; and major campaign donors (corporate, interest group, and private parties).

Supporters of this nature certainly will influence a legislature that must pass on a proposal, and they are even more important when it comes to a ballot measure. Since these measures are generally unavoidably complex and lengthy, many voters do not have the time or background to come to terms with the details and therefore rely on the recommendations of recognized opinion leaders.

While acclaim or disgrace often is the reward or risk for the leadership of an adoption campaign, land preservation ballot measures largely are won or lost during the design of the program. Programs that reflect the values of the community, developed with responsible citizen leadership and built on consensus rather than controversy, generally are met with favor by the voters.

The 1988 King County proposed open space program ballot measure purportedly responded to the strong interests of its citizens to preserve remaining open spaces. However, a sizable percentage of the money it would raise, about 30 percent, was to be dedicated to the restoration of the region's aquarium, a worthwhile but inconsistent element. The measure was not developed with citizen input and there was considerable controversy about its design and the subsequent campaign. While the campaign was well funded with corporate contributions, the measure lost by nine points. In 1989, an open space measure again was placed on the ballot, this time without controversy after it was designed and led by a citizen committee that benefited from considerable public involvement. Several factors that may have seemed to weigh against passage of the second measure actually indicated its strength and likelihood of success. While it was over 33 percent larger than the 1988 measure, it was solely dedicated to addressing the open space losses in the county. The campaign for its passage relied on roughly 50 percent of the 1988 campaign budget, largely due to the fall of corporate support, but the measure enjoyed great community consensus and strong grass-roots support. It passed well above the 60 percent supermajority requirement, receiving a 67 percent majority. With the same campaign manager in both instances—yours truly—this example well illustrates the importance of the right design of an urban land preservation measure over any later campaign wizardry.

Adoption or Passage of the Proposed Program

A manual can be written on designing and implementing a campaign for adoption or passage of an urban land preservation program. Again, the most important element is developing the ballot measure. Several campaign objectives are worth mentioning in this short paper: (1) Design and stick to a campaign strategy based on good research and knowledge of the community. Do not allow the campaign to be constantly whipsawed by inconsequential comments or criticisms. (2) Select a campaign theme or message based on sound research. It must be true and promote the positive results of passage and not just the dire consequences if the measure fails. (3) Make sure that various media are used effectively to get the message to the constituencies the campaign needs to "swing" over to voting yes. (4) Avoid controversies. Remember: People won't commit tax dollars to controversial programs. (5) Work to encourage favorable press attention and strong editorial support. (Don't forget weekly and "shopper" publications. Seniors—a guaranteed swing constituency—read them.) Build on the receptivity of the press to precampaign development of the ballot measure. (6) Sustain a good fund-raising effort and do not incur debt above certain, firm pledges. Unlike candidate races, even a successful ballot measure has difficulty raising dollars after election day. (7) Continue building strong support of civic, interest, and community groups for the ballot measure.

Implementation of the Program

If a program is well designed, its implementation, though arduous, will be far from impossible. Critical issues will remain, however, regardless of the quality of the program's design. The major ones are property selection, determining property values, and speed of implementation.

- *Property Selection.* Selecting the property for preservation is always a sensitive issue. Neighbors, elected decision makers, and interest groups all have their most favored properties, which may not perfectly fit the mission of the program. This issue is certainly less pressing, but by no means avoided, for programs that identify the targeted property prior to voter or legislative approval. Invariably there will be some initial properties that fall by the wayside for which substitutes must be found. In any event, the selection of property is manageable where it is done strictly according to the adopted selection criteria and procedure, with the advice or oversight of a citizen committee, and through a public process that is obviously fair to the many interested observers. There is even less possibility of difficulty where a crisp statement of purpose or vision of the system that is to be preserved has been maintained throughout the design and early implementation of the program.

- *Determining Property Values.* Government acquisition in virtually all jurisdictions is a complex, regulated process with only modest room for negotiation of price on behalf of the taxpayers. A negotiator or adviser experienced in public acquisition is a must to avoid inadvertently clashing with the various regulations and to maximize the buying power of public dollars. While it is possible to create a climate favorable for obtaining a good purchase price on behalf of the public, a program must balance between the often optimistic expectations of landowners and the market value of their property. There also is a need to balance between the voters' sometimes conflicting interests in preserving the urban forest base and not short-changing their neighbors who own the targeted property. During the property negotiations, the public and media will want to make sure the "little guy" is getting a fair shake.

- *Speed of Implementation.* Particularly after the election for a voter-approved urban preservation program, the public will expect rapid action to acquire the targeted land. This anticipation will be moderated if the proponents initially set realistic preservation goals, but the dynamics of a campaign are such that expectations for immediate action will be unavoidably heightened. Consequently, a staffing and implementation plan should be prepared prior to the approved date of funding authorization, and a realistic project time schedule should be publicly presented soon after the funding is authorized. Several major purchases early in the program can provide the breathing room to complete the rest of the acquisition schedule. Through option agreements, these early purchases can be secured in advance of funding authorization. Care should be taken throughout the program, however, to ensure that all transactions are well scrutinized and professionally executed. A sloppy transaction will receive far more media attention and remain in the public's mind far longer than any expeditiously completed effort. Its lasting impression also will severely encumber subsequent efforts to preserve additional lands. A program's administration has the difficult task of moving rapidly but without major error.

Stewardship of the Preserved Properties

Acquisition of the urban forest land base is the beginning of a critical responsibility. The preserved property must be carefully maintained in order to be an ecologically, aesthetically, and recreationally significant element of the urban landscape. The extent to which public access is allowed or facilitated must be balanced against the ecological frailty of the property. In any event, appropriate channeled access should always be considered so that:

- The environmental significance for the preservation effort can be appreciated.
- The demand to create unofficial access that may otherwise occur is minimized.
- The surrounding community's sense of "ownership" and consequently respect for the protected property and the larger program goals are maximized.

The chapter by Springgate and Hoesterey in this volume highlights an innovative public stewardship program by a local government in the Pacific Northwest.

CONCLUSION

Campaigns around the nation indicate that voters are willing to pay for urban land preservation programs. The ballot measure, however, must be cost-effective and address a real concern of the community. The positive changes that the program will produce must be readily apparent to the taxpayer, and implementation must significantly advance the preservation of the urban forest.

Urban land preservation seems to be a game of inches, rather than miles. (Or is that square inches, rather than square miles?) A broad mix of techniques and revenue sources generally must be pursued in order to provide a first-rate land preservation program. Frequently programs are most successful when they are developed collaboratively between the local government, preservation organizations, and general citizens. The reward of a successful program is the permanent preservation of a city's lands most important to the vitality of its urban forest.

8

The Role Economics Can Play as an Analytical Tool in Urban Forestry

JOHN F. DWYER

ABSTRACT Many benefits and costs related to the urban forest can be expressed in economic terms, but their importance varies significantly over the country and as applied to the specific management options and urban forest environments being considered. This paper suggests expanding the use of economics beyond program justification to guidance for improved programs that enhance the contribution of urban trees and forests to the well-being of urbanites. It also suggests methods for integrating economics with information on how changes in the forest environment influence a wide range of forest uses and values. Consideration of perspectives from other social sciences is also recommended.

Supporters of urban forestry programs often advocate that values be expressed in monetary terms, especially to get the attention of decision makers and provide a common denominator for comparing benefits and costs. Foresters and others working with urban forests sometimes feel that dollar values help them make a better case for their programs.

As a forestry economist working in urban forestry, I am often asked how much an urban tree or forest is worth. I usually respond with a series of questions such as: To whom? For what? Under what circumstances? By asking these questions I am trying to convey that the value of urban trees and forests, like any other good or service, depends on the circumstances. In fact, what is a benefit in one instance may be a cost in another. A heavily shaded yard might be highly valued by someone who likes to sit outside on hot summer days, but it might be cursed by a would-be vegetable gardener. I then proceed with another set of questions to establish the framework for discussion of the values that are being sought: What management or policy questions do you want to address? What choices or options do you want to evaluate? What do you want to provide for people? My purpose is to focus attention on the right question. There is an old adage: "A question well defined is half solved."

The heightened interest in dollar values may reflect greater appreciation for the urban forest and its significance to people. Nonetheless, I have some misgivings about this emphasis. First, I am not convinced that dollar values necessarily occupy a dominant position among the considerations for public decisions, and a broader perspective on benefits and values is called for. Second, I do not think that we have focused on the right issues. Finally, I do not believe we are making the most effective use of economic science as an analytical tool to guide efforts to enhance the contribution of urban trees and forests to people.

ACKNOWLEDGING MULTIPLE PERSPECTIVES AND VALUES

Public decision making is complex. Economic efficiency is an important aspect of this process when it concerns urban forestry, but so too are criteria including environmental quality, social well-being, regional development, and a host of others that are weighed in the administrative-political arena. Although estimates of the monetary value of urban trees and forests have helped sustain programs or secure additional funding for urban forestry, in the administrative-political arena it is often difficult to identify what actually influenced public policy decisions. Because the details are not always clear, research should carefully evaluate the role that economic values and other considerations had in key urban forest public policy decisions. Until such an evaluation is made, I am reluctant to conclude that establishing "dollar values for trees and forests" is, in itself, the most effective way to maintain or expand urban forestry programs. During the difficult times being experienced by many urban forestry programs, it would seem appropriate to extend the discussion of the wide-ranging social implications of urban forestry rather than narrow it to those considerations that can be expressed in dollars.

Urban foresters competing with other needed services for available funds sometimes question the wisdom of selling their programs by casting their worth in dollar terms. One such forester in a large city realized that this kind of approach could put his program in the untenable position of competing with a police department that was forced to place a dollar value on a police officer's life in order to receive funding to add an officer to each patrol car, for safety reasons. Along similar lines, officials concerned with upgrading urban wastewater systems might support their proposals with impressive estimates of the possible expenses incurred by homeowners if their sewers backed up into their basements.

Another problem in quantifying a portion of the benefits in dollars is that it can focus attention on aspects that are easily quantifiable at the expense of those that are not, thereby leading to narrowly based decision making. Recent debates over the management and use of public forests are full of examples of the public's unwillingness to accept management programs based on decisions that focused on easily quantifiable benefits such as the sale of wood, or of management that did not look at the interaction of all components of the forest over time and space (i.e., ignored the ecology of the landscape). Urbanites seem even less tolerant of narrowly based urban forest management programs, because these forests greatly influence their lives as the places where they live, work, and spend a large portion of their leisure time. An ecosystem management approach that emphasizes the many interactions between people and the urban forest is critical here, and dollar values provide only partial guidance for that approach.

Some seem to feel that expressing benefits in dollars moves decision making from "emotional" to "rational" arguments. But public decision making often involves emotions. The environmental psychologist Roger Ulrich recently quoted a Swedish public official as saying, "Data without emotion are dust to politicians." Emotional attachment to trees and forests most likely is a very important component of public support for urban forestry programs (Dwyer et al. 1991; Hull 1992). In fact, the emotional attachment may be an important advantage for urban forestry programs.

The values that the public places on urban trees and forests are often much broader than those ordinarily considered by foresters and other tree professionals. The general public and volunteers who work with trees tend to emphasize aesthetics, proximity to nature, and symbolic and spiritual values more than most professionals do (Schroeder and Ruffolo 1993; Westphal 1993). Many of these benefits and costs are best viewed from the perspectives of psychology, physiology, sociology, anthropology, and other sciences.

I have heard that Chicago's former Mayor Jane Byrne, who wanted Chicago to be thought of as an "international city," was persuaded to restore some of the cuts in the urban forestry budget when it was pointed out to her that international cities such as Paris were well known for their tree-lined streets. Chicago's present Mayor Richard M. Daley is a strong supporter of tree planting, particularly in inner-city areas and around schools.

The usefulness of economics, like any science, depends on the issues being addressed. Dollar values are likely to be relatively more useful in addressing some issues than others.

WHAT ARE THE KEY ISSUES?

Our efforts to enhance urban forestry programs have not always focused on the critical issues. Three instances where we need to reevaluate our focus are presented below.

Program Improvement Versus Promotion

It is much easier to build support for programs that are highly effective. In marketing they talk about getting "market ready" before promoting a product or service. This involves being certain that you have the best possible product or service to sell before beginning a sales campaign. There is a lesson here for urban forestry. Economics can play an important role in helping to make our programs more effective, and this is the first step toward maintaining and enhancing those programs. Economic values can tell us a great deal about people's preferences for urban environments and forestry programs, and how much they are willing to give up in order to have particular goods and services. This can be useful guidance for program development. In the long run, the role of enhancing program guidance and improvement is a far more useful one for economics to play than trying to support existing programs. A "proactive" approach is far more effective than "reactive" efforts. If economic efficiency is an important consideration, why not develop a program that is economically efficient rather than attaching dollar values to existing programs to try and make them look impressive?

In this context I am reminded of a conversation with an engineer whose work had included designing forest facilities. At one time it was common practice to design a facility and then ask landscape architects to "shrub it up" to improve its appearance. This was not the most effective use of those landscape architects, and perhaps they should have been involved in the design of the facility as well. The same goes for economists who are called in to make programs "look good" after they have been developed. Economists would often like to contribute to the design of those programs so that they would more effectively meet people's needs. This would go a long way toward "selling" or "promoting" the programs.

Tree Planting Versus Management

We need to look carefully at past efforts to build support for urban forestry programs. Research and advocacy efforts have established that urban trees and forests are valuable, and they have helped generate strong support for urban tree planting. But they have been far less effective in generating support for management of existing trees (even the newly planted ones) or for carefully designed planting and preservation efforts. Management of valuable urban trees and forests is not receiving sufficient attention, and this troubles me as a forester and taxpayer.

I think that I can summarize the thought process that guides a number of municipal programs with which I am familiar: "Trees are valuable. We have a lot of them. When one dies we cut it down and replace it promptly. If people complain about insects, we spray." This approach places little emphasis on key aspects of urban forest management such as species selection, landscape configurations, maintenance, and long-term health of the urban forest. Since many decision makers are apparently unaware of what difference these management and planning activities make to the future of urban trees and forests and the benefits they provide, these activities are seen as unimportant and receive minimal funding.

Part of the problem is that a substantial portion of the work on benefits estimation has been reported in generalities such as the average value of a tree or the total value of the urban forest. There is little information on how the value of a tree or forest is likely to change under different management regimes, hence there are few specific guides for on-the-ground management to enhance the value of the urban forest. It is those on-the-ground recommendations that can increase the benefits to customers/constituents and increase program support. In the long run, satisfied people are the most important form of support for any program.

To estimate changes in values associated with the management of urban trees and forests, we need to address questions concerning the interactions between people and urban trees and forests. How does the forest environment affect values? How does management affect the forest environment? What motivates owners and managers to change the urban forest environment? What difference will urban forest management make to the well-being of urbanites? These are the questions that will tie values to management options and answer the critical questions at the root of the debates concerning the value of management. Fundamental to these questions is the concept of a production function which describes how the attributes of the forest environment interact to provide a particular service from the urban forest. This function links management to benefits that are provided.

There are some encouraging examples of beginning efforts to address these questions of how values change with forest conditions. There are models to predict the scenic beauty of an urban street corridor on the basis of the attributes of trees and other forest resources, as well as other elements along that corridor (Buhyoff et al. 1984; Lien and Buhyoff 1986; Schroeder and Cannon 1983, 1987; Schroeder 1989). We have models to predict the quality of trail corridors based on their attributes (Wiberg-Carlson and Schroeder 1992; Westphal and Lieber 1986). There are models that predict the scenic quality of urban parks on the basis of trees and other resources (Schroeder and Anderson 1984; Schroeder and Green 1985; Schroeder 1986, 1988), as well as other models that predict how changes in the attributes of trees, forests, and other resources will influence individuals' choices among urban parks, as well as their willingness to pay for the use of those resources (Dwyer et al. 1989; Schroeder et al. 1990). There are also guidelines for landscaping homes with trees to achieve energy savings (Akbari et al. 1992; Heisler 1986; McPherson and Rowntree 1993).

But to provide guidance for efforts to enhance the contribution that urban trees and forests make to people we still need more of these models and to extend them to a wider range of urban forest benefits such as human health, well-being, and restoration (Hull and Ulrich 1992).

Much of the discussion in this paper has been directed toward helping managers and planners take a more comprehensive view of urban forest management that reflects the values of all the people they serve. There is also a need to provide individuals with information on the benefits and costs of urban forests so that they can make intelligent choices concerning the management of their own resources and help shape public programs. The information provided to the public should outline the full range of management inputs and outcomes of the options available to them.

Economic Versus Financial Goals

The classic benefit-cost analysis for public goods and services considers all benefits and costs regardless of to whom they accrue or whether dollars actually change hands. Benefits are measured by the willingness of users to pay for goods and services, and costs are measured as compensation required for losses. The basic test of benefit-cost analysis is whether the benefits received by those who gain are enough to compensate those who lose, and still produce a surplus—a net benefit. This surplus is taken as an indication of the increase in national economic development as a result of undertaking the option, and a proxy for improved social well-being (Dwyer and Bowes 1979).

When fees are not collected for goods and services provided by the urban forest, there are no payments or cash flow. This is the case with a large portion of the benefits of urban trees and forests. Fees are not ordinarily charged for the use of forested urban parks, to drive along forested lanes, or to look out over a well-forested city. Hence there is often a significant difference between benefits generated and actual cash flows.

In a few notable exceptions, dollars reflecting the value of urban trees and forests are actually exchanged. Some homeowners receive additional revenue from the sale of their home if the lot is well forested. Communities can receive an actual cash flow in the form of increased property taxes if the value of the trees is reflected in the real estate assessment. Homeowners may receive energy savings if their landscapes reduce the cost of summer cooling or winter heating. Urban residents may achieve a savings in expenditures for travel if they are able to use local parks for outings rather than drive to more distant areas. If trees contribute to the control of runoff and that is reflected in stormwater management programs, municipalities or other groups may be able to achieve savings in stormwater management costs.

Who in local government receives particular benefits and incurs costs usually depends on the structure of municipal government. In many instances, the actual flow of dollars to the group making the investment may be much lower than the estimated total benefits. Many of the benefits that municipalities receive from urban forestry programs are in future savings rather than an immediate payment of dollars to the municipality. This may be a critical concern for cash-strapped municipalities that find it difficult to make investments whose returns are in the future or accrue to other units of government.

Cash flows are a serious problem for many municipalities, and one of the reasons expenditures are not made for maintaining and improving the urban infrastructure (including the trees). Thus in the analysis of urban forest management options it is essential that the distinction between benefits and cash flows be made, and the likely recipients and timing of expected cash flows should be identified.

Economics is certainly not the only science that can be helpful in designing programs that meet people's needs. There are many examples where various physical, biological, and social sciences have produced guidelines that can make substantial improvements in urban forestry programs. Still, economics offers a number of ideas and perspectives that can be helpful in urban forest planning and management. These are discussed below.

ECONOMICS AS AN ANALYTICAL TOOL

In addition to defining the right issues, it is important to make the most effective use of economic concepts in efforts to enhance the contribution of urban trees and forests to the well-being of urbanites. It is probably most useful to think of economics as an analytical tool that can help guide public decisions.

Marginal Analysis

Marginal analysis is the sort of analytical tool that can help deal with some of the current issues facing municipal forestry programs. It is often said that funding for urban forestry is cut rather than police protection since police are more important than urban forestry. This is a case where we must carefully define the question. If the question is whether to eliminate either police or urban forestry, then the appropriate consideration is the relative importance of these two programs to the people who are to be served. I think that in most instances, given that choice, the decision would be to keep police and eliminate urban forestry. However, that is seldom the question facing the municipality.

The issue is most often the relative merits of changes in the funding for various municipal functions. In these instances, the critical consideration is the effectiveness of increments in the budgets for each of these activities. If the choice is between putting an additional police officer on the night patrol or shortening the trimming cycle for street trees, then the decision focuses on the expected outcome of each of these investments and not on the total programs. If there are already many police officers on night patrol, it might be that adding another would contribute little to public safety. And if the trimming cycle for street trees is already quite long, further lengthening might mean serious consequences in subsequent storm damage. While it might be difficult to estimate the benefits of a change in the trimming cycle in dollars, perhaps it would be just as difficult to quantify the benefits of increased public safety and security and reduced property loss associated with the addition of another police officer on the night shift.

Marginal analysis is a key concept that can be applied to a number of decisions in urban forest planning and management. For example, what are the changes in benefits and costs associated with changing the size of trees planted, spacing of trees, or the level of pest management? For a discussion of marginal analysis of urban forest pest management see Dwyer (1982).

Tradeoffs and Production Functions

Analyses of tradeoffs among urban forest benefits have been largely ignored. Given that most benefits are strongly influenced by the location of trees with respect to other resources, and the forest designs required to maximize particular benefits appear to be quite different, efforts to enhance one benefit are likely to result in a decrease in others. For example, landscaping a home for optimal summer cooling may increase the risk of damage from storms and wildfire. Landscaping an urban park for aesthetics may conflict with perceived personal safety (Schroeder and Anderson 1984).

Managing the urban forest for multiple benefits involves a complicated evaluation of tradeoffs, and the value of the resulting benefits may differ substantially from the sum total of the benefits estimated as if each would be derived under optimal conditions. Economists often look at the problem by (1) identifying the different outputs possible with a given input of resources (i.e., the production possibilities), and (2) selecting the combination of outputs that generates the highest value. The analysis focuses on how much of one output must be given up to gain more of another, and it attempts to evaluate these tradeoffs in terms of the relative values of the outputs involved.

The Full Range of Benefits and Costs

Urban forests are complex and provide a wide range of benefits. If we are going to make better choices concerning their management, we need to focus on the important benefits or outcomes of that management. To consider the full range of benefits we must look broadly at the implications of urban forest environments and their management for people. I find that many of the efforts to generate dollar values to provide support for urban forestry fail when they focus on a single easily quantified economic value or outcome—such as increases in property values or energy savings. There seems to be a tendency to overstate these easily estimated benefits in order to justify the program. Under close scrutiny such overestimates may be questioned, and the result is an erosion in support. This can be disastrous if the program is being advocated primarily on the basis of economic efficiency.

We need to look at urban forest benefits across the entire urban environment. For example, we sometimes look at the contribution that trees on a residential lot make to the value of that lot but do not identify the contribution of the entire urban forest throughout the city to the value of a home in that city. The same can be said of the contribution of a particular area of wildlife habitat to wildlife populations across the entire urban area and perhaps the corridors beyond. In Chicago we are currently identifying the role of urban trees and forests throughout the urban environment in moderating urban heat islands, an example of the broader scope that is needed (Nowak and McPherson 1993). For a discussion of the range of benefits that can be provided by the urban forest, see Dwyer et al. (1992).

Estimating Nonmarket Benefits

If dollar values for the wide range of services provided by the urban forest are desired, they can be estimated by a variety of means. All public and private decisions imply values, and we can infer those values from the behavior of individuals and groups. For example, looking at the site choices of individuals engaged in outdoor recreation or their responses to choices between possible sites can help to identify the value of particular sites and the attributes of those sites (Dwyer et al. 1983, 1989; Schroeder et al. 1990).

Looking at the prices paid for a wide range of homes can help infer the value of particular attributes of the landscapes around those homes or in nearby areas (Anderson and Cordell 1985, 1988; Corrill et al. 1978; More et al. 1988; Hammer et al. 1974; Hagerty et al. 1982; Kitchen and Hendon 1967; Weicher and Zerbst 1973; Morales et al. 1976; Payne 1973; Payne and Strom 1975). If actual behavior cannot be observed, then hypothetical choice options can be presented to subjects in carefully controlled experiments and their choices analyzed to develop estimates of value (Dwyer et al. 1989).

Distribution of Benefits and Costs

Economists also give significant attention to who receives benefits or incurs costs and when that takes place. The concern is with the fairness or equity of that distribution. Are some groups incurring an inordinate share of the costs compared to the benefits they receive? Appleyard (1980) identified equity as an important issue in the future of urban forestry.

The distribution of benefits and costs over time is also given significant attention. If benefits are received some time after costs are incurred, there is an additional cost of tying up resources in the effort (interest) that must be considered. This cost is determined by what those resources could be earning in their next most likely use. This cost can be very high for cash-strapped local governments, and in some instances cost reduction will be a prime goal of government decision making.

CAREFUL USE OF AVAILABLE INFORMATION

With the limited information on the economic values of urban trees and forests currently available to guide plans and programs, one must use this information carefully. Unfortunately, in the eagerness to have dollar values to support programs, the available information has often been used incorrectly. A common problem is ignoring the significant variation in values that can accompany differences in the spatial arrangement of the urban forest environment. Some examples of these problems include:

1. Using estimates of the energy savings from trees placed in optimal positions around a single-family suburban home to estimate the benefits of trees in other settings—including street trees in highly urbanized areas. Energy savings, like most other urban forest benefits, depend heavily on the location of trees and associated resources, which should be reflected in any estimates of value.

2. Applying the percentage increase that trees have been shown to make in the sale price of a vacant lot to a property with a home, thereby overinflating the contribution of trees to real estate values. For example, if an analysis indicates that trees in a certain configuration add 30 percent to the value of a vacant lot with no dwelling, it is not appropriate to apply that percentage increment to the price of a lot having the same configuration of trees and a dwelling. This would overstate the contribution of trees to the value of that property by 30 percent of the value of the dwelling.

3. Ignoring differences in urban forest benefits and the conditions that influence them around the country. It is important to recognize regional differences in lifestyles, customs, preferences, climate, and so forth. In northern climates, the potential savings in cooling costs from shade might be much smaller than in warmer southern climates. There are instances in northern areas where trees blocking the sun and reducing solar heating in winter will substantially increase heating bills.

4. Adding up several estimates of tree values without accounting for the fact that they may overlap and the same benefit may be counted more than once. This occurs most frequently with estimates of property values (which may reflect a wide range of benefits, from aesthetics to energy conservation), and the value generated by the Council of Tree and Landscape Appraisers' formula that may also include a wide range of benefits, including aesthetics, energy, and real estate values.

A common theme in these and other misapplications of dollar values in estimating the benefits of urban forestry seems to be one of focusing on a relatively narrow portion of the spectrum of benefits and then overestimating those benefits. There also appears to be considerable misunderstanding about the joint production of benefits as well as what benefits are captured in various estimates of value.

SUMMARY AND CONCLUSIONS

Considerable attention has been given to dollar values of urban trees and forests in efforts to document the significance of urban forestry and generate funding for urban forestry programs. While the usefulness of economics for these purposes may have been overemphasized, considering the multiple perspectives and values involved in public decision making, too little use has been made of economics as an analytical tool for improving urban forestry practices and programs.

If we focus on how the values of urban trees and forests change under alternative management regimes, useful guidance for urban forest management can be developed. These guidelines can lead to increased program effectiveness and a strengthening of public support for stronger programs. They will also help extend the focus of many urban forestry programs beyond tree planting and preservation to other aspects of urban forest management.

Marginal analysis can provide a useful framework for evaluating changes in urban forestry programs in context with other public programs. The key is to focus on the implications of changes in programs for the benefits provided to urbanites. The concept of marginal analysis can be expanded to a wide range of benefits and costs.

If dollar values for the services provided by the urban forest are desired, they can be generated using techniques developed for estimating the willingness of users to pay for environmental services. A significant challenge in that effort is to identify how changes in the forest environment influence the willingness of users to pay for the services provided by those environments.

Analysis of the tradeoffs in production of the various services provided by the urban forest can also offer valuable program guidance. If the combinations of possible outputs of various services at a given level of resources (i.e., production possibilities) can be defined, and values assigned to the outputs, then production can be directed toward the highest value combination of outputs. This analysis can be critical to the development of comprehensive programs, considering that quite different configurations of the urban forest are required to maximize production of each output, and important tradeoffs must be evaluated.

The distribution of benefits and costs over the population (i.e., equity) and over time (schedule of benefits and costs) can be an important consideration in public policy, as can the incidence of actual cash flows required or generated by urban forestry programs. Thus it is often critical that the incidence of benefits and costs be considered.

In view of the limited information on the dollar values of urban trees and forests currently available, particular care must be given in the use of this information to guide decisions. How were the values derived? How well might they fit a particular forest environment being considered? Are the findings appropriate for the issue being addressed?

It is not clear how much emphasis should be placed on dollar values for supporting urban forestry programs. Public decision making addresses many other considerations as well. There is usually no single "bottom line" for public decision making. And if there is a "bottom line" concerning urban forests it is the broad significance of urban trees and forest to people. Perhaps we can do better by listening to our customers/constituents and try to meet their needs rather than trying to impress them with large numbers or dollar values. It is important to consider multiple approaches and criteria for assessing public needs to improve urban forestry programs and increase support for those programs.

I think that the concepts and approaches of economic science can be helpful in addressing key questions and improving the management and use of our nation's urban trees and forests. I am less optimistic about the use of dollar values to establish the significance of urban forestry or shore up support for existing urban forestry and associated programs.

LITERATURE CITED

Akbari, H., S. Davis, S. Dorsano, J. Huang, and S. Winnett. 1992. Cooling our communities: A guidebook on tree planting and light-colored surfacing. U.S. Environmental Protection Agency, Washington, D.C.

Anderson, L.M., and H.K. Cordell. 1985. Residential property values improved by landscaping with trees. Southern Journal of Applied Forestry 9:162-166.

———. 1988. Influence of trees on residential property values: A survey based on actual sales prices. Landscape Planning 15:153-164.

Appleyard, D. 1980. Urban trees, urban forests: What do they mean? In G.S. Hopkins, ed., Proceedings of the National Urban Forestry Conference, November 13-16, 1978, Washington D.C., pp. 138-155. State University of New York College of Environmental Science and Forestry, Syracuse.

Buhyoff, G.J., L.J. Gauthier, and J.D. Wellman. 1984. Predicting scenic quality for urban forests using vegetation measurements. Forest Science 30(1):71-82.

Corrill, M., J. Lillydahl, and L. Single. 1978. The effects of greenbelts on residential property values: Some findings on the political economy of open space. Land Economics 54:207-217.

Dwyer, J.F. 1982. Urban tree and forest pest management: An economic perspective. In B.O. Parks, F.A. Fear, M.T. Lambur, and G.A. Simmons, eds., Proceedings Urban and Suburban Trees: Pest Problems, Needs, Prospects, and Solutions, April 18-20, 1992, pp. 139-143. Michigan State University, East Lansing.

———. 1992. Economic benefits and costs of urban forests. *In* P.D. Rodbell, ed., Proceedings of the Fifth National Urban Forestry Conference, November 15-19, 1991, Los Angeles, pp. 55-58. American Forestry Association, Washington, D.C.

Dwyer, J.F., and M.D. Bowes. 1979. Benefit-cost analysis for appraisal of recreation alternatives. Journal of Forestry 77:145-147.

Dwyer, J.F., E.F. McPherson, H.W. Schroeder, and R.A. Rowntree. 1992. Assessing the benefits and costs of the urban forest. Journal of Arboriculture 18(5):227-234.

Dwyer, J.F., G.L. Peterson, and A.J. Darragh. 1983. Estimating the value of urban trees and forests using the travel cost method. Journal of Arboriculture 9:182-195.

Dwyer, J.F., H.W. Schroeder, and P.H. Gobster. 1991. The significance of urban trees and forests: Toward a deeper understanding of values. Journal of Arboriculture 17:276-284.

Dwyer, J.F., H.W. Schroeder, J.J. Louviere, and D.H. Anderson. 1989. Urbanites' willingness to pay for trees and forests in recreation areas. Journal of Arboriculture 15:247-252.

Hagerty, J., T. Stevens, P. Allen, and T. More. 1982. Benefits from urban open space and recreational parks: A case study. Journal of Northeastern Agricultural Economics Council 11:13-20.

Hammer, T.T., R. Coughlin, and E. Horn. 1974. The effect of a large urban park on real estate value. Journal of American Institute of Planners, July, 1274-1277.

Heisler, G. 1986. Energy savings with trees. Journal of Arboriculture 12(5):113-125.

Hull, R.B. IV. 1992. How the public values urban forests. Journal of Arboriculture 18(2):89-101.

Hull, R.B. IV, and R.S. Ulrich. 1992. Health benefits and costs of urban trees. *In* P.D. Rodbell, ed., Proceedings of the Fifth National Urban Forestry Conference, November 15-19, 1991, Los Angeles, pp. 69-72. American Forestry Association, Washington, D.C.

Kitchen, J., and W. Hendon. 1967. Land values adjacent to an urban park. Land Economics 34:357-360.

Lien, J.N., and G.J. Buhyoff. 1986. Extension of visual quality models for urban forests. Journal of Environmental Management 22(3):245-254.

McPherson, E.G., and R.A. Rowntree. 1993. Energy conservation potential of urban tree planting. Journal of Arboriculture 19(6):321-331.

Morales, D., B.N. Bach, and R.J. Favretti. 1976. The contribution of trees to residential property value: Manchester, Connecticut. Valuation 23:26-43.

More, T.A., T. Stevens, and P.G. Allen. 1988. Valuation of urban parks. Landscape and Urban Planning 15:139-152.

Nowak, D.J., and E.G. McPherson. 1993. Quantifying the impact of trees: The Chicago Urban Forest Climate Project. Unasylva 44:39-44.

Payne, B.R. 1973. The twenty-nine tree home improvement plan. Natural History 82:74-75.

Payne, B.R., and S. Strom. 1975. The contribution of trees to the appraised value of unimproved residential land. Valuation 22:36-45.

Schroeder, H.W. 1986. Estimating park tree density to maximize landscape aesthetics. Journal of Environmental Management 23:325-333.

——. 1988. Perceived quality of urban parks and forests. Trends 25(3):18-20.

——. 1989. Environment, behavior, and design research on urban forests. *In* E.H. Zube and G.T. Moore, eds., Advances in environment, behavior, and design, pp. 87-107. Plenum, New York.

Schroeder, H.W., and L.M. Anderson. 1984. Perception of personal safety in urban recreation sites. Journal of Leisure Research 16:178-194.

Schroeder, H.W., and W.N. Cannon, Jr. 1983. The esthetic contribution of trees to residential streets in Ohio towns. Journal of Arboriculture 9(9):237-243.

——. 1987. Visual quality of residential streets: Both street and yard trees make a difference. Journal of Arboriculture 13(10):236-239.

Schroeder, H.W., J.F. Dwyer, J.J. Louviere, and D.H. Anderson. 1990. Monetary and non-monetary trade-offs of urban forest site attributes in a logit model of recreation choice. *In* B.L. Driver and G.L. Peterson, eds., Forest resource value and benefit measurement: Some cross-cultural perspectives, pp. 41-51. General Technical Report RM-197. USDA Forest Service Rocky Mountain Forest and Range Experiment Station, Fort Collins, Colorado.

Schroeder, H.W., and T.L. Green. 1985. Public preference for tree density in municipal parks. Journal of Arboriculture 11(9):272-277.

Schroeder, H.W., and S. Ruffolo. 1993. Householder's evaluations of street trees in suburban Chicago. *In* P.H. Gobster, ed., Managing urban and high use recreation settings, pp. 68-74. General Technical Report NC-163. USDA Forest Service North Central Forest Experiment Station, St. Paul, Minnesota.

Weicher, J., and R. Zerbst. 1973. The externalities of neighborhood parks: An empirical investigation. Land Economics 49:99-105.

Westphal, L.M. 1993. Why trees? Urban forestry volunteers values and motivations. *In* P.H. Gobster, ed., Managing urban and high use recreation settings, pp. 19-23. General Technical Report NC-163. USDA Forest Service North Central Forest Experiment Station, St. Paul, Minnesota.

Westphal, J.M., and S.R. Lieber. 1986. Predicting the effect of alternative trail designs on visitor satisfaction in park settings. Landscape Journal 5(1):39-44.

Wiberg-Carlson, D., and H.W. Schroeder. 1992. Modeling and mapping urban bicyclists preferences for trail environments. Research Paper NC-303. USDA Forest Service North Central Forest Experiment Station, St. Paul, Minnesota. 11 p.

9

The Urban Forest as a Source of Psychological Well-Being

STEPHEN KAPLAN

ABSTRACT That nature has a special role in improving people's lives has long been suspected but only recently documented. And the understanding of the way in which nature plays this role is more recent still. It turns out that an important component is nature's capacity to restore the mind and spirit—to allow one to recover from mental fatigue and to become once again comfortable, civil, and effective. The enormous importance of this restorative potential is perhaps best illustrated by what happens without it. Untreated mental fatigue leads to risky and impulsive action, to irritability and distractibility, and to a disinclination to reflect on the implications of one's actions. Urban forests have the great and not always realized potential to function as sorely needed restorative environments, thus making possible the management of this pervasive social and individual malady.

The belief that nature plays a special role in terms of its effects on the human mind is by no means of recent origin. Thoreau (1854), for example, showed remarkable insight into the impact of nature experiences on human well-being. Olmsted (1865), another astute observer of the human species, understood the need for fatigued urban dwellers to recover their capacity to focus in the context of nature; he showed this in his writings as well as in his design of parks.

Much as this humanistic insight is both thoughtful and profound, in some quarters it carries little weight. Unfortunately the impact of these poetic accounts has been largely restricted to the realm of arts and letters. In order for such insights to have an impact on land management, resource utilization, and other areas of policy and planning, a more scientific underpinning is required. While solid analysis, based on empirical support, is still in its infancy, considerable progress has been made in recent years.

Rachel Kaplan and I first became involved in this area when we were asked to look at the psychological effects of a community garden (R. Kaplan 1973). Subsequently we were asked to evaluate a wilderness program that was being supported by the Forest Service. This more or less accidental involvement led to our study of the Outdoor Challenge Program over a ten-year period (Kaplan and Kaplan 1989). Despite the many differences in age groups and contexts, the gardening and wilderness studies showed remarkable similarities in the capacity of a nature experience to have a healing effect.

WHAT DOES NATURE HEAL?

Generating empirical support and creating a useful analytic framework for understanding the psychological role that nature plays are clearly important goals. An essential first step is to determine what it is that nature heals. The belief that nature does indeed heal has many adherents; without a more focused understanding, however, progress in research and theory is seriously hampered. Perhaps a useful beginning would be to examine this issue intuitively. If we could identify what it is that leads people to seek a break, a vacation, or a little time outdoors, it may be easier to understand what nature heals.

Koch's (1956) description of two of his colleagues provides some useful imagery for our topic. Both colleagues were faced with a pile of student papers to grade. One of these individuals is described as sitting down at his desk, picking up a paper, reading through it rapidly, making a few marks on it, putting it down, and picking up the next one, and so on. The other individual's behavior might be described as follows: He enters his office, is reminded of the pile of papers on his desk, and decides he can deal with the challenge better with the help of a mug of coffee. Upon his return with the coffee, it occurs to him that he had almost forgotten that there is a colleague he has been meaning to talk with, so off he goes again. Finally back in his office, he observes that the pile of papers is still there. It then occurs to him that he is not entirely sure where he parked his car; he decides that he really should check that out before doing anything else. Koch concludes with the admission that both individuals are in fact the same person—himself.

It is not difficult to empathize with Koch's unfortunate "colleague." Surely all of us have had days like that. It has become common in both lay and professional circles to label any such temporary decline in mental effectiveness as resulting from "stress." But what Koch is talking about does not fit any of the usual symptoms of stress. There are no signs of rapid heartbeat, palmar sweating, or other autonomic indicators. Calling the second individual's distracted behavior "stress" may, in fact, lead to a failure to understand what is going on. Let me offer a different interpretation by suggesting that we provisionally call his condition "mental fatigue."

Many people are familiar with mental fatigue, with feeling "worn thin," not because of bad things, but simply as a result of too many things. Unlike stress, which is defined as a reaction to harm or threatened harm, mental fatigue affects people who are doing what they like to do, but for too long without a break.

There are many consequences of a fatigued state of mind. Impatience and greater distractibility are common symptoms. So is increased irritability. The fatigued individual doesn't necessarily notice the change, but co-workers and family have little trouble recognizing it. One is bothered by things that normally wouldn't have been an issue. Sticking with dull but necessary tasks becomes more difficult. In fact, much of what was once easy is now hard. And as if all that weren't enough, there is a tendency to lose the bigger picture, making it harder to remember that the various aspects of work fit together somehow and make some kind of sense.

For many people, days like this come far too often. There are reasons to believe that this is a pervasive but largely unrecognized problem.

Mental Fatigue and Attention: A Theoretical Analysis

Mental fatigue is a useful label for this syndrome, but it is also somewhat misleading. It does allow one to distinguish this area of difficulty from physical fatigue on the one hand and stress on the other. The difficulty, however, is that the name suggests that the mind as a whole is exhausted, and this is not the case.

A useful handle on what is going on here comes from a distinction made by the great American psychologist and philosopher, William James (1892). He distinguished between two kinds of attention, which in modern terms might be referred to as "directed attention" and "fascination." Directed attention is what it takes to get through a difficult or boring task. It is the kind of attention we call upon when working in distracting surroundings or when trying to make a decision about a complex situation. It takes effort, and it makes one susceptible to fatigue.

Fascination, by contrast, is effortless. It is the kind of attention that is called forth by exciting events or interesting tasks. Far from being hard work, it is often difficult to tear our attention *away* from something fascinating.

Thus the basic distinction is threefold. Directed attention is effortful, it is subject to voluntary control, and it is susceptible to fatigue. Fascination, by contrast, is at the opposite pole on each of these dimensions. In terms of our analysis of mental fatigue then, it is more useful to name the syndrome according to what is becoming fatigued —hence we would call it directed attention fatigue.

It may seem strange that so important an aspect of the human mind as directed attention should be so fragile. Yet, in evolutionary perspective, this apparent limitation might have been quite reasonable. To be able to pay attention by choice to one particular thing for a long period would make one vulnerable to surprises. The capability of being vigilant, of being alert to one's surroundings, may have been far more important than the capacity for long concentration. Further, much of what was important to the evolving human—wild animals, danger, caves, blood, to name a few examples—was (and still is) innately fascinating and thus does not require directed attention. It is only in the modern world that the split between the important and the interesting has become extreme. All too often the modern human must exert effort to do the important while resisting distraction from the interesting. Thus the problem of directed attention fatigue may well be of recent vintage.

Some Implications of Directed Attention Fatigue

How serious a problem is directed attention fatigue? If it is a minor annoyance, a mere sniffle in the sea of health, it hardly requires major consideration. If, however, people suffering from it are seriously impaired, or if it is a pervasive problem, then it becomes a matter with implications for policy and planning. One way to think about the issue of seriousness is in terms of the impact directed attention fatigue can have on basic psychological processes.

Directed attention fatigue has many, substantial impacts on the capacity to think. It leads to difficulty in sustaining a line of thought; one is readily deflected or distracted. There is limited ability to analyze, to plan, to decide. Not only are these abilities diminished, the interest in a reflective stance declines also. There is a strong bias toward acting rather than thinking. It is difficult to listen to the opinions of others. Thoughtfulness is replaced by impatience. In fact, a major cost of directed attention fatigue may be the tendency to act impulsively, to take unnecessary risks. Recent findings on pilot errors, for example, implicate the role of disturbed sleep patterns, a clear cause of directed attention fatigue (Moore-Ede 1993; Public Citizen 1992).

Not only are thinking and taking action implicated, but feelings are influenced as well. Individuals suffering from directed attention fatigue tend to be irritable. Research evidence suggests that they are resistant to helping others in need (Cohen and Spacapan 1978). And although this syndrome is distinct from stress, if it persists it can certainly lead to stress. Over extended periods, as one becomes progressively less competent, the awareness of one's reduced ability to handle difficult situations is bound to grow. Then the anticipation of potential harm, a classical basis for the stress reaction, becomes a likely consequence.

Even if directed attention fatigure can have potentially serious consequences, it need not become a matter worthy of consideration if it is a relatively rare condition. Quite to the contrary, however, it is far from rare. Although frequently unnoticed or mislabeled, it is widespread. Leading the list of individuals for whom it is a likely pattern are those suffering from serious illnesses and those who are caretakers of the ill. While to date directed attention fatigue has been documented only in cancer patients (Cimprich 1990) and AIDS caregivers (Canin 1991), there is every reason to believe that this phenomenon is quite general. People experiencing grief over a major loss, whether it be of a significant other, a job, or one's home, are also highly susceptible. Overwork, sleep loss, and coping with prolonged attention-demanding situations (like urban traffic) also lead to fatigue of this important capacity.

WHAT HELPS: RESTORATIVE ENVIRONMENTS

In order to counteract this process, it is necessary to find an alternative basis for maintaining one's focus. Fortunately there is such a source, and it is widely available. Fascination, the other form of attention, is itself resistant to fatigue and permits directed attention to rest.

There are many sources of fascination. Fascination can come from *content* of various kinds. It can be noisy, like watching auto racing, or quiet, like walking in a natural setting. Fascination can also come from *process*. Birdwatching, for example, is a process that allows one to pay attention without effort. Predicting, as practiced by gamblers, is another process example. Quiet fascination—characteristic of certain natural settings— has a special advantage in that it provides an opportunity for reflection, which can further enhance the benefits of recovering from directed attention fatigue. I will refer to such opportunities as "restorative experiences" or "restorative environments."

Fascination is thus a central component of a restorative environment. By itself, however, it is not sufficient. Three additional components have been identified (Kaplan and Kaplan 1989):

1. *Being away* is useful, but by itself does not guarantee a restorative environment. People often use the term as a shorthand for going to a restorative place. Nonetheless, there are many places that are "away" but would not permit the necessary relief from directed attention fatigue. A prison cell is a vivid example.

2. The environment should have *extent* rich enough and coherent enough to constitute a whole other world. Restorative environments work best when one can settle into them, when they provide so much to see, experience, and think about that they take up the available room in one's head.

3. There should be substantial *compatibility* of the environment with one's purposes and inclinations. In other words, the setting must fit what one is trying to do and what one would like to do. Compatibility is a two-way street. On the one hand, a compatible environment is one where one's purposes fit what the environment demands. At the same time the environment must provide the information needed to meet one's purposes. Thus in a compatible environment one carries out one's activities smoothly and without struggle. There is no need to second-guess or to keep a close eye on one's own behavior. What one does comfortably and naturally is what is appropriate to the setting (Kaplan 1983).

The Role of Pleasure and Enjoyment

All other things being equal, an environment that is enjoyable is likely to be more restorative than one that is not. There is, however, reason to doubt that enjoyment is a requirement of a restorative experience. At present there are no research results bearing on this question, so the issue is not clear. A few anecdotal findings, however, may offer some useful perspective.

A colleague who suffers from multiple sclerosis continued to fish for several years, despite his handicap, because of his great love for the sport. Ultimately, however, he found that the amount of help required from his fishing buddies was more than he could tolerate. Weekend fishing trips turned out to be disagreeable and quite distressing. Yet, to his surprise, when he returned to work the following week after a trip, he found himself at his desk working with greatly enchanced concentration and effectiveness.

Another colleague, whose husband had died recently, characteristically was paying more attention to the needs of others than to her own, and I was concerned that she might tend to overlook problems created by directed attention fatigue. She was, in fact, upset to find herself less energetic and competent than usual. Because of this, although resistant to the idea of "indulging" herself by taking daily nature outings, she agreed to give it a try. She subsequently reported that they do help, that they work best when one is alone, and that being sad does not undermine their effectiveness.

Environmental Dimensions

There are some environmental properties that should be kept in mind in planning for a setting that will be effectively restorative. (1) *Proximity:* People hesitate to go out of the way for restorative experiences, despite their importance. (2) *Scale:* A setting need not be large to be effective. (3) *View:* Having an engaging view of nature is important, whether the view is from the window or while on a trail in a natural area. (4) *Preference predictors:* A substantial amount of work on environmental preference has pointed to the significance of mystery, legibility, complexity, and coherence (Kaplan and Kaplan 1989). The relationship of these predictors to the restorativeness of a setting has not yet been demonstrated, but anecdotal evidence suggests their importance.

Social and Cultural Dimensions: The Issue of Legitimacy

Even when an individual is convinced that recovery from directed attention fatigue is important, and appropriate environments are available, pursuit of restorative experiences might still not occur. An important factor in this failure of self-help is the social climate in which we live. There is little social support available for such behavior. On the contrary, our culture tends to frown on so-called frivolous activities. This is perhaps a carryover of the puritan perspective, which H.L. Mencken characterized as "the haunting fear that someone, somewhere, may be happy." The tendency to frown on not obviously productive activities was neatly captured by a donor of a park bench at a park near where I live. The inscription on the plaque reads:

Park Bench Donation: "Gary L. Krause—
You should be home studying."

EMPIRICAL SUPPORT

Thoreau, Olmsted, and many others who have written of nature's role in mental health were surely speaking from firsthand experience. They did not address the issue of mental fatigue, nor cast the need for restorative settings in terms of the consequences of the overuse of directed attention. The theoretical analysis proposed here offers a different kind of input, suggesting a framework for understanding why nature may be a powerful agent in healing. Further corroboration for the poetic, the anecdotal, and the theoretic, however, would be most desirable. This section offers an overview of some of the empirical research that addresses this issue.

A number of studies point to the beneficial effects of nature on physical and mental health. Studies have been carried out in a variety of settings, including hospitals (Ulrich 1984; Verderber 1986), prisons (Moore 1981; West 1986), and home (Kaplan 1985). Recent studies in the workplace indicate that people who can view the natural environment during their workday have fewer ailments and higher job satisfaction (Kaplan 1993).

There have also been studies that explicitly measured directed attention. The first of these was carried out by the Irvine group (Hartig et al. 1991), who compared wilderness vacationers with two other groups: urban vacationers and a nonvacationing control group. Following their trip, the wilderness group showed a significant improvement in their ability to proofread, a task that is highly demanding of directed attention. Comparable improvement was not found for the other groups. In a second study, participants first completed a task that led to directed attention fatigue. The next forty minutes were spent either walking in an urban setting, walking in a natural setting, or reading magazines (random assignment), followed by completion of a series of tasks. The results supported the hypothesis: superior proofreading was performed by the natural environment group.

Another study employing specific measures of directed attention examined the incidence of mental fatigue in recovering cancer patients. Cancer patients are generally instructed in self-care when they leave the hospital. They not only tend to have difficulty remembering such information; some even deny that they ever received it. It has also been observed that cancer patients with a clean bill of health from a medical point of view often suffer persistent coping problems of many kinds, including marital difficulties and severe limitations in returning to their former activities (Obrist and James 1985).

Feeling that these observations suggested serious mental fatigue problems, Cimprich (1990, 1992) studied recovering breast cancer patients, using a wide range of attentional and other measures. Participants were randomly assigned to either the experimental or the control group. In the former, each person signed a contract agreeing to participate in three restorative activities (of at least twenty minutes each) per week. The control group was not told about restorative activities until the study was completed. While the notion of restorative activities was explained in broad terms with numerous examples, participants generally selected nature-based activities (such as walking in nature and gardening) to fulfill their contracted time.

Cimprich reported that the participants in both groups showed severe attentional deficits shortly after surgery. The experimental (restorative) group showed gradual but steady improvement in their capacity to pay attention during the four times they were measured in the twelve weeks following surgery; the control group did not. Further, in the restorative group the participants went back to work sooner and were more likely to go back full time. Another striking difference was the inclination of members of the restorative group to start new projects (like learning a language or losing weight). No new projects were reported by the control group participants. And finally, experimental group members showed significantly greater gains on quality-of-life ratings.

What is particularly remarkable about this study is the effect of a very modest intervention (three activities of at least twenty minutes a week) on a problem that, according to the literature in this area, has the capacity to undermine people's lives for years.

CONCLUSIONS

Cost Effectiveness: Restorative experiences produce large benefits for a relatively small investment, with few negative side effects. Performing such activities is a way to help otherwise impaired individuals regain their effectiveness and go on with their lives. Restorative activities can also play a preventive role by reducing work pressures and encouraging reflection, a mental bookkeeping activity with long-term implications for health and effectiveness. Such small differences can have remarkably large effects.

Special Landscapes: If everyone who could benefit from the restorative potential of nature experiences were to put this knowledge to use, it could create an enormous pressure on the landscape. It thus behooves us to consider ways in which each kind of special landscape could be designed or managed to serve as a restorative environment. This may be a particularly challenging task for certain kinds of landscapes, such as those emphasizing water conservation or fire safety. On the other hand, it is likely to be well worth the effort, since meeting this challenge could bring increased public acceptance as a substantial fringe benefit.

Institutional Implications: A comparable challenge faces experts knowledgeable about institutional influences on the landscape. Legal, political, administrative, and economic factors have the potential, if approached with insight and ingenuity, both to protect landscapes with restorative potential and to foster their creation. If restorative settings are even half as significant as preliminary research suggests, such efforts will be well rewarded.

ACKNOWLEDGMENTS

Work on this paper and on the research that led to it was supported, in part, by the U.S. Forest Service, North Central Forest Experiment Station, Urban Forestry Project, through several cooperative agreements. I would also like to thank Rachel Kaplan for her many and substantial contributions to this paper.

LITERATURE CITED

Canin, L.H. 1991. Psychological restoration among AIDS caregivers: Maintaining self care. Doctoral dissertation, University of Michigan, Ann Arbor.

Cimprich, B. 1990. Attentional fatigue and restoration in individuals with cancer. Doctoral dissertation, University of Michigan, Ann Arbor.

———. 1992. A theoretical perspective on attention and patient education. Advances in Nursing Science 14(3):39-51.

Cohen, S., and S. Spacapan. 1978. The aftereffects of stress: An attentional interpretation. Environmental Psychology and Nonverbal Behavior 3:43-57.

Hartig, T., M. Mang, and G.W. Evans. 1991. Restorative effects of natural environment experiences. Environment and Behavior 23:3-26.

James, W. 1892. Psychology: The briefer course. Holt, New York.

Kaplan, R. 1973. Some psychological benefits of gardening. Environment and Behavior 5:145-152.

———. 1985. Nature at the doorstep: Residential satisfaction and the nearby environment. Journal of Architectural and Planning Research 2:115-127.

———. 1993. The role of nature in the context of the workplace. Landscape and Urban Planning 26:193-201.

Kaplan, R., and S. Kaplan. 1989. The experience of nature: A psychological perspective. Cambridge University Press, Cambridge and New York.

Kaplan, S. 1983. A model of person-environment compatibility. Environment and Behavior 15:311-332.

Koch, S. 1956. Behavior as intrinsically regulated: Work notes towards a pre-theory of phenomena called "Motivational." In M.R. Jones, ed., Nebraska Symposium on Motivation, pp. 42-89. University of Nebraska Press, Lincoln.

Moore, E.O. 1981. A prison environment's effect on health care service demands. Journal of Environmental Systems 11:17-34.

Moore-Ede, M. 1993. The twenty-four hour society. Addison-Wesley, Reading, Massachusetts.

Obrist, M.T., and R.H. James. 1985. Going home: Patient and spouse adjustment following cancer surgery. Topics in Clinical Nursing 7(1):46-57.

Olmsted, F.L. 1865. The value and care of parks. Report to the Congress of the State of California. (Reprinted 1976 in R. Nash, ed., The American environment, pp. 18-24. Addison-Wesley, Reading, Massachusetts.)

Public Citizen. 1992. Pilot fatigue could kill you. 8(5):1-3.

Thoreau, H.D. 1854. Walden, or Life in the woods. Ticknor and Fields, Boston.

Ulrich, R.S. 1984. View through a window may influence recovery from surgery. Science 224:420-421.

Verderber, S. 1986. Dimensions of person-window transactions in the hospital environment. Environment and Behavior 18:450-466.

West, M.J. 1986. Landscape views and stress responses in the prison environment. Master's thesis, University of Washington, Seattle.

PART THREE
Special Purpose Landscapes

10

Scenic Value in the Urbanizing Landscape

PATRICK A. MILLER

ABSTRACT During the 1980s major North American cities developed at an unprecedented rate, causing a variety of complex environmental problems. One was the loss of scenic value in the urbanizing landscape. The concern over this problem has been expressed in numerous instances by citizen groups opposing proposed development. Yet scenic values are still not being incorporated in the planning process in a comprehensive way. Some of the reasons for this are examined, including misconceptions about what scenic values are and the extent to which they can be planned for, difficulties that those involved in other aspects of landscape planning have in understanding and dealing with scenic values, and the responsibility of design professions to provide supportive and comfortable environments for people. The recent evolution of public concern related to planning for scenic values is also discussed. Lastly, several simple but important considerations in scenic value planning are described.

The decade of the 1980s was a period of unprecedented growth and development for American cities (Garreau 1991). Much of it occurred around the edges of large cities, spurred by a yearning for a different lifestyle than was available in the city—a lifestyle reflecting the more spacious, tranquil countryside. As a result, much of the agricultural and forested land around most major North American cities has been chopped up. The development of sprawling suburbs and associated commercial enterprises is a phenomenon that has been termed "edge cities." Ironically, this type of rapid, sprawling development is destroying the qualities that attracted people to these places initially. A backlash of concern over the environmental damage caused by this type of development has begun to emerge. At the same time it has focused attention on the root problem of urban sprawl: the need to make cities more livable.

With this increased concern and attention has come an adjustment or redefinition among certain disciplines. The field of landscape ecology emerged during the 1980s, first in Europe and then in North America. The central difference between landscape ecology and traditional ecology is the inclusion of human use and habitation of the landscape as part of the ecological process. The profession of landscape architecture has also made some changes. Authors such as Michael Hough (1984) and Anne Whiston Spirn (1984) have extended the concept of "designing in response to ecological processes," originally developed in Ian McHarg's *Design with Nature* (1969), into the urban environment. The forestry profession has begun to build a new branch, called urban forestry, by shifting its land stewardship philosophy and strong heritage in the natural sciences to a new setting, the urban environment. The complex problems and issues which must be dealt with call for a multidisciplinary approach—an approach that includes a holistic under-standing, as well as the ability to deal substantively with individual aspects of the landscape, including such things as urban forest stand management; wildlife manage-ment; economic, political, and social issues; and human safety as well as human behav-ioral issues.

An aspect of landscape management that is of increasing concern, and is the focus of this paper, is the scenic value of the landscape. One has only to read the newspaper of any major North American city on almost any day to see this concern expressed repeatedly. People are speaking out against unwanted development (see Figure 10-1), and high on their list of concerns is the "way the development will look," or the effect it will have on the character of their community. Even so, few communities are involved in planning for scenic values in a comprehensive way. This chapter proposes to start with a discussion of what constitutes scenic value, then explore some of the reasons for the reluctance to include scenic value considerations in planning and management of the landscape. Current trends in scenic value planning will be examined, and the chapter will conclude with some relatively simple things that can be done in most communities to improve planning for scenic values.

Figure 10-1. Eco-graffiti offers an anony-mous expression of disapproval (above) over the development of a Kmart store (left) in Christiansburg, Virginia, on land that was previously used for agri-cultural purposes. (Photos by the author)

SCENIC VALUES: A BROADER DEFINITION

What are scenic values in the landscape? They are those aspects of a place or landscape that people like or value. They are more than simply things to "look at." People do more than look at the landscape as if it were a painting or a piece of art; they live in it. When people look at a landscape, they sense whether it would appear to be safe, easy to find your way around in, and an interesting place. People read and interpret these things from the landscape in a natural way, often not involving much conscious thought. These are things that make a landscape a supportive and comfortable place for people. Scenic value, then, is very much about how comfortable and supportive people perceive a landscape to be.

What is happening to those places we like, particularly in urbanizing or developing areas? Increasingly our world is becoming more visually homogenous. Our ability to recognize those places in a community that reveal its social and natural functions is being lost; and along with this we are losing a physical structure that affects our ability to understand, find our way around, and engage in activities. With respect to built features, it used to be that the town square, the church steeple, and the solid granite structure of a bank were all icons conveying meanings about various activities and functions. Likewise, communities were built around natural features such as rivers and streams, hills, ravines, meadows, swampy areas, and woods. The role that they played in the ability to distinguish one place from another is evident in the map of almost any community, in names such as Mercer Slough, Magnolia Hill, Sand Point, Drapers Meadow, and Westwood. Such names not only help us locate and distinguish one landscape from another, but also convey something about the original character of the area. The name conveyed what the landscape was like, what it might be used for, and whether there might be hazards. Unfortunately, development often destroys or alters these natural distinguishing characteristics. This is particularly true where high land values and modern technology have made it both profitable and possible to literally move mountains. Not only does this have disastrous environmental consequences, but it also destroys a useful way for people to understand and relate to the landscape.

But are people *really* concerned about the loss of scenic values? Hardly a day goes by when there is not some article in the newspaper about a controversial land development project. Often the stated objections to the project are not visual ones. They range from concerns over water quality and destruction of natural systems to the loss of historically significant resources (see Figure 10-1). Even though visual or scenic value may not even be mentioned, it is clear from how people talk about the development that a strong motive for opposition is "how it will look." This was the case recently in Blacksburg, Virginia, when a landowner along a major roadway in the community marked a large number of trees with bright-colored surveyor's tape in preparation for cutting the trees and subsequently developing the property. The next morning, "Save Our Trees" signs mysteriously appeared on the property as citizen opposition was almost instantly galvanized. Ostensibly the opposition was organized to save the trees, which were neither rare species nor significant specimens. I believe it was the thought of losing the sight of this lovely grove along a major roadway in the community that moved people to act. In fact, if the landowner had not marked so visibly all the trees that were to be cut, people in the community would probably not have realized the magnitude of the loss, and opposition would have been much slower to form.

People are concerned about the appearance of their everyday environment. Despite the level of concern people exhibit over the appearance of their community, there is a reluctance to insist that the planning process give scenic values equal consideration to other aspects of the landscape. When scenic values are considered, they are often a "shadow concern" secondary to a "real" issue like water quality or habitat destruction. There are two reasons for this: misconceptions about scenic values, and difficulty in accommodating visual concerns in the traditional planning processes.

IS BEAUTY IN THE EYE OF THE BEHOLDER?

One reason scenic values are difficult to include as a planning consideration is their subjective nature. Human preferences for the landscape are like many other human phenomena. They reflect individual differences, but there are also a great many areas of agreement. If we take human appearance, for example, we have very little difficulty distinguishing one individual from another. So, each person is different. But if an individual were to walk into a room with two heads or three eyes, people would gasp in disbelief. So, people are also similar. Aesthetic aspects of the landscape are the product of a complex experiential phenomenon—the interaction between human beings and the world they live in. While individual human reactions to the landscape are difficult to predict precisely, they are not a random or spurious phenomenon either. In fact, there is an amazing amount of agreement on landscape preferences. And there is much evidence that people care tremendously about how the landscape around them appears and that this appearance has an influence on their well-being. Certainly, enough agreement exists to provide a sound basis for including scenic values in the planning process.

Often when scenic values are considered as part of the land planning process, they are treated as an afterthought—a decoration to be applied after the really important problems have been solved. This occurs for two reasons: (1) the conception of scenic values in the landscape held by many is of a kind of picture or work of art, rather than an experiential phenomenon; and (2) it is difficult to incorporate scenic values into the traditional planning decision processes. This is indeed unfortunate, for the users of the landscape, for other uses of the landscape, and for the quality of the environment.

Scenic Value as a Picture or Art

When scenic values are treated like artistic renderings, something to be passively looked at, their management is simply the expressive artistic manipulation of a visual composition. But scenic values in the landscape are more than simply things to "look at." They involve people's ability to make sense of the landscape and function in it. A supportive landscape provides opportunities for visual interest or involvement, as well as opportunities for reflection and mental restoration. The visual experience is a pervasive aspect of almost any use of the landscape. Moreover, it is an important aspect of people's well-being. When viewed this way, it is easy to see why scenic values should not be treated as a cosmetic afterthought.

Difficulties with Traditional Decision Making

Efforts to incorporate scenic values into traditional planning decision making encounter three difficulties: first, there is the traditional separation of science and art, an extension of the "scenic value as art" problem discussed above; second, scenic value is generally not recognized as a legitimate function in the landscape; and third, planners find themselves uncomfortable dealing with scenic values. In the traditional division between the artistic/qualitative world and the scientific/quantitative world, there is a reluctance of individuals on either side to cross the divide. Traditional planning is grounded in the scientific/quantitative world. While scenic values are neither a random and spurious phenomenon nor simply an artistic expression, they are difficult to quantify and generally are dealt with on a qualitative basis. There is a need for those involved in traditional planning decision making to reach out and encompass this type of information in the planning process. Appleton (1975:23) summarizes this difficulty well: "As long as the men of taste scorn the Philistines of science, and as long as the scientists fear the verdict of guilt by association with such shady characters as art historians, so long shall we each feel obliged to opt either for studying the landscape as the subject of rational analysis or for enjoying it as the source of aesthetic satisfaction. Are these two kinds of experience really irreconcilable?"

Often associated with the scientific/quantitative view is a lack of recognition of scenic value as a legitimate function or purpose of the landscape. Sometimes this is not a consciously stated approach, but more of an attitude reflected in the relative priority given to scenic values. If a tree is serving as an important "visual element" in a landscape, is it really doing something important or useful? If it is just passively sitting there "looking pretty," how can it be serving an important purpose? In the minds of people who hold this view, enhancing scenic value is not really something "truly useful," like providing habitat, filtering air, or modifying the climate. This is not to say that these other purposes are not important, but that the visual role deserves equal recognition as a legitimate landscape function. A recent personal experience makes clear the importance of this role of trees to people. In my neighborhood the streets are lined with large trees. When a flyer was sent by the city to all neighborhood residents indicating that they were supposed to trim the street trees, it had about the same effect as poking a hornet's nest. People were not concerned about losing the air-filtering, climate-modifying, or habitat aspects of these trees. They were primarily concerned about how the trees were going to look and the affect that it would have on the character of their neighborhood. Scenic values are important to people's well-being and satisfaction with their own environment. It is important that planners recognize scenic value as a legitimate purpose of the landscape and work toward incorporating such considerations into the planning process.

But scenic values are imprecise and not easily accommodated within our traditional technological and scientific ways of thinking. Traditional science and engineering thinking places a premium on precision and predictability. Although there is enough agreement on landscape preference to provide a sound collective basis for planning, there are still individual differences. These differences mean that it is difficult or impossible to predict precisely the reaction of every individual to a given landscape. For some, the lack of precision makes scenic values unpleasant and difficult to deal with. Planners need to be aware of the biases in their own training and views, and make a conscious attempt to understand and incorporate scenic values into the planning process.

It is important that those involved in planning landscapes for other purposes not confine themselves to a myopic and technical understanding of the landscape, but also develop an understanding of the richness of the visual experience. Our ability to include scenic values in the planning process will be greatly enhanced if those who have expertise in the scientific/quantitative aspects of the landscape will not be reluctant to recognize and deal with scenic values as an important landscape concern. While this is not easy, it is clearly something that is necessary and can be dealt with.

CREATIVE EXPRESSION OF LANDSCAPE DESIGNERS

Complicating the task of explaining scenic values to lay people, and planners of other aspects of the landscape, is the behavior of certain landscape designers. These are members of the "landscape as art" approach, which seems to be a reaction to the lack of a strong, unified design theory for landscape aesthetics. It includes works such as Christo's *Running Fence*, Smithson's *Spiral Jetty*, Irwin's *Nine Spaces, Nine Trees*, Bayer's *Mill Creek Canyon Earthworks* (Figure 10-2), and a number of works by Schwartz (see Figure 10-3). This approach encompasses an "if it is art anything goes" attitude and a "different is better" axiom for design quality. The result is what I refer to as the tabloid version of aesthetics—gaudy and geared for shock effect, but not containing much substance to sustain the viewer. Included in this category are several of Schwartz's works, such as *Splice Garden* and the *Rio Shopping Center*, as well as SWA's *Harlequin Place*. This type of behavior by designers only reinforces many misconceptions other planners have about scenic value. While there may be a place for this extreme artistic expression in the landscape, it must be carried out with an eye to ethical obligations to provide landscapes for the public that are comfortable to be in.

Figure 10-2. Designer Herbert Bayer uses creative expression in the design of *Mill Creek Canyon Earthworks* in Kent, Washington. Geometric forms are combined with natural elements and well-articulated spaces necessary for a comfortable and supportive environment for people. (Photo by the author)

Figure 10-3. The three-dimensional, mathematical symbols in *Jail House Garden* in downtown Seattle are the creation of landscape architect and artist Martha Schwartz. While these sculptural forms provide visual novelty, they are so abstract that viewers may have no way to make sense of their surroundings. There are also few other elements to make this entry plaza a comfortable place for people. (Photo by the author)

Landscape architects must find ways to accommodate the needs of people in their design of landscapes, thus achieving a creative expression that is not reactionary but based on an understanding of the intricacies of the landscape and people's relationship to it. The Kaplans (1982) have pointed out the human need for landscapes that are both involving and make sense. The creative expression of a designer can provide a poetic aspect to the landscape that can be very involving (Figure 10-2). However, if this creative expression causes the landscape to become nonsensical (Figure 10-3), the result will be an uncomfortable or unsupportive environment.

SOME BROADER IMPLICATIONS OF VISUAL EXPERIENCE

One of the primary ways people take in information about the world around them is through visual experience. This has important implications for other ways we use the landscape and for the quality of the environment itself. This happens in two ways: in terms of what people infer about the landscape and activities that are taking place there; and in terms of a sense of connectedness to a place or environment that people obtain as a result of their experience of the environment.

What people see in the landscape is also important for public support of other landscape uses, such as wildlife management, woodlots, open space, and heritage preservation. When lacking the expertise to technically evaluate the management of the landscape for other purposes, people often rely on their visual experience of the landscape. Does it look like a pleasant place to be? Does it appear to be interesting to explore?

Are some elements incongruent with its purpose? Does it look neglected? The answers to these questions can be very influential to the public perception of whether the landscape is well managed.

The visual experience of the natural environment contributes to a sense of connectedness to the environment. This is important in finding solutions to broader environmental problems faced by the world today. Other writers, such as Hiss (1990), have lamented the lack of a sense of connection to the land that has resulted from increased urbanization. Most people today have few opportunities to connect with nature firsthand—to feel and contemplate the wonder of the natural environment. For most people, the natural environment and related environmental problems are simply mental constructs, not unlike other political or economic issues. The visual experience is the primary way in which a sense of connection to nature is obtained—a sense of connection necessary to fully comprehend the magnitude of environmental loss faced by our world today. The success of humankind in dealing with these larger scale environmental problems lies not simply in a rational understanding of the problem but in a commitment to the natural environment that comes from the experience of nature. It is not enough for this experience to happen once or twice a year, several hundred miles from home. It must be available to all in the environment in which they live.

The visual experience of the landscape is too important to be a decorative afterthought. It is an integral part of human life and important to the health of those who use the landscape, to other uses of the landscape, and to the long-term health of our environment.

CURRENT TRENDS IN PLANNING FOR SCENIC VALUES

There seems to be a resurgence under way of interest in scenic issues in landscape planning. This interest in landscape aesthetics follows a lull that occurred after the heyday of visual management activity stimulated by the ecology movement of the 1960s. Those initial activities reached a peak in 1979 when 112 papers on the subject were delivered at a conference entitled Our National Landscape (USDA Forest Service 1979). It was during that period that such terms as VRM (visual resource management) and VQOs (visual quality objectives) came into use. Planning activities were largely focused on public lands and tended to try to blend natural resource management with the visual characteristics of the natural landscape. In this arena the landscape assessment procedures which evolved placed a premium on objectivity. While these earlier efforts at landscape assessment broke new ground in often hostile environments, they tended to ignore many of the broader experiential or visual aspects of the landscape.

The more recent interest in scenic landscape planning has a different emphasis. While the preservation of natural beauty is still a primary concern, the current activities stress cultural aspects of the landscape as part of a broader concern for community character. These efforts are directed at lands mainly in private ownership. The approaches used are more descriptive and better able to take into account a broad range of visual or experiential aspects of the landscape.

There seem to be several reasons for this recent interest in the visual aspects of the landscape. Partly, there is a reaction to the rapid growth and development of the 1980s. People have become alarmed at how fast their surroundings have changed, more often than not for the worst. Another reason is a more pervasive concern for traditional values.

The search for traditional values has even created a professional design market 1 a number of architectural design firms that specialize in neotraditional village This is part of a broad reaction against the fast pace of modern society. Peo searching for values that they perceive to be more lasting. Many also yearn for a simpler but more meaningful way of life. These attitudes manifest themselves in the landscape in an interest in heritage landscapes, rural landscape planning (Yaro et al. 1989), and the preservation of agricultural landscapes (Nassauer 1992). The scenic aspect alone is not the stated purpose, but it is an important part of what is driving people's expressed concern. Clearly, planning for scenic values is not going to resolve all the anxieties of modern society, but the provision of supportive environments is one way to help people cope.

The institutional support for this increased concern for scenic values is coming from some unusual places. For example, the 1990 Food, Agriculture, Conservation, and Trade Act, or Farm Bill, included provisions aimed at improving the scenic characteristics of agricultural landscapes by requiring certain actions of farmers desiring to participate in government farm programs (Nassauer 1992). A more recent example is the Intermodal Surface Transportation Efficiency Act, better known as the 1991 Highway Bill, which includes provisions for $80 million to be spent over six years in developing a National Scenic Byways Program. This follows the efforts of the Forest Service and the Bureau of Land Management over the past three years in developing scenic byway programs. These efforts are placing less attention on visual assessment, as in the past, and more on the experience, preservation, and interpretation of scenic landscapes.

HOW DO WE PLAN FOR SCENIC VALUE?

The thought of planning for scenic values brings to mind the words of the landscape painter and student of human nature, Elmore Morgan, in a lecture entitled "Man's Marks," delivered in 1993 at the College of Architecture and Urban Studies at Virginia Polytechnic Institute, Blacksburg. When asked about preserving what is valuable in the landscape, he advised, "Know what you have before you fool around with it." His instructions were simple, "Look up, look down, look straight ahead. Be alert for what you already have." The first step then in planning for scenic value is to ask the people who live in a landscape, "What is special about this place?" Morgan notes, "It is interesting how people share perceptions about the spirit of a place." A second common, but important, influence is vegetation. Vegetation can influence the scenic value of a place in several ways, both as a preferred content of the landscape and as an important spatial delineator and place attribute.

A place in the landscape can be special for a variety of reasons. It may contain features of cultural or natural significance, such as a historic structure or specimen tree (see Figure 10-4). Special places often have meanings associated with them. In the case of historic places (see Figure 10-5) they symbolize past cultures and times, which tend to fascinate people, thus contributing to their preference for the landscape. In the case of historic or natural features it is important to note that significance depends not just on the features themselves but also on the surrounding landscape. This is evidenced in the procedures for nominating a historic structure to the National Register of Historic Places. The procedure requires a discussion of the "integrity" of the historic structure, including the extent to which the surrounding environment impinges on the historic significance of

Figure 10-4. A special place is created by a specimen live oak in Charleston, South Carolina. (Photo by the author)

Figure 10-5. Another special place is created by viewers' fascination with the past culture and way of life represented by historic Mabry Mill on the Blue Ridge Parkway in Virginia. (Photo by the author)

Figure 10-6. The historic integrity of Old Salem Church is adversely affected by incompatible adjacent land uses that have grown up around the historic site. (Photo by H. Miller)

the structure. Clearly, it is possible to preserve a historic structure but lose its historic significance if its integrity is compromised (see Figure 10-6). This is true of all special places. When other activities in the landscape are visually discordant with the reasons that people perceive a place to be special, then the scenic value of that place is going to be lessened. Good planning should protect special places from the development of incompatible adjacent uses.

Special places are often taken for granted in the rural landscape, where the threats from discordant development are few. As the urbanizing edges of cities creep over the landscape, the synergistic role of multipurpose planning seems to present particular opportunities. Special places, wildlife habitats, open spaces, heritage landscapes, wetlands, and woodlots are all examples of landscape uses that are likely to have difficulty competing economically in the urbanizing landscape if considered individually. Once the special places of the landscape are lost to urban development, they are almost never reclaimed. It is therefore imperative that scenic values and the preservation of special places be a consideration in all types of landscape planning and management if the urbanizing edges of all of our cities are not to become an amorphous, anonymous, landscape goo.

THE ROLE OF VEGETATION IN SCENIC VALUE

The relationship between nature and preferred human environments is well established (Kaplan and Kaplan 1989). The preference for greenness and lush landscapes is probably an innate reaction within the human species (Kaplan and Kaplan 1982). While people may learn to adapt and even like landscapes that are devoid of vegetation, it is easy to imagine that a natural attraction to green and lush landscapes would be an evolutionary advantage for the ancestors of the human species, in terms of both food and shelter. Vegetation also plays other roles in landscape preference, especially in fulfilling the dual human needs for "involvement" with the landscape and "making sense" of the landscape (Kaplan and Kaplan 1982).

At a larger scale, vegetation can give structure to the landscape. This is important in people's ability to make sense of the landscape. Strong structuring elements make it easier to form a cognitive map. People prefer landscapes that have a strong cognitive image. This structure can take a variety of forms. It may be a street tree planting that marks pathways through the landscape or serves as a delineator of different neighborhoods. Natural riparian vegetation also provides structure as natural drainage ways pass through the landscape (see Figure 10-7). Or the use of vegetation in a characteristic manner may help distinguish one area of a community from another. Vegetation works in many ways to tie a larger landscape together—to allow it to make sense as a whole to people.

Figure 10-7. As this greenway (stream and riparian vegetation) runs through the city of Boulder, Colorado, it becomes part of the physical structure of the community and helps people make sense of the landscape by becoming a strong element in their cognitive map of the community. (Photo by the author)

Figure 10-8. In this view, vegetation forms an enclosure, suggesting a comfortable human scale space and a sense of safety or shelter. The break in the vegetation, with a glimpse of what lies beyond, creates a sense of mystery. (Photo by the author)

As a landscape becomes increasingly urbanized, the chance that this structure will be disrupted becomes greater. Drainage ways are placed underground and forests are chopped into unrelated pieces. Preserving vegetation which serves to structure the landscape naturally can go a long way toward preserving scenic quality. It would seem reasonable that these natural structuring elements would also be valuable for other landscape purposes such as open space, wildlife habitat, groundwater recharge zones, and water filtration areas. Also, as the area becomes increasingly urbanized, creation of landscapes or large-scale plantings becomes more important. Large-scale street tree plantings and reforestation of denuded areas serve to form the future structure of an urbanizing landscape. Landscape ordinances that require liberal plantings for new development can help establish a new character for urbanizing areas.

At a site scale, vegetation plays a different role. As a delineater of outdoor spaces it serves an important function in helping us distinguish one place from another and make sense of the landscape. The use of a particular species of vegetation, or combinations of species, can impart a distinguishing character to a place. Places that are clearly defined are likely to be preferred. The use of vegetation to enclose spaces can also provide a sense of human scale or a sense of safety and shelter. Both are attributes of supportive and comfortable environments and enhance scenic value.

Vegetation can also play a role in the important human need for involvement with the landscape. Landscapes that offer this potential are likely to be preferred. Vegetation arranged so that it partly blocks views into adjacent areas, but does not block potential access, can create a sense of mystery in a landscape (Figure 10-8). Mystery, which plays upon human curiosity or the need for involvement, is one of the most powerful attributes of scenic value in the landscape and one that has been used for centuries by garden designers to enhance scenic value. Vegetation as an important structuring element in the landscape enhances our ability to understand and make sense of our surroundings, both at a community and a site scale. It is also the single most important building block that designers can use in creating comfortable, supportive, and interesting places for people.

RELATIONSHIP TO OTHER LANDSCAPE PURPOSES

Scenic values have an intrinsically positive relationship to most landscape purposes that involve preserving or managing the natural environment. There may be some conflicts, but in general, if a landscape is used for open space, wildlife habitats, natural heritage, agricultural, or forestry purposes, rather than being developed for housing, commercial, or industrial uses, its scenic value will be greater. In fact, in many instances when landscapes are managed for ecological diversity, the scenic value is also enhanced. For

Figure 10-9. Wildlife management activities in the Lake Hills Greenbelt of Bellevue, Washington, also enhance the scenic value of the landscape. Previously (left) there was no aquatic habitat. Addition of water to create that habitat (below) also produced a more visually diverse landscape. (Photos by R. Hoesterey)

Figure 10-10. A stormwater retention area in Christiansburg, Virginia (below) serves only the engineering function of holding rainwater runoff, while one in Ann Arbor, Michigan (left) serves a dual engineering and scenic function.

example, a wildlife management objective may be to provide more habitat diversity partly by creating openings in a thickly forested landscape. This is likely to make the landscape more visually accessible and improve scenic value (see Figure 10-9). In addition, cultural landscape management has an intrinsically positive relation to scenic value. The preservation of historic structures and artifacts is likely to increase viewer interest, and thus the scenic value of a landscape. This does not mean that greater consideration of scenic values necessarily results in greater scenic value enhancement, but simply that there are few conflicts between scenic values and these other landscape purposes.

There may be some potential for conflict between scenic values and the management of landscapes to prevent fire or to conserve water. The management of landscapes to prevent fires involves the removal of fuel (vegetation) around human habitation, and management to conserve water in arid landscapes often means less lush, green vegetation. While such restrictions theoretically interfere with scenic value, there is currently so little consideration given to scenic values in these types of landscape management that the opportunities for visual enhancement by other means far outweigh the potential losses.

One area of tremendous potential for improving the scenic value of landscapes being managed for other purposes lies in areas used for public utilities and infrastructure. A great deal of land is used for utility rights-of-way, power substations, pipelines, flood drains, and stormwater retention. Much of this land lies neglected and is often an eyesore, but many of these areas have the potential to be attractive green spaces (see

Figure 10-10). It is important for those who manage landscapes for such purposes to be aware of and take advantage of their scenic value potential.

CONCLUSIONS

Scenic values are more than just an artistic composition. They are important to human well-being and are a pervasive aspect of almost all activities occurring in the landscape. In spite of this, planning for scenic values lags behind planning for other environmental purposes. This is due to misconceptions about scenic values on the part of many who are involved in traditional planning, as well as difficulties in incorporating scenic values into traditional planning decision making. It is critical that those involved in all aspects of landscape planning endeavor to broaden their perspective to include these concerns. This is important not only in improving the scenic value of the landscape but in gaining public support for other purposes for which the landscape is being managed, as well as increasing public awareness of environmental problems in general.

Support for scenic value planning is increasing. Much of this support is related to other landscape purposes, such as scenic byways, heritage preservation, and agricultural landscapes. These current efforts are different from the visual resource management efforts of the 1970s and 1980s. They are less quantitative and more descriptive, drawing on the broader experiential aspects of the landscape. Two fairly easy things can be done to improve or preserve the scenic value in most communities: identify and protect those special places in most communities that people find interesting and that impart meaning to the landscape; and take advantage of the powerful role that vegetation can play in enhancing the scenic value of the landscape at both the community and site scale. There are few conflicts between scenic value planning and planning for other landscape purposes. In those instances where potential conflicts exist, there are still ample opportunities to improve scenic value before conflicting with the other purpose.

Scenic values are important to the future of the landscape and the people who inhabit the landscape. Since the visual experience is a pervasive aspect of almost all uses of the landscape, and since there are so few opportunities to plan for just the scenic values, it is imperative that those involved in planning for other landscape purposes also address scenic value concerns, or the view of the future will be in doubt.

LITERATURE CITED

Appleton, J. 1975. The experience of landscape. John Wiley and Sons, New York. 293 p.

Garreau, J. 1991. Edge city: Life on the new frontier. Doubleday, New York. 546 p.

Hiss, T. 1990. The experience of place. Knopf, New York. 233 p.

Hough, M. 1984. City form and natural process. Van Nostrand Reinhold, New York. 281 p.

Kaplan, R., and S. Kaplan. 1989. The experience of nature: A psychological perspective. Cambridge University Press, Cambridge and New York. 340 p.

Kaplan, S., and R. Kaplan. 1982. Cognition and environment: Functioning in an uncertain world. Praeger Publishers, New York. 287 p.

McHarg, I. 1969. Design with nature. Natural History Press, Garden City. 198 p.

Nassauer, J. 1992. In the Midwest, new opportunities help farmers express the beauty of conservation. Landscape Architecture, April 1992, p. 136.

Spirn, A.W. 1984. The granite garden: Urban nature and human design. Basic Books, New York. 334 p.

USDA Forest Service. 1979. Our national landscape. Proceedings of Our National Landscape Conference. General Technical Report PSW-34. USDA Forest Service Pacific Southwest Forest and Range Experiment Station, Berkeley, California. 752 p.

Yaro, R., R. Arendt, H. Dodson, and E. Brabec. 1989. Dealing with change in the Connecticut River Valley: A design manual for conservation and development. Lincoln Institute of Land Policy and Environmental Law Foundation, University of Massachusetts, Amherst.

11

Management of Greenbelts and Forest Remnants in Urban Forest Landscapes

JAMES K. AGEE

ABSTRACT Greenbelts and forest remnants are valued landscapes in urban settings, conveying a sense of nature in largely developed areas, and simultaneously serving a wide variety of uses and values. They represent a spectrum ranging from pristine/native species to previously managed/alien ones, and any point on this spectrum may be a desirable management objective. Options are a function of scale and structure. Scale is typically measured by reserve size and fragmentation. Structure is usually characterized as remnant (a residual patch of a formerly larger landscape) or emergent (a new patch designed after the reserve was created). These landscapes will change over longer time scales than we usually think about, with implications for planning and the need for patience in obtaining desired landscape structure.

Greenbelts and forest remnants are highly valued landscapes in urban settings. They represent pieces of nature in a matrix of development, and although they may be highly fragmented and difficult to sustain over the long run, they justify unusual investments in comparison to rural wildlands. These areas usually consist of native vegetation, but for the purposes of this chapter they are defined broadly as containing either native or introduced (alien) vegetation that may be pristine or in some state of recovery after past disturbance. In the urban setting, perception of nature may be more important than reality. If a particular vegetation composition and structure meets the objectives for which a greenbelt or forest remnant was established, it need not be native, virgin forest. Having provided a broadened definition, I will nevertheless use mostly native examples to illustrate the major points here.

The management of greenbelts and forest remnants is complicated by the multitude of objectives for which these landscapes are managed. Most public wildland management agencies are finding that the days of single-use management are over. Urban forest managers found this out long ago. Greenbelts and forest remnants serve a wide variety of objectives: they provide stable cover and erosion protection in geomorphically sensitive areas; they protect water quality and quantity (Perry, this volume); they provide habitat for wildlife species (Milligan and Raedeke, this volume); they provide visually attractive areas (Miller, this volume), which may also be used for restorative landscapes (Kaplan, this volume); and they may also be used to conserve energy (McPherson et al., this volume), although greenbelts and forest remnants are rarely managed directly for energy values. These objectives are not always compatible with one another. For example, one person's idyllic restorative landscape may also harbor native animals, such as coyotes, that prey on another neighbor's pets (Quinn 1992). Greenbelts and forest remnants are nevertheless highly valued landscapes, and management of sustainable species composition and structure is essential if they are to function as producers of the desirable outputs for which they were established.

THE KEY PRINCIPLES OF MANAGEMENT

The first key principle in managing greenbelts and forest remnants is that ecological change is inevitable. In any wildland ecosystem, the only constant is change. Today's desirable conditions may evolve into tomorrow's undesirable ones.

The second key principle is that scale is a critical variable in designing management plans. Many greenbelts and forest remnants are in patches much smaller than those found in nature. Permanently fixed and quite contrasting edges are common, and rarely are any buffers present. The buffer, if any, must be built into the greenbelt or forest remnant. Nevertheless, there are some urban forest landscapes large enough so that edge effects can be effectively managed within the unit. A good example of this is the Tiger Mountain State Forest (discussed by McClelland, this volume). Occupying over 10,000 acres, this working forest can include timber harvesting at the same time that it represents wild forest values. The other end of the spectrum is the greenbelt or forest remnant of several acres, or one which is very long and narrow, so that the entire unit is composed of edge environments. Both the intensity and type of management must vary along this spectrum.

The third key principle is that of time: ecological processes generally take longer than social processes. An example of this is the evolution of a forest patch twenty miles east of Seattle. For thousands of years it went through a cycle of fire and rain, with new forest replacing old every several hundred years after catastrophic forest fires, and the ample rainfall encouraging relatively fast and abundant regeneration of Douglas-fir (*Pseudotsuga menziesii*) trees. With stable climate, the ecological rate of change has been relatively predictable and slow.

Near the beginning of the twentieth century, the patch came under private ownership and was logged and burned, a disturbance close enough to its natural cycle that the process of natural recovery started as it had in the past. By the 1930s, little economic value was yet present within the patch, and it was abandoned for nonpayment of taxes and reverted to county ownership. By 1960, when the patch was fifty years old, development began to occur as the suburbs of Seattle broadened. At first, development consisted of small patches of housing in a largely forested matrix. By 1980, urban encroachment was so pervasive that the forest patches became isolated within a sea of development. Some areas, like Tiger Mountain, were designated as "working forests," with forest industry trading lands to public agencies and receiving more rural parcels in return. By 1990, parts of the working forest were designated "natural resource conservation areas" where recreation is a primary focus, and other nearby urban forest landscapes were designated "wildland parks."

The eighty years described here represent but a third of the natural fire cycle for this forest, and about 10 percent of the potential life span of an individual Douglas-fir tree. In these eight decades, the social definition of these areas has changed incredibly, from essentially worthless land to a highly valued urban forest landscape. We must recognize that the social equation will continue to change at a rate faster than these trees can grow, and incorporate this into long-term greenbelt and forest remnant planning.

SIZE AND STRUCTURE OF GREENBELTS AND FOREST REMNANTS

The management opportunities in greenbelts and forest remnants can be analyzed through an evaluation of appropriate size and structure in the design of these areas. Of course, management must often occur in the midst of design constraints already in place, but such an evaluation can be helpful in designing sustainable ecological conditions even if the preserve's size and shape are already fixed.

An old truism in preserve design is the bigger the better (Noss 1987). Recent debates have centered on whether, given the constraints on total preserve area, one to several large reserves are in fact better than a larger number of scattered reserves (Soule and Simberloff 1986) for the purposes of biodiversity, and whether corridors between preserves actually function as intended (Simberloff and Cox 1987). For the purposes of greenbelts and forest remnants, biodiversity may not be a dominant or even an appropriate objective, so these debates, although pertinent to natural area design, may not be specifically of any help in managing greenbelts and forest remnants in urban settings.

Nevertheless, large greenbelts and forest remnants offer the opportunity to have natural processes operate to a greater degree than in small areas. The "wild" end of the ecological spectrum can express itself in large areas, where visual, acoustic, and ecological buffering are maximized. Where a more natural environment is desired, large units are generally better than small ones. Natural processes may not always be enjoyed while being experienced, however. Large units can harbor predators on humans (including other humans) as well as enable "destructive" processes like forest fires to move readily across the landscape through continuous fuels.

Edge may be a desirable characteristic of a greenbelt or forest remnant. Substantial edge, such as in a linear greenbelt, is a very efficient viewing design. It may possess high opportunity for restorative environments because of visual and physical accessibility. Areas with extensive edge may also be good investments, providing high return for acquisition dollars compared with less accessible areas. Biologically, edge in greenbelts or forest remnants may be desirable because desired landscape elements may not always be found in circular arrangements (e.g., riparian areas). Topographically sheltered locations may be linear, providing better protection to the unit than a circular design. Edge in landscapes may be desirable for certain wildlife species (Thomas et al. 1979; Agee et al. 1989). However, edge can be detrimental to opportunities for solitude and may have a number of biological costs associated with sustainable forest structure over time. Some interior forest may be useful to buffer undesirable social or biological impacts associated with edge.

One simple way to evaluate buffer capability is to calculate the area/perimeter (A/P) ratio for a given greenbelt or forest remnant. Larger areas usually have higher capability to provide buffer within their core. Both larger and more circular areas will have higher A/P ratios compared with smaller or more linear areas. For a circle of one acre, the A/P ratio is 58.5; while for a circle of 1,000 acres, the ratio is 1,861. One is less likely to be bothered by traffic noise or fumes, or the sight of development, in the larger area. The A/P ratios for squares, a more likely property boundary configuration, are slightly less than for circles. Long, narrow areas have much lower ratios.

Shape is also important in buffering capability. Shape buffering for an area of a given size may be quantitatively expressed by comparing its A/P ratio to that of an equal-area circle (Agee 1975). This buffer ratio is essentially a perimeter comparison that can be interpreted as an edge effect, with ratios near 1.0 (more circular) having least edge and smaller ratios having more edge. This ratio is independent of size of area, which may have significant effect on actual buffering capability. A greenbelt in a residential development (Figure 11-1B) has a buffer ratio of 0.42, while one portion of a national park in which edge effects were deemed significant has a buffer ratio of 0.43 (Figure 11-1C). The "open space" of another proposed development has a buffer ratio of 0.03 (Figure 11-1D). The contact edge for people is much higher, but the biological edge may require intensive management.

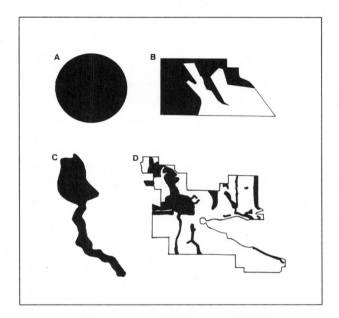

Figure 11-1. Buffer ratios are the ratio of the area/perimeter of an area divided by the area/perimeter of an equal-sized circle. (A) The circle has a buffer ratio of 1.0. (B) A development with a sensitive area greenbelt, with a buffer ratio of 0.42. (C) A riparian strip in a park, with a buffer ratio of 0.43. (D) A proposed development with substantial "open space," with a buffer ratio of 0.03.

REMNANT AND EMERGENT LANDSCAPES

The management of a greenbelt or forest remnant depends not only on management objectives but on the state of the landscape. The landscape may be a fresh one, such as bare soil, from which a new greenbelt may emerge. Alternatively it may be a remnant of a former landscape, in dictionary terms "what is left over..., a fragment..., a trace." Salvaging a sustainable landscape character from such pieces requires imaginative strategies.

Predictable patterns of stand development occur in natural landscapes. These have been described in most general form as *single cohort* or *multiple cohort* patterns depending on intervening disturbances during the development period. These patterns can be mimicked by urban forest managers in developing or retaining greenbelt or forest remnant structure over time. It should be emphasized that such planning (1) involves long periods, so that quick-fix approaches may not work, and (2) may involve an intensive, hands-on approach that can conflict with social expectations for wild urban forest areas.

The single cohort stand development (Figure 11-2) goes through four stages: the stand initiation or establishment phase; the stem exclusion or thinning stage; the understory reinitiation or transition stage; and the old-growth or steady-state stage (Oliver and Larson 1990; Peet and Christensen 1987). In very large, "wild" urban forests, such stages may be allowed to occur through natural succession. Usually, though, management may be desirable to modify natural stand development sequences to more quickly attain or maintain a desirable landscape structure. For example, in the stand initiation stage, forest stands are often too dense, so that many stems compete for growing space. Thinning can increase the growth of desirable residual trees and remove slower-growing, less desirable trees before they are removed by nature in the stem exclusion stage of forest development. Windthrow may be decreased and fire hazard lessened by this more "proactive" stance. As with most treatment, side effects may be undesirable. Opening the stand too early may encourage even more tree regeneration, or allow undesirable understory plants to invade the growing space. In the stem exclusion stage, thinning may also be used to concentrate growth on desirable stems but can also open a stand to accelerated windthrow. Patch thinning can be used to open growing space for a new cohort of young trees, essentially beginning the understory reinitiation stage. This may be desired for visual diversity, for screening purposes, or to replace a stand in stages that for reasons of disease, potential windthrow, or old age may not be sustainable over the long run.

The second major stand development sequence is the multiple cohort pattern (Figure 11-3), where several age classes coexist over a small area. In natural stands, this has been caused by disturbance opening up gaps in the forest while leaving a substantial component of the existing age classes. Fire and wind have been responsible for historical multiple cohort stand development patterns on the landscapes that become greenbelts and forest remnants.

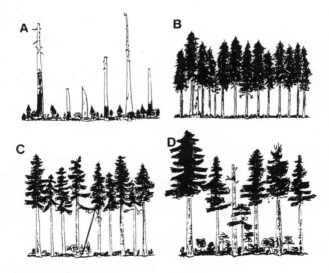

Figure 11-2. A single cohort stand development scenario after major disturbance. Forest remnants can be in any of these stages: (A) stand establishment; (B) stem exclusion; (C) understory reinitiation; (D) old growth. In the Pacific Northwest, progression through to the old-growth stage may take hundreds of years; most lowland forest remnants are in the stem exclusion stage.

Figure 11-3. A multiple cohort stand development scenario. Disturbances open the canopy but do not kill the entire stand, allowing initiation of a new cohort. This pattern, repeated several times, creates a several-aged stand.

Figure 11-4. Without management of edge effects, wind damage can work its way progressively into the stand.

Remnant Landscapes

Most remnant forest patches, whether they begin with a single or a multiple cohort structure, will eventually become multiple cohort stands because of increased edge, recreational use, and disturbance by wind or human-caused fire. The manager's choice is to plan for multiple cohort forest stands, or to accept those that nature will provide, possibly in a catastrophic manner, given the remnant condition of the patch. Multiple cohort, multiple species stands are more likely to function effectively, in a social sense, if they are varied enough to be resistant to insects and diseases (which are often species specific), wind, and possibly fire (if fire-resistant trees are part of the species mix).

In most remnant landscapes in the Pacific Northwest, hardwoods such as alders (*Alnus* spp.), cottonwoods (*Populus* spp.), or maples (*Acer* spp.) are an early successional component that will be replaced by conifers. They are commonly found in young-growth forests that got their start after logging but before development occurred in the area. The hardwoods tend to represent a higher recreational hazard than conifers because their limbs are heavier and they often break in summer windstorms, when people are more likely to be in the area. Thinning hardwoods and planting trees such as western redcedar (*Thuja plicata*), which grow well in small gaps, is a good way to make the transition between the stem exclusion and understory reinitiation stages of a single cohort stand, and begin the transition to a multiple cohort stand. Hardwoods can be very desirable in emergent landscapes or at the edges of remnant forests, but within stands they are eventual losers in the successional sequence to conifers, which are genetically programmed to grow taller and overshadow their broadleaved competitors.

The biggest challenge in remnant landscapes is to mitigate biological edge, particularly that associated with wind. In "wall" edges, one of two outcomes is likely with no mitigation. The wall blows down at its edge, and the blowdown progresses over time toward the interior of the stand, or edge trees are thinned by the wind and branches on residual trees are "pruned" off by breakage (Figure 11-4).

Three mitigation strategies may be employed to lessen this edge progression. The first is the most common, and that is to do nothing. It may be biologically appropriate where edge effects are assumed to be less significant than elsewhere. In most cases, it is legally or politically the only feasible option, given regulations on "sensitive areas." The second is rarely employed but can be effective, and that is to create a transitional edge that is less abrupt than the typical "wall" of trees next to graded land. Some trees are removed and others are pruned at every other whorl (Figure 11-5) to ensure that wind will enter and

Figure 11-5. Selective whorl pruning of the tree on the left creates a crown pattern on the right which is less vulnerable to windthrow.

Figure 11-6. A forest edge management strategy to reduce wind impact. Whorl pruning on trees near the edge, and creating a "stepped" wall by planting vegetation that will deflect wind up and over a stand, will reduce forest edge impacts.

shake, rather than blow over, the edge trees. The idea is to create a defensible edge in advance of nature. A third option is to create a deflective device in front of the edge. Buildings can serve this function, but so can fast-growing trees. Hardwoods in particular will grow well along the edge (Figure 11-6), and if species such as hybrid poplars (e.g., *Populus trichocarpa* x *deltoides*) are planted, the buffer can be in place within several years. Even though most hardwoods are out of leaf in winter when conifers are most at risk, their stem and branch structure will buffer a "wall" edge of conifers. Along especially exposed edges, a stepped planting of shrubs, alders, and cottonwoods can "push" winds over the tops of adjacent conifer forest remnants.

Most natural forest remnants harbor pockets of endemic disease. In the Pacific Northwest, laminated root rot (*Phellinus weirii*) is a common disease in lowland forests west of the Cascades. Where such pockets exist, the most sensitive species, such as Douglas-fir, will be killed or susceptible to windthrow. Surveys by forest pathologists can identify such pockets, and species more resistant to that disease—such as western hemlock, red alder (*Alnus rubra*), or western redcedar for laminated root rot—may be planted in the gaps created if tree cover is desirable. Such pockets can be used to encourage a multiple cohort, multiple species stand.

Figure 11-7. In a small forest remnant, traffic impact can vary from: (top) little impact, where understory vegetation and tree regeneration are healthy; (middle) substantial impact, where understory is clumped around tree stems and elsewhere absent; to (bottom) where traffic is heaviest, no understory exists.

Gaps in the forest cover created by disease, windthrow, or patch thinning are important to encourage shrub and herb cover. However, management of traffic is critical if understory vegetation is to survive. An example of managed versus unmanaged traffic in the same small urban park (Figure 11-7) suggests that excessive trampling can eliminate future vegetation management options as well as destroying current understory plants and lowering the vigor of overstory trees through soil compaction and root damage. Hardening trails, using thinned or downed hazard trees as barriers, and adequate signing are important ways to mitigate direct recreational use. Sometimes thorny vegetation such as devil's club (*Oplopanax horridum*) in wet areas, or wild roses (*Rosa* spp.) or blackberries (*Rubus* spp.), will effectively deter unwanted use adjacent to trails.

Emergent Landscapes

Emergent landscapes are those built from scratch. They may occur as a product of the development process, or after a natural catastrophe such as a hurricane-force wind or a fire. They present unique opportunities and challenges. Rather than taking what is left of a remnant landscape, one can build a new forest or greenbelt. Planned use in the future must be a part of the emergent landscape design process. Emergent landscapes almost always begin as single cohort stands, because of the typical flush of start-up funds that allows complete planting of a site. Eventually, a multiple cohort structure will result from management or nature unless the emergent landscape is very large.

In the Pacific Northwest, conifers and hardwoods can be intermixed in plantings to provide complementary mixes of form, line, color, and texture (e.g., Litton 1968) during the stand establishment stage on the landscape. Recognizing the differential growth rates and life spans of these trees, alders and Douglas-fir may be interplanted, but control on alder density must be done early in the stand establishment stage, because Douglas-fir is very intolerant of shade. Eventually alder should be removed from interior forest locations after its nitrogen-fixing abilities have been utilized by the interplanted firs. Alder is relatively short-lived and becomes a recreational hazard within twenty-five to thirty years. One alternative to taller red alder is Sitka alder (*Alnus sinuata*), which provides the same nitrogen-fixing ability but is much shorter. Using Sitka alder can help the conifers and reduce later management costs of removing or managing tree hazards (Harrington and Deal 1982). On poor sites, Douglas-fir needs to be given a head start of several years so it is not overtopped by the Sitka alder. Western redcedar or western hemlock can be interplanted under red alder, as they are tolerant of the shade, but since the cedar is more disease-resistant it is generally favored. Obviously, control over recreational use is important to prevent tree scarring, removal, or soil compaction. True firs should be avoided because of their propensity to be pirated as Christmas trees.

Underplanting of smaller native trees, such as vine maple (*Acer circinatum*) or Pacific yew (*Taxus brevifolia*), can be done during any thinning operation. Simulating the understory reinitiation stage by patch thinning to create small gaps is an excellent way to vary the structure of a single cohort stand, and create sustainable diversity in forest species composition and structure.

CONCLUSIONS

The suggestions in this chapter for active management of forest remnants and greenbelts follow from the almost inevitable and often undesirable changes that occur in forest greenbelt and remnant areas after establishment. Certainly there are few mandates for such active management and usually no maintenance funds. In some cases the desire for a "wild" landscape may override hazard-tree or windthrow management plans.

The desire for urban forest landscapes, along with the fact they will be forced into smaller and more "unnatural" configurations within urban environments, suggests that active management may be more common in the future. Forward-looking managers must start thinking of the landscape character desired in those future times, as such character cannot be created overnight.

Several obvious problems confront the forward-looking manager: (1) reconciling the many objectives for forest greenbelts and remnants; (2) defining desired future landscape conditions as targets for urban silvicultural practices; and (3) dealing with continuing unwillingness to make management investments today for benefits that will accrue to future generations. The constituency for acquisition is much more vocal than the one for management, even though we buy these areas once yet manage them in perpetuity. Overcoming these practical difficulties may be impossible until we face increasing problems of greenbelt and forest remnant damage, necessitating some form of management. The 1990s may well be the era of a new urban forestry capable of projecting the state of the forest into future decades and managing to achieve societal objectives.

LITERATURE CITED

Agee, J.K. 1975. Management options for Redwood Creek, Redwood National Park. National Park Service, Western Region, San Francisco, California.

Agee, J.K., S.C.F. Stitt, M. Nyquist, and R. Root. 1989. A geographic analysis of historical grizzly bear sightings in the North Cascades. Photogrammetric Engineering and Remote Sensing 55:1637-1642.

Harrington, C.A., and R.L. Deal. 1982. Sitka alder, a candidate for mixed stands. Canadian Journal of Forest Research 12:108-111.

Litton, R.B. 1968. Forest landscape description and inventories: A basis for land planning and design. Research Paper PSW-49. USDA Forest Service.

Noss, R. 1987. Protecting natural areas in fragmented landscapes. Natural Areas Journal 7:2-13.

Oliver, C.D., and B.C. Larson. 1990. Forest stand dynamics. McGraw-Hill, New York.

Peet, R., and N. Christensen. 1987. Competition and tree death. Bioscience 37:586-595.

Quinn, T. 1992. The distribution, movements, and diet of coyotes in urban areas of western Washington. Ph.D. dissertation, University of Washington, Seattle.

Simberloff, D., and J. Cox. 1987. Consequences and costs of conservation corridors. Conservation Biology 1:63-71.

Soule, M., and D. Simberloff. 1986. What do genetics and ecology tell us about the design of nature reserves. Biological Conservation 35:19-40.

Thomas, J.W., tech. ed. 1979. Wildlife habitat in managed forests: The Blue Mountains of Oregon and Washington. USDA Forest Service Agriculture Handbook 553.

12

Wildlife Habitat Design in Urban Forest Landscapes

DOROTHY A. MILLIGAN RAEDEKE and KENNETH J. RAEDEKE

ABSTRACT Wildlife habitat is greatly altered in the process of urbanization, and maintenance of wildlife populations is often a controversial element of the development process. The objective of wildlife habitat management in urban environments is to maintain biological diversity by retaining sufficient habitat for the maximum number of wildlife species. Landscape design issues that must be considered are the size, composition, connectivity, and dynamics of the habitat patches, and human perceptions of the habitat areas. There are also important constraints in incorporating wildlife habitat into urban environments, such as human health and safety issues and allocation of both land and monetary resources. For example, if land or funds are allocated for an extensive linear corridor system, it may not be possible to retain patches of sufficient size to provide adequate habitat for the targeted wildlife species. The design of wildlife habitat should reflect the general context of the area. Recommended design elements in an urban landscape will be different from those in a transitional landscape, thus providing habitat for different species across a gradient from urban to rural areas. Design objectives must clearly recognize these constraints, and expectations must be consistent with the potential of the area to incorporate wildlife.

In the process of urbanization, wildlife habitat is altered. Some areas are totally converted to intense urban uses and most wildlife habitat values are lost, while others are altered to lesser degrees. The value of what remains depends on how the habitat is treated in the development process. With proper consideration and understanding of basic concepts of landscape design, high quality wildlife habitat can be maintained within the urban forest landscape.

Several review articles have summarized the results of studies of urban wildlife habitat (see Stenberg and Shaw 1986; Adams and Dove 1989). In this paper we discuss the importance of the different elements of wildlife habitat design within urban forests, and provide recommendations for improving habitat in the process. These elements include patch size, shape, and composition, the connection between patches (connectivity), and patch dynamics and viability. It must be recognized that each decision directing land use allocation is a compromise between the different disciplines and resources. And even within the wildlife management discipline, land and resource allocations are a compromise; for example, if land is allocated to a corridor, there may be less land dedicated to habitat patches. The question is, What are the best allocations of these limited resources?

LANDSCAPE MANAGEMENT OBJECTIVES

The objectives of wildlife habitat management within urban forest environments are similar to general wildlife management objectives. We want to provide adequate habitat (food, cover, and water) for the greatest variety of wildlife by maintaining the greatest diversity of habitats. These habitats must also be viable in the long term, and ideally would be sustainable with little or no management intervention. But we must recognize the need to undertake management to meet specific habitat objectives.

Maximizing biodiversity includes a recognition of three components: within-patch (*alpha*) diversity, between-patch (*beta*) diversity, and regional or landscape (*gamma*) diversity (Whittaker 1972, 1977). Alpha diversity is determined by the characteristics within the habitat patch: structural complexity, patch size, patch shape, composition of the plant communities, and the presence of special habitat features, such as snags (dead, standing trees), downed logs, and water. Alpha diversity is lower in small habitat patches (with minimal structural and plant species diversity) than in larger habitats (with multilayered vegetation).

Beta diversity is the species richness found at the juncture of two patches; it is what wildlife biologists refer to as the "edge effect" (Leopold 1933), created whenever two different environments meet. Edges provide a high degree of habitat diversity because of the additive results when two plant communities or patch conditions come together. Along habitat edges, species common to either plant community may be found, as well as other species that may be the product of the edge itself. For example, edges provide the habitat requirements for bird species that nest in forest canopies and feed in the air over open fields, or for deer that rest in forest stands and feed in adjacent shrublands.

Gamma diversity is the degree of habitat diversity across the landscape, and is the product of the alpha and beta diversity for all the patches and communities within the region. Gamma diversity is greater in areas where a variety of habitat patches are

Table 12-1. Species pool for the habitats in the Puget Sound lowlands of King County, Washington.

Habitat	Number of species			
	Birds	Mammals	Amphibians, reptiles	Total
Shrub wetland	8	3	4	15
River and stream	11	6	3	20
Riparian forest	59	22	11	92
Grass/forb	17	20	9	46
Grasslands	38	8	3	49
Shrublands	32	22	11	65
Conifer forest	57	25	14	96
Deciduous forest	54	24	14	92
Mixed forest	48	22	14	84
Urban/Suburban	60	16	4	80
Urban/Suburban	37	11	2	50

Source: King County (1987).

interspersed across the landscape, individual patches are larger, and connecting areas are more substantial. This is demonstrated by Table 12-1. Using King County, Washington (1987), as an example, we calculated the number of vertebrate species that find adequate habitat conditions in the cover types found in the county. The results clearly demonstrate the potential increase in species diversity when a mosaic of different habitat cover types are retained.

MANAGEMENT APPROACHES

There are three basic approaches to providing wildlife habitat in urban forests: preservation of specific habitat areas on a case-by-case basis, restoration of specific habitat areas, and design of wildlife habitat on a landscape basis. The approach that one will adopt is generally dictated by the existing conditions, the degree of urbanization, and the regulatory opportunities to direct land use on a landscape scale.

Preservation of special habitat areas during the process of urbanization is a common practice. Habitat preservation is most commonly employed for special habitat areas, such as wetlands and streams. In some jurisdictions there are also requirements for retaining open spaces and provisions for protecting some types of wildlife habitat. The King County Sensitive Areas Ordinance of 1990 is an example of the types of habitat protection that can be expected through current regulatory approaches.

Habitat restoration is most appropriate for valued habitats, such as wetlands, mature forests, riparian systems and streams, or even pastoral grasslands. Restoration of such habitats is a difficult and expensive process with no guarantees of success. In general it is easier to preserve habitats than to restore or recreate them at a later time. However, in many instances restoration can be an effective means of providing high quality wildlife habitat in urban environments; see, for example, Milligan (1985) for a discussion of habitat values of created wetlands in urban environments.

Effective wildlife habitat is often created in urban settings as part of the development design process. Urban design features can produce wildlife habitat even when their primary function is not habitat creation. For example, ponds for stormwater runoff control can be designed to provide wildlife habitat in addition to stormwater detention (Milligan 1985; Adams et al. 1986), and similar results can be achieved in powerline right-of-way corridors (Leedy et al. 1980), golf courses, cemeteries (Howard 1987), aesthetic landscape plantings and water features (Ziebell 1986), and rockeries.

LANDSCAPE DESIGN ISSUES

Not all landscape and wildlife habitat management issues are relevant to urban forest design, nor are all wildlife species appropriate for urban forest habitats, even though they may be found in the surrounding forest lands. In the urban forest landscape we are most concerned with providing suitable habitat patches within an urban context. Thus we focus on these individual habitat patches and their relationship to other patches in the urban forest mosaic. This section discusses the management aspects and characteristics most relevant in the urban forest landscape.

Patch Size and Shape

Many studies have found that the size of habitat patches is a major determinant of the number of species that an area can support; see Adams and Dove (1989) for a review. In general, as the patch size increases, so do the number and type of species that can find adequate habitat in the patch. Small urban forest patches can support a variety of small birds and mammals, such as songbirds, mice, voles, shrews, squirrels, rabbits, and some small predators. With larger forest patches one can also find larger mammals such as deer and coyotes.

Dickman (1987) studied fifty isolated habitat patches in an urban area to determine their use by mammals, reptiles, and amphibians. He found that patch size and nearness to open water influenced amphibian and reptile use. Habitat patches of at least 1.4 acres were required to support amphibians and reptiles. For small mammals, a minimum patch size of 1.6 acres was required.

Vizyova (1986) found that the size of the habitat patch was the best predictor of the number of terrestrial and avian species. He concluded that to manage for land vertebrates, the minimum patch size should be 12.5 acres, with an optimum of 50 to 70 acres.

Larger forest patches also provide interior habitat for those species that avoid the edge habitat. For example, many species of birds prefer the interior of forests, and will not successfully nest in small forest patches that consist almost entirely of edge habitat. These birds generally avoid areas within 100 meters of the edge of the patch. Hence, if a forest patch is to provide interior habitat for these species, it must be a minimum of 200 meters in diameter.

Levenson (1981) classified woodlots of less than 5.7 acres as edge communities due to the high abundance of shade intolerant plants. Species richness was highest in woodlots of about 5.7 acres because of the mixing of shade tolerant and intolerant species.

The amount of edge for a given size of patch can be greatly affected by the shape of the patch. For example, linear patches have much more edge per unit area than square patches do, and circles have the least amount. Varying the patch shape can be used as a tool to create edge or, conversely, to maintain interior habitat.

Patch Composition

All else being equal, habitat patches with greater structural and habitat complexity will support a larger number of species. Increased structural diversity allows for greater resource partitioning (MacArthur 1965). Birds, for instance, often partition a given habitat by using different layers or strata, such as forest floor, low shrubs, tree trunks, lower canopy, and upper canopy. More bird species will find adequate habitat in a patch that includes these various structural features.

Numerous studies have demonstrated the value of habitat complexity in urban forest environments. Gavareski (1976) compared bird communities in forested urban parks with those in a larger natural area in Seattle. She found that large urban parks with a natural diversity of vegetation supported bird populations similar to the natural area used as a control. She also found that the number and diversity of birds declined as vegetation was removed.

Habitat complexity can to some degree compensate for small patch size. Linehan et al. (1967) found very dense populations of a large variety of breeding birds in urban woodlots as small as 20 acres when they included an adequate shrub understory, mature trees, and standing dead trees (snags). However, Whitcomb et al. (1981) noted that interior forest species were absent from the smaller habitat patches.

Habitat suitability for wildlife can be increased in a given patch through the presence of special habitat features, such as downed logs, natural debris piles, snags, rock piles and talus, floating logs and islands in wetlands, perches and roosts, and cavities. The importance of snags is probably the most well known of these features. In western Washington, approximately fifty species of forest wildlife (including birds, mammals, reptiles, and amphibians) are considered to be dependent on snags and downed logs for nesting in cavities and on limbs, as feeding sites, for perching and roosting, and for denning (Brown 1985).

PATCH DYNAMICS AND VIABILITY

As noted by Agee (in this book), the only constant landscape feature is change. Habitat change occurs primarily through the process of natural succession or through disturbance. Disturbance can be planned or unplanned, and can occur as a result of human actions or natural events. Some habitat patches within the landscape are more vulnerable to disturbance and change than others.

The patterns of succession after disturbance of coniferous forests in the Pacific Northwest are well documented (see Brown 1985 and Kruckeberg 1991). After fire, timber harvesting, or other disturbance, the forest is rapidly invaded by early successional communities such as the initial grass-forb communities. As these plant communities change over time, the wildlife community also changes, with new species replacing those found in earlier successional stages (see Table 12-2).

The successional patterns of plant communities must be considered when evaluating habitat potential in urban forest landscapes. Many highly desirable communities may not be maintained or even achieved in the long run through simple preservation. Continued management or disturbance may be required to prevent the reinvasion by trees, and eventual succession to forest stands. For example, in western Washington where conifer forests dominate the landscape, grasslands and pastures are a pleasant change in the landscape, and provide habitat for a variety of wildlife not found in the forest stands. However, most of these grasslands were formerly forest stands, and are

Table 12-2. Numbers of wildlife species in stages of forest succession following clearcutting. Changes are given as the number of species present in a given stage relative to the previous stage.

Successional stage	Number of species			
	Total	Gained	Lost	Net
Old-growth forest	152	—	—	—
Grass-forb	177	74	49	+25
Shrub-seedling	187	35	25	+10
Pole-sapling	157	13	43	−30
Young forest	161	17	13	+4
Mature forest	167	16	10	+6
Old-growth forest	152	1	16	−15

Source: Modified from Raedeke (1988).

maintained only through constant grazing or mowing, and without these activities will rapidly revert to forest. Typically there would be an invasion of shrubs, followed by deciduous trees such as red alder (*Alnus rubra*), maples (*Acer* spp.), and cottonwoods (*Populus* spp.), and then finally by conifers (see Kruckeberg 1991).

As noted by Agee (this volume), habitat features that result from retention of forest patches are vulnerable to windthrow, fire, disease, and other natural disturbances. Some of these changes may be beneficial to wildlife, while others may reduce the habitat's value. Fire or insects may kill trees and hence create snags. These are generally limited features in urban forests. Windthrow would create downed logs and organic debris for the forest floor and for riparian and stream corridors. However, windthrow and fire can totally eliminate a forest patch or corridor.

Connectivity

Corridors are usually considered to be linear strips of habitat serving as links between habitat areas (Adams and Dove 1989). They are widely acclaimed as key elements for maintaining wildlife populations and diversity in the process of landscape design and management. The corridor concept is largely derived from the equilibrium theory of island biogeography (MacArthur and Wilson 1967). Corridors are considered to play an important role in maintaining healthy, reproducing plant and animal populations, assisting in maintaining species that require more resources than are available in a single patch, and perhaps constituting important habitat in their own right (see Simberloff and Cox 1987).

While the corridor concept is widely accepted by many land use planners, there is still scientific debate about the value and function of corridors. Simberloff et al. (1992) notes that much information on corridors is "outside the bounds of mainstream science," and questions the allocation of scarce resources, such as land (i.e., habitat) and conservation funds, to maintain or restore corridors in urbanizing environments.

Corridors may also pose conservation problems by facilitating transmission of contagious diseases, fires, or other catastrophes, and increasing exposure of animals to predators, domestic animals, and poachers (Simberloff and Cox 1987). Quinn (1992) noted in his research that urban coyotes were most commonly associated with greenbelts (e.g., corridors), and that these greenbelts facilitated the movement of coyotes through the area. In turn, the coyotes were important urban predators that ate a variety of other urban wildlife and substantial numbers of domestic dogs and cats. Coyote predation actually improved conditions for some urban wildlife as the predation pressure by dogs and cats was reduced. By definition, corridors are composed entirely of edge habitat, and support mainly edge species.

Human Perceptions and Safety

Wildlife habitat retained in urban forest landscapes must be perceived by the community as an amenity and not as a source of pests, disease, or waste. Lands that are not valued by the community are commonly degraded and used to dump urban refuse and lawn wastes (Adams and Dove 1989). This topic is discussed in other contributions to this volume.

Concern for human safety in urban environments is a potential constraint to development of effective wildlife habitat. In urban parks the understory vegetation is often cleared to reduce cover for muggers and other criminal elements. This loss of understory vegetation reduces the value of such areas for wildlife (Gavareski 1976).

Some habitat features are also considered to be safety hazards. Current health and safety regulations in Washington State often require that snags be removed. They are considered to be a hazard to people working in the woods, or safety hazards within development areas. Loss of snags can greatly reduce the number of woodpeckers that feed on insects in snags, and cavity nesting birds that excavate cavities in snags.

Some species of wildlife are not desirable in urban areas, and provision of habitat or corridors for them is not warranted. Problem species in western Washington include bears (*Ursus americanus*), cougars (*Felis concolor*), and to a lesser degree, coyotes (*Canis latrans*), beaver (*Castor canadensis*), deer (*Odocoileus hemionus*), and elk (*Cervus elaphus*). Raccoons (*Procyon lotor*) and some other species can be potential carriers of rabies and other disease. In Washington, the Department of Wildlife has active programs to deal with "pest" species and other wildlife that are incompatible with urban lands. Considerable effort is required to capture and remove species such as beavers, bears, and the occasional cougar from urban areas.

WILDLIFE HABITAT AND THE URBAN FOREST GRADIENT

The wildlife habitat features appropriate for incorporation into the urban landscape will depend on the degree of urban development, and the eventual degree of urbanization in the final landscape. Priorities for wildlife habitat features in these landscapes will also vary with the degree of urbanization. In the following sections, we contrast two ends of this urban forest gradient: urban areas and the transitional forest lands that are in the process of urbanization.

Urban Lands

In this discussion, urban lands are defined as those areas that are largely developed but still have some undeveloped patches of habitat. Parks, golf courses, cemeteries, and other types of open space are also located within the developed areas. Much of the urban open space is likely to be disturbed and degraded, or else previously developed land that has been abandoned. These areas are the primary potential habitat patches for incorporation into a wildlife landscape plan.

Patch size and shape will be largely dictated by the existing conditions, as will potential for effective corridors linking existing patches. Corridor and patch composition may conflict with concerns for human health and safety. Plant community succession will be a minor concern, since these are largely managed areas in which natural plant community succession has been truncated by management.

Parklike habitats with limited understory but high aesthetic value will be the most acceptable habitats. While these areas will provide habitat for common species typically adapted to urban environments, they can also support substantial populations of less urban-associated wildlife, including waterfowl, squirrels, and other small mammals, and passerine and other bird species.

Wildlife habitat management in urban areas should seek to preserve more natural habitat patches where possible, retain habitat features within urban parks and open space, and restore habitats in abandoned and disturbed areas. Retention or addition of complex layers of vegetation, where possible, will increase wildlife species diversity (see Penland 1984; Milligan 1985), but concerns for human safety must be considered. Nest boxes and other artificial habitat features can also be provided in such managed landscapes if maintenance of these features is included in the management program.

Transitional Urban Forest Landscapes

We define transitional urban forest lands as rural forest and agricultural lands that are under conversion to more intense urban uses such as residential, business, or planned community developments. These are the lands on the urban forest fringe. In western Washington they are characteristically lands that have been altered by forestry practices and by some limited conversion to agricultural uses. Urbanization takes the form of a patchwork of residential blocks within the mosaic of a variety of forest stands and agricultural lands. Alpha, beta, and gamma diversity for wildlife habitat can be quite high due to the intermingling of habitats, with many substantial patches in a fairly natural forest condition.

In this landscape, there are opportunities to design for specific resource purposes, since much of the land has not been developed. Unlike the urban setting, where many patch characteristics are relatively fixed or are limited by human safety concerns, the transitional landscape can be designed to meet specific objectives within the constraints of property ownership rights, available resources for land purchase and management, and the regulatory framework.

The approach to landscape design for maximum wildlife habitat in this setting would be to retain as much of the variety in habitat patches as possible, to retain and enhance key habitats (such as wetlands and stream systems), and to maximize habitat patch size where possible. Since human safety is not an intense issue in this landscape, habitat patches should be retained in their "natural" condition, or allowed to develop into vegetatively and structurally complex habitats if they have been disturbed.

Grasslands and shrublands require active management to prevent their eventual conversion to forest stands through natural succession. Table 12-2 shows that retention of these habitats increases the variety of wildlife species in this landscape. Habitats such as grasslands have high appeal to local residents, but active management may not be practical or feasible, depending on ultimate landownership.

If special habitat areas (such as wetlands and riparian areas) are retained and a full range of the existing habitat patches are maintained in fairly large blocks, we expect that transitional urban forest landscapes can continue to support the complete array of resident species. The exception would be large mammals, especially elk, cougars, and bears. Provision of corridors in the transitional landscape should be of secondary concern. While the corridor concept has been widely accepted in the popular literature, many ecologists question their efficacy (see Simberloff et al. 1992), and suggest that limited resources would be more productive if allocated to other habitat uses. Many of the species most commonly considered to benefit from corridors may not be appropriate for urban forest landscapes (such as cougars, bears, deer, and other large mammals).

MANAGEMENT OBJECTIVES

As noted above, there are potential limitations to providing effective wildlife habitat in the urban environment. The objectives of a wildlife habitat management program must be consistent with human safety and perceptions regarding habitat values. The species intended for the landscape must also be consistent with the capabilities of the habitat patches.

It is inappropriate to provide habitat or corridors that would encourage movement of some species of wildlife into urban areas. Bear, cougar, deer, and elk have been determined by state wildlife departments as inappropriate urban species. In addition to concerns for human safety, substantial property damage can result from interaction with these species. And once established, they can be very difficult to manage and control.

In a recent land use project in King County, Washington, we were asked to recommend the amount of stream buffer that would be adequate to provide a movement corridor for black bears through a proposed subdivision down to a stream that supported salmon. Our recommendation, which was supported by the Washington Department of Wildlife, and ultimately by the county planners, was to provide only minimal buffers along the stream to meet water quality and fish habitat protection needs, and to discourage bear movement through the area (Raedeke Associates 1990). Bears were considered to be an inappropriate species within this urban forest habitat.

Thus the objective should be to maintain habitat for the greatest variety of wildlife species that are compatible with urban uses. One must recognize the constraints imposed by human health and safety, and the habitat requirements of the species.

WILDLIFE HABITAT DESIGN PRIORITIES

The following recommendations for habitat design in the urban forest landscape are given in general order of priority for implementation, based on our evaluation of cost effectiveness and the potential for providing effective, sustainable wildlife habitat. They also assume that the resources available to provide habitat will be limited, and that land managers will be required to make allocations to potentially conflicting uses, such as affordable housing, parks, schools, hospitals, and other urban uses, as well as wildlife habitat.

The first priority should be to retain or restore special habitats that support high numbers of species or those with special conservation status. These habitats include many types of wetlands, mature forests with abundant snags and downed logs, and riparian vegetation and stream corridors. Restoration of some of these habitats may also be recommended, especially when there is a high probability of success.

The second priority would be to maximize patch size. This could be accomplished by grouping habitat patches into a single larger habitat area. Mitigation banking as a model for loss of wetlands could also be explored for upland communities. Combined mitigation banking of uplands and wetlands would provide larger and more complex habitat areas and support a disproportionately higher number of wildlife species than smaller or isolated habitat patches. Larger patches are also less vulnerable to natural disturbance such as windthrow, and are likely to be more sustainable without requiring active management. Retention of very small habitat patches within individual developments will provide habitat only for species adapted to urban conditions.

Third, we recommend that a variety of patch types be retained within the urban forest landscape. Retention of a habitat mosaic will increase beta and gamma diversity by providing edges and will increase the potential wildlife species pool for the landscape.

Fourth, where human health and safety allow, habitat management efforts should promote within-patch complexity (alpha diversity).

Finally, if resource allocation allows for corridors between habitat areas, such corridors should be incorporated. While there is no definitive proof that corridors function as is often claimed, they may well be an important landscape feature that would allow for movement of some wildlife between patches.

LITERATURE CITED

Adams, L.W., and L.E. Dove. 1989. Wildlife reserves and corridors in the urban environment: A guide to ecological landscape planning and resource conservation. National Institute for Urban Wildlife, Columbia, Maryland.

Adams, L., T. Franklin, L. Dove, and J. Duffield. 1986. Design considerations for wildlife in urban stormwater management. Trans. North Am. Wildl. and Nat. Resource Conf. 51:249-259.

Brown, E.R., ed. 1985. Management of wildlife and fish habitats in forests of western Oregon and Washington. USDA Forest Service Pub. R6-F&WL-192-1985. Portland, Oregon.

Dickman, C. 1987. Habitat fragmentation and vertebrate species richness in an urban environment. Journal of Applied Ecology 24:337-351.

Gavareski, C. 1976. Relation of park size and vegetation to urban bird populations in Seattle, Washington. Condor 78:375-382.

Howard, J. 1987. The garden of earthly remains. Horticulture 65:46-56.

King County. 1987. Wildlife habitat profile. King County Open Space Program. Parks, Planning, and Resources Department, Seattle, Washington.

Kruckeberg, A.R. 1991. The natural history of Puget Sound country. University of Washington Press, Seattle.

Leedy, D., L. Dove, and T. Franklin. 1980. Compatibility of fish, wildlife, and floral resources with electric power facilities and lands: An industry survey analysis. Edison Electric Institute, Washington, D.C.

Leopold, A. 1933. Game management. Charles Scribner's Sons, New York.

Levenson, J.B. 1981. Woodlots as biogeographic islands in southeastern Wisconsin. *In* R.L. Burgess and D.M. Sharpe, eds., Forest island dynamics in man-dominated landscapes, pp. 13-39. Springer-Verlag, New York.

Linehan, J., R. Jones, and J. Longcore. 1967. Breeding-bird populations in Delaware's urban woodlots. Audubon Field Notes 21:641-646.

MacArthur, R. 1965. Patterns of species diversity. Biological Review 40:510-533.

MacArthur, R., and E. Wilson. 1967. The theory of island biogeography. Princeton University Press, Princeton, New Jersey.

Milligan, D. 1985. The ecology of avian use of urban freshwater wetlands in King County, Washington. M.S. thesis, University of Washington, Seattle.

Penland, S. 1984. Avian responses to a gradient of urbanization in Seattle, Washington. Ph.D. dissertation, University of Washington, Seattle.

Quinn, T. 1992. The distribution, movements, and diet of coyotes in urban areas of western Washington. Ph.D. dissertation, University of Washington, Seattle.

Raedeke Associates. 1990. Wildlife habitat evaluation study for the Anstalt property, King County, Washington. Final Report RA-89-177. Seattle, Washington.

Raedeke, K. 1988. Forest management and wildlife in the Pacific Northwest. Northwest Environmental Journal 4:263-278.

Simberloff, D., and J. Cox. 1987. Consequences and costs of conservation corridors. Conservation Biology 1(1):63-71.

Simberloff, D., J. Farr, J. Cox, and D. Mehlman. 1992. Movement corridors: Conservation bargains or poor investments. Conservation Biology 6(4):493-504.

Stenberg, K., and W. Shaw, eds. 1986. Wildlife conservation and residential developments. University of Arizona, Tucson.

Vizyova, A. 1986. Urban woodlots as islands for land vertebrates: A preliminary attempt on estimating the barrier effects of urban structural units. Ecology (CSSR) 5:407-419.

Whitcomb, R.F., C.S. Robbins, J.F. Lynch, B.L. Whitcomb, M.K. Klimkiewicz, and D. Bystrak. 1981. Effects of forest fragmentation on avifauna of the eastern deciduous forest. *In* R.L. Burgess and D. M. Sharpe, eds., Forest island dynamics in man-dominated landscapes, pp. 125-205. Springer-Verlag, New York.

Whittaker, R. 1970. Communities and ecosystems. Macmillan, New York.

——. 1972. Evolution and measurement of species diversity. Taxon 21:213-251.

——. 1977. Evolution of species diversity in land communities. Evolutionary Biology 10:1-67.

Ziebell, C. 1986. Ponds and their associated habitat in residential settings. *In* K. Stenberg and W. Shaw, eds., Wildlife conservation and residential developments, pp. 102-104. University of Arizona, Tucson.

13

Energy-Efficient Landscapes

E. GREGORY McPHERSON, ROWAN A. ROWNTREE, and J. ALAN WAGAR

ABSTRACT A 25 foot tree reduces annual heating and cooling costs of a typical residence by about 8 to 12 percent ($10-$25). Assuming savings of $10 per household, a nationwide residential tree planting program could eventually save about $1 billion each year. Direct shade on the building will account for most of these savings in hot climates, while heating and cooling savings from reduced wind speeds and evapotranspirational cooling will be relatively more important in cooler climates. The energy conservation potential of landscapes is greatest in residential and commercial land uses, where planting space is most available and buildings consume large amounts of energy for heating and cooling. The greatest cooling savings can be obtained by shading the west side of air-conditioned buildings located in areas with the hottest climates. In cool climates the need for wind protection tends to result in a more "closed" landscape structure than in hot climates, where an "open" landscape enhances cooling breezes. The structure of energy-efficient landscapes can complement landscapes designed for wildlife, visual quality, sustainability, and buffering. Careful design can minimize potential conflicts with fire-safe and water conserving landscapes. Tree plantings for energy conservation are likely to become more commonplace due to their relatively flexible structural requirements, cost-effectiveness, and growing support from utilities and federal agencies.

As we enter the twenty-first century, the continued heavy consumption of fossil fuels for energy looms as a major problem. Dwindling petroleum supplies and the effects of climate change can have a devastating impact on our ecology and economy. A few degrees of warming may change ocean currents, global air circulation patterns, rainfall regimes, and agricultural capabilities enough to cause mass starvation in some regions. Hopefully, we will avoid such worst-case scenarios, and in working toward that goal energy-efficient landscapes are one means of conserving energy and creating a more sustainable society.

This chapter addresses several questions about energy-efficient landscapes. How can they improve environmental quality and conserve energy? Are they a cost-effective approach to conservation? In what ways do they conflict with or complement other types of landscapes within a city and a region? Answers to these questions should assist policy makers, urban foresters, utility and natural resource managers, design and planning professionals, and concerned citizens who are working to improve their local environments.

VEGETATION AND THE URBAN CLIMATE

Rapid urbanization in the United States during the past fifty years has been associated with a steady increase in downtown temperatures of about 1°F (0.8°C) per decade. The demand for electricity in U.S. cities increases abut 2 percent for every degree F (3-4% per °C) rise in temperature, and approximately 3 to 8 percent of the electricity used for cooling is needed to compensate for this urban heat island effect (Akbari et al. 1992). The warmer temperature in cities compared to surrounding rural areas has other implications, such as increases in carbon dioxide emissions from fossil fuel power plants, municipal water demand, unhealthy ozone levels, and human discomfort and disease. These problems could be accentuated by global climate change, which may double the rate of urban warming. The accelerating world trend toward urbanization, especially in tropical regions, hastens the need for energy-efficient landscapes.

Buildings, paving, and vegetation measurably affect the ambient temperatures of different sites within a city. Maximum temperatures within the green space of individual building sites may be 5°F (3°C) cooler than outside the green space (Saito et al. 1990-91). At the larger scale of urban climate (6 miles or 10 kilometers square), temperature differences of more than 9°F (5°C) have been observed between city centers and more vegetated suburban areas (Mizuno et al. 1990-91).

Urban forests ameliorate climate and human comfort through (1) shading, which reduces the amount of radiant energy absorbed, stored, and radiated by built surfaces, (2) evapotranspiration, which converts radiant energy into latent energy, thereby reducing sensible heat that warms the air, and (3) airflow modification, which affects transport and diffusion of energy, water vapor, and pollutants.

The relative importance of these effects depends on the area, surface roughness, and configuration of vegetation and other landscape elements (Wilmers 1990-91). Generally, large green spaces affect climate farther away than smaller ones do (areas of 10,000 square feet affect a relative distance of 600 to 900 feet) (Honjo and Takakura 1990-91). Tall trees influence surface roughness, and deciduous trees contribute to seasonal differences in turbulence (Oke 1989). Tree spacing, crown spread, and vertical distribution of leaf area influence the transport of cool air and pollutants along streets by advection, and out of urban canyons by turbulent mixing from above (Oke 1989; Barlag and Kuttler 1990-91).

For individual buildings, solar angles and infiltration are often important. Because the summer sun is low in the east and west for several hours each day, shade to protect east and especially west walls helps keep buildings cool. Rates at which outside air infiltrates into a building can increase substantially with wind speed. In cold, windy weather the entire volume of air in a poorly sealed home may change two to three times per hour (DeWalle and Heisler 1988). Even in newer or tightly sealed homes, the entire volume of air may change every two to three hours.

ENERGY SAVINGS FROM LANDSCAPES

Seven percent of the total energy consumed in the United States during 1987 was used for household heating and cooling, at a cost of $180 billion (EIA 1989). The average household spent $350 for heating and $109 for air-conditioning. These expenditures accounted for 32 percent and 10 percent of the typical annual energy bill ($1,090), respectively (EIA 1989). Results of experimental studies and computer simulations reviewed in the following section suggest that energy savings from a 25 foot tree range from $10 to $25 yearly. A nationwide residential tree planting program could eventually save about $1 billion each year, assuming a savings of $10 per household. Additional savings would accrue from effects of lower summertime temperatures on energy used by commercial buildings, many of which are air-conditioned. Electric utility customers could also benefit from reduced capital investment in peak electric generating capacity or power purchases and power plant emission controls.

Measured Savings

Relatively few studies have monitored effects of landscapes on building energy use. Monitoring studies are expensive and somewhat risky because factors such as occupant behavior, thermostat settings, and changing weather make it difficult to isolate the effects of landscapes on heating and air-conditioning. In a review of measured cooling savings from landscapes, vegetation was reported to consistently lower wall surface temperatures by about 30°F (17°C) (Meier 1990-91). Air-conditioning electricity savings ranged from 10 to 80 percent. In the Arizona studies (McPherson et al. 1988; Simpson 1991), turf alone provided cooling savings of 10 to 25 percent, largely due to evapotranspirational (ET) cooling. Shading from shrubs and trees in Florida (Parker 1983) and Pennsylvania (DeWalle et al. 1983) resulted in greater cooling savings.

Studies dating back to the 1930s have monitored heating savings from windbreaks and more recently have measured wind speed reductions in residential neighborhoods resulting from the combined effects of buildings and landscapes (Heisler 1990). Reported heating savings from windbreaks have ranged from 3 to 40 percent (Heisler 1986), with 10 to 12 percent savings found for a mobile home and detached houses in Pennsylvania and New Jersey, respectively.

Simulated Savings

The effects of landscapes on energy use in buildings are easier to simulate than to measure because all variables can be kept constant except the landscape. To date, most simulation studies have assumed mature trees and near optimum locations of vegetation around a limited number of building types. In reality, it may take five to fifteen years before trees grow large enough to provide the savings reported, or else additional expense is incurred by planting larger trees. And the opportunity to plant trees in optimal locations is constrained by the presence of utilities, narrow sideyards, paving, buildings, and existing vegetation. Therefore, the assumptions used in simulation studies should be as carefully scrutinized as the results. Simulations are best used to compare the relative impacts of different landscape treatments.

Recent simulation studies have used shading models and empirical data to incorporate effects of trees on solar gains, wind speed reductions, and air temperatures in building energy analysis (Wagar 1984; Huang et al. 1987, 1990; McPherson and Dougherty 1989; Akbari et al. 1990; Heisler 1991; Sand 1991; McPherson and Sacamano 1992). Results vary because of different assumptions regarding tree numbers, size, and locations; building insulation levels; and local climate. Generally, annual air-conditioning savings from a deciduous tree (25 feet tall and wide), near a well-insulated home, ranged from 10 to 15 percent (200-400 kWh, $15-$25) (McPherson and Rowntree 1993). Savings during peak cooling periods ranged from about 8 to 12 percent (0.4-0.5 kW).

Higher percentage air-conditioning savings for cities in cool climates compared to those in warm climates can be misleading, since estimated annual cooling energy (kWh) and dollar savings are greatest in warm climate cities. Reduced solar gains from tree shade account for most of the cooling savings in warm climate cities. The effect of ET cooling on air-conditioning is poorly understood. It was estimated to account for 25 to 50 percent of total cooling savings in one study (McPherson and Rowntree 1993), but found to be 60 to 80 percent in another (Huang et al. 1987).

For both heating and cooling, annual residential energy savings from a single 25 foot yard tree generally ranged from 2 to 8 percent, with the greatest dollar savings ($10 to $25 per year) in warm climates. As expected, reduced wind speeds from increased tree cover resulted in greatest heating savings in cool climate cities. For instance, in Boston and Minneapolis heating savings that were attributed to reduced wind speeds accounted for over 50 percent of the total annual energy savings (McPherson and Rowntree 1993). However, deciduous trees located to shade east and south walls can obstruct winter irradiance and provide little summer shade in cool climate cities. The result is increased energy costs compared to an unshaded condition (Thayer and Maeda 1985; Heisler 1986; Sand 1991). Therefore, the potential energy costs of trees improperly located near buildings are greatest in cool climates, while their potential energy savings are greatest in warm climates. In all climate zones, a tree shading the west-facing wall provides about twice the energy savings of the same tree shading a similar east-facing wall (McPherson and Rowntree 1993).

These monitoring and simulation studies suggest that landscape vegetation around individual buildings can provide heating savings of 5 to 15 percent and cooling savings of 10 to 50 percent. Despite our incomplete understanding of the aggregate effects of neighborhood trees on air temperature and wind speed, these indirect effects appear to be just as important as direct shading effects.

COST-EFFECTIVENESS OF ENERGY-EFFICIENT LANDSCAPES

Studies by scientists and electric utilities have reported that proper planting and care of trees to maximize building energy savings and mitigate heat islands can be more economical than other methods of reducing electrical demand, carbon dioxide emissions, and heat islands (e.g., light-colored surfaces; modifying urban geometry) (McPherson 1994). An increasing number of utility-sponsored tree planting programs for energy conservation indicate their cost-effectiveness.

The Arizona Corporation Commission (1990) staff recommended that utilities fund the development of consumer guides on energy-efficient landscaping and tree planting rebate programs. These recommendations were based on the results of a benefit-cost analysis that found the present value of net benefits for planting 180,000 trees to be $2.9 million. The analysis assumed planting costs of $45 per tree, annual water costs of $4 to $6 per tree, a 7 percent discount rate, and a 20 year planning horizon. Each tree was assumed to shade the west-facing wall and provide annual and peak savings of 250 kWh and 0.33 kW, respectively, after the fifth year. Trees were found to be an economical conservation measure because they met the need for cooling energy services at a lower cost than generation of electricity. Arizona utilities now support tree planting programs that are delivered through nonprofit groups such as Trees for Tucson/Global ReLeaf.

American Forests and the U.S. Environmental Protection Agency have implemented a Cool Communities Program to capture the potential of volunteerism with the goal of improving energy conservation through community tree planting and light-colored surfacing. Currently there are seven Model Cool Communities, with possible expansion to 250 cities as part of the Clinton administration's Global Change Action Plan.

The Energy Policy Act of 1992 requires utilities to include environmental externalities and other social costs associated with different energy supplies when evaluating the costs of alternative energy sources. Because energy-efficient landscapes can be cost-effective energy conservation measures and provide other economic, environmental, and aesthetic benefits that extend beyond the site where each tree is planted, utility and public sector investment in tree planting is likely to grow (Dwyer et al. 1992).

STRUCTURE OF ENERGY-EFFICIENT LANDSCAPES WITHIN A CITY

The physical structure of energy-efficient landscapes will differ within a city due largely to different land use characteristics. For instance, windbreaks are more suitable in low-density suburban residential areas than in high-density residential zones near the city center. This section examines how the potential for energy-conserving landscapes changes with land use and existing tree cover. A strategy is presented for identifying locations that are likely to provide the greatest return on investment in new tree planting for energy conservation.

Energy Conservation Potential of Different Land Uses

Land use is perhaps the single most important variable related to urban forest cover, because different land uses have characteristic development patterns that influence tree planting and survival (Rowntree 1984). Land use refers to the primary activity occurring on the land (e.g., commercial, residential, industrial), while land cover refers to the physical surface material covering an area (e.g., tree, building, paving, grass). Many city and county planning agencies map land use, but few map land cover. Both land use and land cover can be interpreted from aerial photographs and other remotely sensed imagery.

The potential of new tree plantings to conserve energy depends on the amount of plantable space within land uses. The amount of available growing space (AGS) is defined as land covered by grass, bare soil, shrub, and tree cover. Canopy stocking level (CSL) is defined as the percentage of AGS covered by trees and reflects the degree to which potential tree planting spaces have been filled (McPherson and Rowntree 1989). Areas with low CSL indicate relatively high tree planting potential. This definition is an approximate indicator of plantable space because some areas without tree cover are not suitable for trees due to other incompatible uses (e.g., ball fields, utilities, vehicular use), while some paved areas excluded from the index are actually plantable (e.g., sidewalks, parking lots, playgrounds).

To evaluate citywide tree planting potential it is necessary to consider the relative magnitude of land use types across a city, as well as CSL associated with each land use. A poorly stocked area occupying half of the city's land should support more new plantings than a similarly stocked area occupying only 10 percent of city land. A simple indicator of tree planting potential (TPP) by land use can be calculated, if percentages of CSL and area (A) are known, using the equation:

$$(1 - CSL) \times A = TPP.$$

Tree planting potentials have been estimated for one region based on data obtained from the Chicago Urban Forest Climate Project (McPherson et al. 1993). Differences in TPP span the urban-to-rural gradient: from densely populated Chicago, to the older suburban communities of Cook County, to the rapidly urbanizing farmlands of DuPage County. In all three sectors, TPP is greatest in the one-to-three-family residential land use category. Large commercial land uses are a second potential planting location. In Chicago, significant opportunities for tree planting exist in higher density residential, small commercial, and park land uses. The conversion of vacant and agricultural land to urban land uses provides substantial potential for tree planting in Cook and DuPage counties. Parks and forest preserves also have potential for increased tree numbers in suburban communities near Chicago. Although the values for CSL and area will differ for land uses across cities of varying size, age, and location, the relative ranking of tree planting potential will probably remain relatively constant.

Prioritizing New Planting Locations for Energy Conservation

The potential for tree planting in residential and commercial land uses is especially significant because buildings in these areas consume most of the heating and cooling energy used in a city. Therefore, adding vegetation is likely to provide the greatest net benefits when planting and maintenance costs and energy savings are calculated. At least two other factors need to be considered to further specify areas within these land uses where new tree plantings can achieve the greatest energy savings.

First, energy savings are likely to be greatest in areas where climate is most extreme. For example, cooling savings will be greater from trees shading homes in the hot interior valley of Los Angeles than from trees near homes in the clement coastal zone. Second, greater cooling savings will come from shaded buildings with air-conditioners or heat pumps than from shaded buildings with evaporative coolers or no mechanical cooling. Other building-related factors that influence potential energy savings include construction type (e.g., wood frame, masonry, slab, basement), floor area, building orientation, and the thermophysical properties of walls, windows, and roof. Also, setback distances of buildings from the street and other buildings influence the potential space for addition of new trees, as well as their shading impact.

Greater absolute energy savings can be obtained from older homes that are poorly insulated or loosely constructed than from new homes that are energy efficient. However, traditional energy conservation measures (e.g., double pane windows, insulation) may be more cost-effective than tree planting for older homes. Energy-efficient landscapes are likely to be more cost-effective for new construction, because most traditional conservation measures are already installed and the marginal costs of additional measures are relatively high compared to trees.

Finally, it is important to reiterate that sizable energy savings can be obtained from vegetation that does not directly shade buildings. The magnitude of indirect effects on air temperature, airflow, and radiation generally increases with increasing leaf surface area. Forest belts, riparian corridors, woodlots, and other "natural" landscapes contain large amounts of leaf surface area per unit land area. The salubrious influence of these vegetated masses on climate can extend well into the adjacent built environment, although further research is needed to document this impact on energy use.

To summarize planting priorities, residential and commercial land uses offer the greatest potential for new tree planting, and, coincidentally, these buildings consume the largest percentage of energy for heating and cooling. As a first priority, energy-efficient landscapes should be targeted to shade buildings and paved surfaces within these areas, while providing solar access and wind protection during winter. A more refined approach to maximize energy savings will further subdivide these areas based on factors such as local climate and pertinent characteristics of the building stock. Secondary opportunities for energy-efficient tree plantings are more likely to vary from city to city depending on land use patterns and canopy stocking levels.

STRUCTURE OF ENERGY-EFFICIENT LANDSCAPES IN DIFFERENT CLIMATIC ZONES

The ideal structure of energy-efficient landscapes in different climatic regions of the United States follows from principles of bioclimatic architectural design (Olgyay 1973). For instance, tree shade on the east side of buildings is a net benefit in warm climates but often a net cost in cold climates because of reduced winter solar heat gain, even from deciduous trees and shrubs. Generally, requirements for winter wind protection and solar access in cold climates result in residential landscapes with the following structural characteristics:

- Dense evergreen foundation plantings.
- Tall, dense evergreen and deciduous windbreaks, hedges, and buffers.
- Deciduous shade trees, shrubs, and vines shading west walls and air-conditioners (and in more temperate zones, east walls).
- Unobstructed sky space to the south for solar access.
- Deciduous trees shading sidewalks, parking lots, streets, and other paved surfaces.
- Multistory buffer plantings between neighborhoods.

Usually, energy-efficient landscapes in hot climates are more "open" than landscapes in cold climates, because airflow cools building surfaces, thereby minimizing air-conditioning use when temperatures are below 90°F (Givoni 1981). Structural characteristics of landscapes in hot climates can be generalized as follows:

- Evergreen shade trees, shrubs, and vines shading west and east (deciduous trees for south shade in areas without heating loads and solar collectors) building surfaces and air-conditioners.
- Open understory for natural ventilation.
- Trees shading sidewalks, parking lots, streets, and other paved heat sinks.
- Dispersed vegetated parklike oases for local climatic amelioration.

Of course, desert areas subject to extreme winds and dust storms will benefit from shelterbelts and a more "closed" landscape structure. Extensive damage to homes from trees felled by recent tropical storms suggests the need for more judicious selection and location of shade trees in hurricane-prone regions.

Landscapes designed for energy conservation in temperate climate zones combine principles listed above depending on the relative need for heating and cooling. The greatest challenge in temperate zones lies in resolving sometimes conflicting needs for wind protection and solar access (Oke 1988) or shading and cooling breezes (Westerberg and Glaumann 1990-91).

CONFLICTING AND COMPLEMENTARY USES
WITH OTHER URBAN LANDSCAPES

Landscapes are seldom designed to optimize a particular function such as energy efficiency. The extent to which new landscapes will be devoted to conserving energy will be related to how well they can provide other functions required by city dwellers. This section notes some of the ways that energy-efficient landscapes complement or conflict with other landscapes.

The structure of energy-efficient residential landscapes can conflict with design recommendations for fire-safe landscapes. Shading geometry is such that plants close to a building provide greater shade than similar plants away from the building. However, plants near buildings can carry fire to the structure, thereby increasing the fire hazard. Application of the following guidelines can reduce conflicts between energy-efficient and fire-safe landscapes:

- Do not shade roof surfaces (most attics are well insulated anyway, so little is saved).
- Use fire-resistant species to shade walls.
- Irrigate plants near the structure on a regular basis (this mini-oasis also enhances ET cooling).
- Avoid continuous vegetation from property boundaries to the buildings.

A conflict between energy and water conserving landscapes is possible because reduced landscape irrigation results in reduced ET cooling. Also, as overall leaf area is reduced to conserve water, direct and indirect energy benefits diminish. Research to evaluate energy and water tradeoffs has shown that lowering city temperatures can reduce landscape water consumption, and cooling energy savings can reduce water consumed at power plants (McPherson 1991). However, the cost of irrigation water for high water use trees such as mulberry can offset the energy savings from shade (McPherson and Dougherty 1989). The following guidelines can be applied to promote the conservation of both water and energy:

- Create a mini-oasis near the building to provide wind protection, ET cooling, and strategically located plants for shading windows, walls, and air-conditioners.
- Shift to more xeric plant associations away from the building.
- Use water-efficient irrigation systems and landscape management practices.
- Plan a citywide system of water-efficient oases designed to mitigate urban heat islands (e.g., some parks, cemeteries, golf courses, riparian areas).
- Shade streets, parking lots, and public buildings with low water use tree species to mitigate the urban heat island and demonstrate xeriscape design principles.

Energy-efficient landscapes have potential to complement other functions required of landscapes. Although the "open" character of energy-efficient residential landscapes in warm climates can conflict with the multilayered structure of landscapes valued by certain types of wildlife, community-scale greenbelts that provide important wildlife habitat can simultaneously contribute to energy conservation. Through judicious design, energy-efficient landscapes can increase species, age, and genetic diversity of the urban forest, thus enhancing the sustainability of natural organisms and processes within our cities. Residential landscapes can express individual aesthetic preferences while conserving energy. Energy-efficient landscapes on public land can be designed to reflect "sense of place" within a city, as well as the city's overall identity.

CONCLUSION

As the need for cost-effective urban forest management grows, multipurpose landscapes will expand because they produce more net benefits than single-purpose landscapes. The structure of energy-efficient landscapes can complement the structure of most other urban forest landscapes. Careful planning and design will minimize structural conflicts when fire safety, water conservation, and other functions are high priority. Given the ease with which energy-efficient landscapes can be integrated with other landscapes, and the burgeoning support of tree planting programs that is coming from utilities and government agencies, their future looks bright.

In this chapter we have described methods for planning energy-efficient landscapes at a citywide scale. What is needed now are examples that apply and evaluate these ideas. With research findings and demonstration results in hand, citizens, policy makers, planners, and utilities will be better equipped to create more energy-efficient landscapes and more sustainable cities.

LITERATURE CITED

Akbari, H., S. Davis, S. Dorsano, J. Huang, and S. Winnett, eds. 1992. Cooling our communities: A guidebook on tree planting and light-colored surfacing. U.S. Environmental Protection Agency, Washington, D.C.

Akbari, H., A.H. Rosenfeld, and H. Taha. 1990. Summer heat islands, urban trees, and white surfaces. ASHRAE Transactions 96(1):1381-1388.

Arizona Corporation Commission. 1990. Resource Planning Staff Report. Utilities Division, Arizona Corporation Commission, Phoenix.

Barlag, A., and W. Kuttler. 1990-91. The significance of country breezes for urban planning. Energy and Buildings 15-16:291-297.

DeWalle, D.R., and G.M. Heisler. 1988. Use of windbreaks for home energy conservation. Agriculture, Ecosystems, and Environment 22-23:243-260.

DeWalle, D.R., G.M. Heisler, and R.E. Jacobs. 1983. Forest home sites influence heating and cooling energy. Journal of Forestry 81:84-88.

Dwyer, J.F., E.G. McPherson, H.W. Schroeder, and R.A. Rowntree. 1992. Assessing the benefits and costs of the urban forest. Journal of Arboriculture 18:227-234.

Energy Information Administration. 1989. EIA household energy consumption and expenditures, 1987, vol. 1. Energy Information Administration, Washington, D.C.

Givoni, B. 1981. Man, climate, architecture. 2nd ed. Van Nostrand Reinhold, New York.

Heisler, G.M. 1986. Energy savings with trees. Journal of Arboriculture 12:113-125.

——. 1990. Mean wind speed below building height in residential neighborhoods with different tree densities. ASHRAE Transactions 96, part 1:1389-1396.

——. 1991. Computer simulation for optimizing windbreak placement to save energy for heating and cooling buildings. *In* Trees and Sustainable Development: The Third National Windbreaks and Agroforestry Symposium Proceedings, pp. 100-104. Ridgetown College, Ridgetown, Ontario.

Honjo, T., and T. Takakura. 1990-91. Simulation of thermal effects of urban green areas on their surrounding areas. Energy and Buildings 15-16:433-446.

Huang, J., H. Akbari, H. Taha, and A. Rosenfeld. 1987. The potential of vegetation in reducing summer cooling loads in residential buildings. Journal of Climate and Applied Meteorology 26:1103-1116.

Huang, Y.J., H. Akbari, and H. Taha. 1990. The wind-shielding and shading effects of trees on residential heating and cooling requirements. ASHRAE Transactions 96, part 1:1403-1411.

McPherson, E.G. 1991. Economic modeling for large-scale tree planting. *In* E. Vine, D. Crawley, and P. Centolella, eds., Energy efficiency and the environment: Forging the link, pp. 349-369. American Council for an Energy Efficient Economy, Washington, D.C.

McPherson, E.G. 1994. Cooling urban heat islands with sustainable landscapes. *In* R. Platt, R.A. Rowntree, and P.C. Muick, eds., The ecological city: Preserving and restoring urban biodiversity, pp. 151-171. University of Massachusetts Press, Amherst.

McPherson, E.G., and E. Dougherty. 1989. Selecting trees for shade in the Southwest. Journal of Arboriculture 15:35-43.

McPherson, E.G., D.J. Nowak, P.L. Sacamano, S.E. Prichard, and E.M. Makra. 1993. Chicago's evolving urban forest. General Technical Report NE-169. USDA Forest Service Northeastern Forest Experiment Station, Radnor, Pennsylvania.

McPherson, E.G., and R.A. Rowntree. 1989. Using structural measures to compare twenty-two street tree populations. Landscape Journal 8:13-23.

——. 1993. Energy conservation potential of urban tree planting. Journal of Arboriculture 19:321-331.

McPherson, E.G., and P.L. Sacamano. 1992. Energy savings with trees in Southern California. Research Report. USDA Forest Service Western Center for Urban Forest Research, Davis, California.

McPherson, E.G., J.R. Simpson, and M. Livingston. 1988. Effects of three landscape treatments on residential energy and water use in Tucson, Arizona. Energy and Buildings 13:127-138.

Meier, A. 1990-91. Strategic landscaping and air-conditioning savings: A literature review. Energy and Buildings 15-16:479-486.

Mizuno, M., M. Nakamura, H. Murakami, and S. Yamamoto. 1990-91. Effects of land use on urban horizontal atmospheric temperature distributions. Energy and Buildings 15-16:165-176.

Oke, T.R. 1988. Street design and urban canopy layer climate. Energy and Buildings 11:103-113.

——. 1989. The micrometeorology of the urban forest. Philosophical Transactions of the Royal Society of London 324:335-349.

Olgyay, V. 1973. Design with climate. Princeton University Press, Princeton, New Jersey.

Parker, J.H. 1983. Landscaping to reduce the energy used in cooling buildings. Journal of Forestry 81(2):82-84.

Rowntree, R.A. 1984. Forest canopy cover and land use in four eastern United States cities. Urban Ecology 8:55-67.

Saito, I., O. Ishihara, and T. Katayama. 1990-91. Study of the effect of green areas on the thermal environment in an urban area. Energy and Buildings 15-16:493-498.

Sand, M.A.P. 1991. Planting for energy conservation in the North: Modeling the impact of tree shade on home energy use in Minnesota and development of planting guidelines. Master's thesis, University of Minnesota. 111 p.

Simpson, J.R. 1991. Simulating effects of turf landscaping on building energy use. In E. Vine, D. Crawley, and P. Centolella, eds. Energy efficiency and the environment: Forging the link, pp. 335-347. American Council for an Energy Efficient Economy, Washington, D.C.

Thayer, R.L., and B. Maeda. 1985. Measuring street tree impact on solar performance: A five climate computer modeling study. Journal of Arboriculture 11:1-12.

Wagar, J.A. 1984. Using vegetation to control sunlight and shade on windows. Landscape Journal 3:235-245.

Westerberg, U., and M. Glaumann. 1990-91. Design criteria for solar access and wind shelter in the outdoor environment. Energy and Buildings 15-16:425-431.

Wilmers, F. 1990-91. Effects of vegetation on urban climate and buildings. Energy and Buildings 15-16:507-514.

Portions of an earlier version of this chapter were published in the November 1993 issue of the Journal of Arboriculture.

14

Water Conserving Landscapes

ROBERT C. PERRY

ABSTRACT This paper presents a range of ideas and guidelines coming from the study of ecology and design practices that lead to the conservation of water in urban landscapes. Such approaches are helping to shape the composition and character of landscapes in dry climate regions, including the southwestern United States. Especially effective is the use of a water budget in designing and managing landscapes.

Conserving water in urban areas is an important goal in landscaping, particularly in the dry climates of the southwestern United States. In these regions it has been customary to design and install a wide variety of landscapes and simply provide supplemental water, as needed, through permanent irrigation systems. As a result, it is estimated that more than half the water used in urban areas throughout the Southwest is applied to landscapes. Investigations into this water use also reveal a great deal of waste and inappropriate consumption.

Ongoing population growth and recurring drought cycles have increased our concern for conserving water in urban landscapes. Questions about the availability of water and the costs associated with its use are becoming more important in the design and management decisions. This pressure has stimulated renewed efforts to identify the best methods of conserving water and making the most of its use. During this process, many types of water conserving landscapes have been conceived. The stereotypical image of such a landscape is one made up of cacti and rocks. This paper attempts to dispel that image and to show that such landscapes can be rich and diverse and still conserve water.

FRAMEWORK FOR DESIGNING WATER CONSERVING LANDSCAPES

The foundation for designing and managing water conserving landscapes can be discovered by developing a sensitivity to the regional environment and through the application of specific design actions. This approach initially encourages us to study the large-scale climate, topography, and soils in combination with the native plant species. Such information provides a context for understanding the issue of water conservation and many other aspects of ornamental landscapes, and also brings attention to several key concepts of ecology. It is the ecological approach that allows us to see the landscape as a functioning system of many parts well suited to its particular region and individual site. The ecological approach also offers guidelines and ideas that can be applied to urban landscapes successfully. Several of these are noted in the paragraphs below.

The regional climate, topography, and soils provide the basic framework for landscape plants to adapt and grow. Rainfall patterns, temperature extremes, sun exposure, and basic soil properties are the key parameters. This macro-scale view helps to evaluate the adaptability of certain plant species to arid conditions or drought stress. The seasonal nature of moisture and temperature in a region indicates the natural cycles and rhythms that affect plants. The availability of moisture, daylight, and warmth bears directly on plant growth, rest, and flowering habits. The design and management of a landscape need to reflect these rhythms in order to achieve optimum performance by making appropriate decisions about watering, pruning, and mulching.

Plants evolve and adapt in groups or associations. Instead of treating plants as individual garden elements in a landscape, a sense of overall association is needed that enables plants to interact and complement each other while adapting to moisture, sun, soils, space, and other considerations. Native and exotic plant species should not be introduced without some idea of their origin and natural habitat. Do they come from subtropical, Mediterranean, arid, or temperate climates? Do they grow in coastal, foothill, or valley habitats? This background information enables us to bring together plants with greater levels of compatibility and suitability in the landscape.

There are many natural patterns among plants. Physical characteristics include the size, shape, foliage color, texture, and fragrance; cultural adaptations include preferences and tolerances of sun, shade, moisture, and soil fertility. A successful landscape will develop plant associations that combine many layers or patterns of physical and cultural characteristics. Natural landscapes demonstrate a strategy of species diversity that leads to flexibility and adaptability to many environmental conditions and changes. Greater plant diversity also increases the wildlife value of landscapes. These observations provide ideas for use in urban landscapes.

A landscape is dynamic. The microclimate conditions in particular are always changing and thus contributing to the evolution of the landscape. Where possible, landscapes should be reviewed and amended or adjusted to reflect the process of maturing.

DESIGN ACTIONS PROMOTING WATER CONSERVATION

Although understanding regional conditions and the ecology of natural environments provides many insights for conserving water in landscapes, additional criteria and guidelines are needed. In recent years, the idea of using a water budget has been recommended as a basis for designing and managing urban landscapes. This budget indicates the total amount of water that can be used by a landscape over a one-year period. From the outset, landscapes must be designed and managed to survive and perform successfully within this budget allocation.

A water budget is determined on the basis of the evapotranspiration loss of moisture in a region. In states such as California, a network of weather stations provide evapotranspiration data for many sites throughout the state. The data are referenced to the evapotranspiration loss of moisture from tall fescue turf grass that is well irrigated. This calculation is based on instrument readings and is considered to be the maximum amount of water the turf grass needs to survive in a healthy and attractive form.

The water budget currently adopted by the California Department of Water Resources is set at 80 percent of the annual evapotranspiration loss of tall fescue turf grass. In a coastal region near Los Angeles, the annual loss averages 50 inches, resulting in a water budget allocation of 40 inches of supplemental moisture for urban landscapes. The annual loss in Palm Springs is 71 inches, resulting in a water budget of 57 inches. Thus the water budget approach provides the overall water conservation goal for the landscape. The concept also allows the designer and landscape manager a wide range of choices in meeting this goal and considerable flexibility from project to project. The clarity of the conservation goal and flexibility in attaining it are the key advantages of the water budget approach.

With experience, a number of specific design actions have emerged that help to achieve the landscape water budget. These include:

- Landscape plantings should be organized into groupings that have similar water needs. This is often described as hydrozoning. Three hydrozone categories are commonly recognized, based on the percentage of annual evapotranspiration loss: low (10 to 30 percent), moderate (40 to 60 percent), and high (70 to 90 percent). A landscape must be designed with hydrozones that will not exceed the overall annual water budget.

- Landscape plantings should emphasize the use of plants closely adapted to the climate and soil conditions of the site. Turf grass areas in arid regions in particular should be carefully considered for functional and aesthetic merit.

- Landscape areas should be efficient to irrigate. Narrow turf grass areas, steep slopes, and oddly shaped plots need special consideration.

- Landscape areas should be designed to capture and infiltrate irrigation water and seasonal rainfall. On-site capture and infiltration of water can be of greatest benefit to established trees and natural areas that do not receive supplemental irrigation.

- Irrigation design practices should emphasize the efficient application of water to root zones of plants, consistency within hydrozones, exposure, infiltration rates, and topography.

- Use should be made of water-saving products, including matched precipitation heads and emitters, rain guards, and low elevation check valves.

- Water conservation should be increased through soil preparation and maintenance practices, including the use of composted organic humus during the soil preparation process, and ongoing surface mulching around trees and shrubs.

CONCLUSION

Water conservation in landscaping requires an understanding of the regional ecology as well as design practices that can be adapted to each project site. The regional view provides a broad perspective to the design program, while specific design practices can be helpful in conceiving many individual and successful landscape areas. The most recent development in landscape water conservation is the concept of the water budget. A budget that is based on regional climate can prove useful as a conservation goal to direct design and management efforts.

15

Fire-Safe Landscapes

JAMES R. CLARK

ABSTRACT Urbanization of forest lands in regions where fire is an important part of the natural landscape places people and homes in jeopardy. In such areas, the conditions of fuel, weather, and ignition are common enough for fire to occur with regularity. One goal for both landscape design and management in fire-prone locations is to minimize the spread of a fire, and thereby limit its potential to become a major conflagration. Achieving fire-safe landscapes involves a basic understanding of fire behavior and management. The principals involved are well defined, using fuel separation and management as key elements.

In many natural ecosystems, fire is an integral component. The health and continued functioning of the system require periodic fire, even though its aftereffects are temporarily devastating. In sharp contrast, fire is regarded as a complete evil in human-dominated environments. Every effort is made to prevent its ignition and spread. As long as the lines dividing natural areas and forests from residential communities are well defined, the dichotomy of our regard for fire is acceptable. But when communities and natural areas become intermixed, our expectations about fire come into conflict. While we might regard fire as a part of nature and its function, we ignore the risk to our homes and lives; we don't believe it can happen to us.

Nowhere is this conflict more evident than at the urban-forest interface, a place where natural environments and development overlap. The boundary between wild forest and city-suburb becomes indistinct. In such locations the concentration of people, along with the mix of jurisdictions, landownership, and resource management practices, makes the problem of preventing fire both difficult and complex.

The urban-forest interface comes in many different forms. In California, the interface may be a vacation home on a ten acre lot in the Sierra Nevada range, a new residential development in foothills of the Central Valley, or an isolated ranch in the chaparral zone. Similar types of development may be found across the United States.

Along the urban-wildland interface, fire is to be expected. The purpose of this paper is to introduce the concepts and practices that may reduce the danger associated with fire in these areas as well as discuss the relationship of fire-safe landscapes to other types of landscape development.

GENERAL ASPECTS OF WILDFIRES

Given the deadly nature of fire, the science of understanding and predicting its occurrence is relatively well developed. Thus the creation of a fire-safe environment is not limited by information. This contrasts with some of the more recent interests in landscape development, such as creating energy-conserving or low water-use landscapes.

Fire requires fuel, heat, and oxygen. In terms of preventing the spread of fire, the primary determinants are fuel, weather, and topography. Movement will be more rapid under conditions of high wind, high temperature, and low humidity. Fire moves uphill as much as sixteen times faster than across flat ground (R. Pike, pers. comm.). The most significant fires along California's coastal areas are associated with an excessive fuel load and Diablo or Santa Ana weather conditions: air temperatures of 75°F or above, winds from the east (or otherwise offshore) with speeds over 25 miles per hour, and relative humidity in the area of less than 30 percent.

Only the fuel load can be managed. The weather conditions are likely to occur every year and in any season. Thus the potential for fire is limited only by the amount of fuel and the presence of the initial combustion. Resource managers and homeowners have little influence over weather and topography and must focus their attention on fuel management. By regulating the quantity, fuel type, and its continuity, we attempt to prevent the initiation and spread of fire. In landscape settings, this involves reducing the overall fuel volume and creating breaks in fuel continuity.

Fire moves across a landscape in two ways: linear spread and spotting (Figure 15-1). The former is the continuous progression of flame across an area. Since this requires continuous fuel, creating fuel breaks disrupts the continuity of fuel and restricts linear spread.

But breaking fuel continuity does not prevent fire spread by spotting. In this form, firebrands or other sources of ignition are transported through the air on the wind and may move far ahead of the flame front. Spotting is severe when the crowns of trees or other tall objects ignite. Since crown fires move three to eight times faster than ground fires, it is critical to prevent the vertical spread of combustion. Under intense combustion conditions, crowns may literally explode and firebrands will be carried across a wide portion of the landscape. In the Oakland Hills fire of 1991, the explosion of tree crowns and the wide dispersal of firebrands contributed significantly to the rapid and extensive spread of the fire.

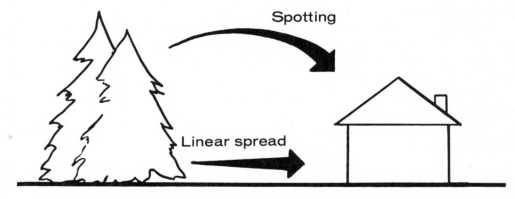

Figure 15-1. Movement of fire across the landscape.

Campaigns to raise awareness of fire prevention are well established in American society. In natural areas, Smokey the Bear has been overwhelmingly successful. While such programs do reduce the number of accidental fires, they do not address fires that have been set intentionally. Arson cannot be ignored in either urban or wildland locations. Estimates of the number of forest fires resulting from arson may range up to 33 percent. In California, the Department of Forestry and Fire Protection reports that 13 percent of the fires it managed in 1991 were started by arson (R. Pike, pers. comm.). However, arson fires have traditionally resulted in 80 percent of the fire damage.

FIRE-SAFE LANDSCAPES

A fire-safe environment is one in which the threat of fire to property and people is minimized. It is rooted in some of the fundamental concepts of fire management: prevention of ignition and spread of the fire itself, and separation of the fire from people and property. In developing a fire-safe environment, preventing fire from either entering or exiting a property is achieved by removing a continuous source of fuel.

A fire-safe landscape is a truly integrated environment, for it involves aspects of design and maintenance for both plants and structures. Vegetation management alone cannot ensure survival, but when it is integrated with structural design, the prospects are enhanced. Experience in Southern California's chaparral environment has demonstrated that even where clearance of 100 feet is maintained, homes with wood roofs are twenty-one times more likely to burn than those with nonwood roofs (Los Angeles County Department of Forester and Fire Warden 1990).

Fire-safe landscapes attempt to minimize both forms of fire spread. Linear spread is controlled by creating and maintaining gaps and breaks in fuel. Spotting is prevented by breaking fuel ladders that allow ground fire to move into tree crowns. This may include removing low-hanging limbs and associated understory plantings. Such an approach also separates trees and vines from structures. Breaking fuel ladders includes removal of bark, loose debris, dead and fallen branches, and leaves from the crown and trunk. One of the reasons eucalyptus (*Eucalyptus* spp.) is a significant fire hazard is the large amount of branches, leaves, bark, and so forth, each tree produces. This fuel provides a well-developed fuel ladder. If the debris and low-hanging branches are removed, the fire potential is reduced significantly.

The basic components of a fire-safe environment are (adapted from Baptiste 1992):

- Separating vegetation from structures.
- Reducing the overall amount of fire fuels on the property.
- Preventing vertical spread by eliminating fire ladders.
- Reducing the continuity of fire through fuel breaks.
- Integrating fire management across both landscape and structures.
- Being familiar with fire potential, including topography.

The approach that best embodies fire-safe landscape concepts is that of *defensible space*—the separation of fire (and fuel) from structures. The idea of an area that can provide defense against fire is a simple one. It clearly assumes that fire will occur and steps must be taken to respond to that reality.

Fundamentally, a fire-safe landscape and its associated defensible space create a patchy landscape. This reduces the likelihood of fire spreading either into or away from

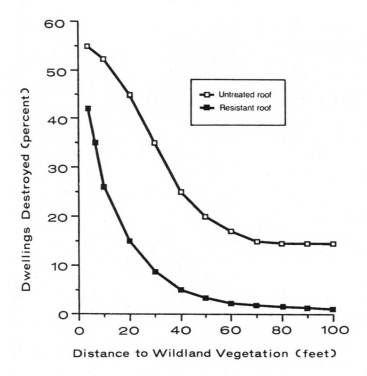

Figure 15-2. Relation of roof composition and vegetation clearance to survivability of dwellings. From Davis (1990); reprinted from the *Journal of Forestry* (vol. 88, no. 1) published by the Society of American Foresters, 5400 Grosvenor Lane, Bethesda, MD 20814-2198. Not for further reproduction.

a structure. The value of distance between vegetation (the fuel) and structures is seen repeatedly in postfire analysis (Figure 15-2). Where defensible space is present, the odds for survival are vastly increased (R. Martin, University of California at Berkeley, pers. comm.). During the Atlas Peak fire in 1981, of 111 structures with adequate defensible space, only 5 were destroyed. In contrast, where such space was lacking, 86 structures (out of 111) were destroyed (Davis 1990).

While fire-safe landscapes are usually discussed at the scale of the single-family residence, it is possible to apply these concepts at the community or large development scale. The ideas of separation, structural integrity, and fuel management remain applicable. And since small lot sizes prevent meeting the requirements for defensible space, successful fire-safe landscapes may be developed only through community-wide cooperation (see Baptiste 1992; Frady 1992).

DESIGN OF FIRE-SAFE LANDSCAPES

The design of fire-safe landscapes integrates regional information into a local environment. While it is possible for an individual residence to completely isolate itself from the regional and surrounding landscape, this is a rarity and should not be seen as the standard. More commonly, residential developments, vacation homes, commercial developments, ranches, and other communities at the urban-rural interface exist in tandem with their surroundings.

Fire-Safe Landscapes in a Regional Context

Fire exists as a natural component for a wide range of environments. Therefore, at a fundamental level, a regional context considers the potential for fire to occur. Put another way, there are places which will experience significant fire on a frequent and recurring basis. For example, the Berkeley Hills area of the San Francisco Bay region has had fourteen significant fires since 1923. Diablo weather conditions occur every year. Intensive planting of trees and other plants across the landscape provides a fuel source.

The general predictability of fire in forested areas is quite high. The Forest Service (Intermountain Region) has developed a Wildland Home Fire Risk Meter which considers slope, vegetation type, and roof composition in making a relative risk rating (National Fire Protection Association 1991). In California, the Department of Forestry and Fire Protection is in the process of establishing fire hazard severity zones across the state (1993).

As part of awareness campaigns, resource managers often designate fire danger on a relative scale. Where it is high, activities such as campfires may be restricted. Similar programs should become part of urban-wildland interface areas. On "red flag" or high danger days, some activities, such as use of open burning, barbecues, and lawn mowers, may be limited.

In addition, regional considerations for fire safety involve development of the urban infrastructure. In both urban and urban-wildland interface areas, land use is regulated by a tangled mosaic of jurisdictions and management. Issues such as emergency planning and communication as well as fuel management programs must be addressed on a regional scale. For example, simple matters such as incompatibility of hose connectors or inadequate residential addresses may become the critical weak link in an overall fire management plan.

Within a region, fire-safe landscapes facilitate fire fighting. The design of roads for access and turning radius is a significant aspect of fire safety on a regional level. If fire-fighting personnel cannot safely enter *and exit* an area, the chances for defending it against fire are greatly reduced. Similarly, construction requirements for fire retardant materials are based on local ordinances. Placement of electrical utilities underground and maintenance of adequate clearance above ground will reduce the potential for ignition and hazards from live wires.

The components of a fire-safe landscape may simply be incompatible with the design and management of residential neighborhoods. During the Oakland Hills fire, vegetation was often continuous from home to home; dense, unmanaged buffer strips were composed of trees and located at the top of ridges; equipment could not negotiate narrow, winding roads that were blocked by cars and fallen residences. Given the nature of the fire and the problems in fighting it, there seems little possibility that any residence could have been completely fire-safe. Only through concerted regional effort can an area like Oakland Hills begin to develop a fire-safe character.

Fire-Safe Landscapes at the Residential Level

Fire-safe landscapes create a relationship between vegetation and structures that reduces ignition of fire through fuel management and structural composition, prevents or otherwise minimizes lateral and vertical spread through creation of defensible space, and provides the potential for defending the site from fire.

The single most important component of a fire-safe structure is a fire-retardant roof. The California Department of Forestry and Fire Protection notes that the roof is most vulnerable part of the house (CDFFP, no date). In Oakland, trees were often set on fire by the structure rather than the other way around. Additional aspects of structures important in fire safety are the exterior finish, topographic position, roof gutters, windows, attic vents, exposed stilted foundations, and presence of a deck.

In the design of fire-safe landscapes, providing space between plants and buildings is the key ingredient for vegetation management—not selecting plant species for their ability to resist ignition or burning. A reliance on "fire-retardant" plants for safety seems misguided and doomed to failure. While evergreen, highly resinous plants are more hazardous than deciduous, non-oily species, this knowledge is not easily implemented. Moreover, plant selection issues must not obscure the reality that ongoing maintenance is the key element.

Questions about plant selection should be seen in the context of fuel management rather than flammability. The East Bay Municipal Utility District (Baptiste 1992) referred to some plants as "pyrophytes" and suggested that these "almost attract fire." Yet information on species-specific flammability is sketchy at best. Where large trees are planted at high densities and left unmanaged for decades, as is the case in eucalyptus and pine forests of the East Bay hills, the potential for fire is large whatever the species.

A more appropriate general rule for plant selection would be the arrangement, management, and use of native species whose growth and development patterns are adapted to the region's patterns of fire. Situations where spatial arrangement, planting density, and species selection respond to the theme of defensible space are far more likely to be fire-safe. Examples include:

- Maintaining an area of well-irrigated turf adjacent to a structure.
- Using a mix of trees, shrubs, and ground covers, under variable irrigation regimes, to create a patchy mosaic of vegetation.
- Using native plants under nonirrigated conditions at the edge of the defensible space.
- Maintaining active programs of pruning and dead plant and debris removal to reduce fuel volumes.

MANAGEMENT OF FIRE-SAFE LANDSCAPES

As with any landscape design, successful fire-safe landscapes can be achieved only when reasonable management is applied.

Regional Awareness

The key element in fire safety is public and professional awareness and responsiveness. As long as the public and their leadership refuse to accept the potential for a catastrophic fire, little can be done to create a safe environment. The sense of "it can't happen to me" is simply one of denial. Information on the inevitability of fire within a region can enhance public awareness, but may be useful only when followed by a clear plan of action that includes individual site visits by fire professionals, followed by recommendations for specific actions. This may involve both structural and vegetation inspections.

On a more comprehensive scale, landscape and resource managers must see fire as a regional threat and not simply a local problem. In the East Bay hills area a mosaic of landownership includes several cities, unincorporated county lands, the East Bay Regional Park District, and the East Bay Municipal Utility District. These groups, along with several other agencies, have formed an interagency working group to deal with fire management policies and practices.

Fuel Management and Defensible Space

Since fuel is the one manageable element required for fire, it becomes the primary tool in maintaining fire-safe landscapes. Fuels management operates on two levels. First, creating defensible space separates vegetation from structures. This disrupts the continuity of fuel and reduces its linear spread. Such defensible space also involves moving debris and firewood away from the home. The Sierra Front Wildfire Cooperators (Frady 1992) describe maintaining defensible space as removal, reduction, and replacement of vegetation.

Second, fuel management creates space between large fuel elements. Thinning trees so crowns do not touch, lifting crowns from the ground, and removing understory plants are all methods of breaking fuel ladders. In so doing, the likelihood of a fire crowning out is reduced and the spread of the fire by spotting is also reduced.

Creation and management of defensible space includes several specific practices (taken from California standards):

- Clearing trees, shrubs, and other brush 30 feet away from houses.
- Removing overhanging limbs and branches within 15 feet of a roof.
- Thinning dense vegetation 100 to 200 feet away from the structure.
- Providing 10 feet of vertical clearance between the ground and branches or vegetation.
- Removing woodpiles from near structures.
- Removing dead vegetation.
- Clearing all vegetation within 10 feet of a chimney.
- Creating a workable access plan for entry and exit to the property.

RELATION TO OTHER LANDSCAPE FORMS

Creation and management of fire-safe landscapes could hardly be more antagonistic to the goals of most special purpose landscapes:

- Cities and towns strive to plant more trees, often seeking continuous canopies. Fire-safe landscape management views dense plantings of trees as a significant fire hazard.
- Communities preserve remnant forest strips, patches, and buffers as a way to retain the values associated with natural forests. Fire-safe landscape management considers that such assemblages may permit ground fires to move vertically, thus contributing to their spread.
- Control of erosion requires good vegetation cover, especially on steep hillsides. Fire-safe management reduces vegetation in such situations.

- Energy-conservation programs promote the placement of trees directly adjacent to structures. Fire-safe landscapes require separation between vegetation and structures.
- Water-conserving landscapes minimize the amount of water applied to vegetation. In fire-safe landscapes, maintenance of well-watered vegetation near structures is urged.

The conflicts between fire-safe landscapes and other special purpose designs are most severe on small residential lots. There is simply not enough space to adequately meet the diverse landscape goals. But these conflicts can be reconciled, especially on larger lots. In cases where defensible space can be created and maintained on a single lot, it may be possible to strategically place a small number of trees near a structure to provide for energy conservation. Similarly, a well-conceived hydrozoning plan may allow for a water-conserving landscape to be fire-safe.

Fire-safe landscapes may also be developed at the scale of the development or neighborhood. This requires a more intense level of cooperation among property owners and local government. But it allows for other landscape purposes to be developed on individual lots.

What appears to limit the ability to resolve these apparent conflicts is our collective experience with diverse landscape goals. There seems to be an adequate information base for a number of landscape types. Rarely have the precise needs of landscape forms been integrated into a coherent whole. However, as resource managers define the need to meet a wide range of goals for their land, the ability to successfully combine several purposes will only increase.

SUMMARY

Creating and maintaining fire-safe landscapes is a complex process that must take into account the character of structures, the infrastructure, and vegetation. Management must involve property owners of individual residential lots as well as large regional resources. The following appear to be the key elements in a fire-safe landscape:

1. *Public and professional awareness.* In some areas, fire is inevitable. Both property owners and public officials must be prepared to address this reality. Before any action will be taken, such awareness must be created. Regional resource managers and communities must develop cooperative fire management and fighting plans. Property owners cannot deny the risk of fire.

2. *Physical infrastructure.* A plan for engaging a large fire requires access for and compatibility of equipment.

3. *Structural design.* Codes regulating design of structures should require fire-resistant building materials, especially for roofs, support members, and decks.

4. *Defensible space.* Fire fuel and structures must be separated within individual lots or the community as a whole.

5. *Fuel management.* Fire fuel must be reduced and managed. Pruning, tillage, and selective plant removal will disrupt the continuity and supply of fuel across a larger landscape. Programs of prescribed burning must be included, despite adverse air quality effects.

ACKNOWLEDGMENTS

Thanks very much to Nelda Matheny, HortScience, Inc., as well as Herb Spitzer and Paul Rippens, Los Angeles County Fire Department, for their thoughtful comments and review of the manuscript.

LITERATURE CITED AND ADDITIONAL REFERENCES

Baptiste, L. 1992. Firescape: Landscaping to reduce fire hazard. East Bay Municipal Utility District, Oakland, California. 16 p.

California Department of Forestry and Fire Protection. No date. Fire safe—inside and out. Sacramento, California.

——. 1993. Bates Bill AB 337 progress information. Sacramento, California.

Davis, J.B. 1990. The wildland-urban interface: Paradise or battleground? Journal of Forestry 88(1):26-31.

East Bay Regional Park District. 1992. Regional Parks Newsletter. March 1992. Oakland, California.

Frady, S. 1992. Wildfire protection for homeowners and developers: A guide to building and living fire safe in the wildlands. Sierra Front Wildfire Cooperators, Carson City, Nevada. 26 p.

Los Angeles County Department of Forester and Fire Warden. 1989. Fire hazard vs. erosion control: A homeowner's guide. Los Angeles County Department of Forester and Fire Warden, Los Angeles, California. P6-89. 12 p.

——. 1990. Homeowner's guide to fire and watershed safety at the chaparral-urban interface. Los Angeles County Department of Forester and Fire Warden, Los Angeles, California. 34 p.

National Fire Protection Association. 1991. Wildfire strikes home. 2nd ed. National Fire Protection Association, Quincy, Massachusetts. 80 p.

Svihra, P. 1992. The Oakland-Berkeley hills fire: Lessons for the arborist. Journal of Arboriculture 18: 257-261.

Washington Department of Natural Resources. 1991. Defensible space: Planning and managing your fire defensible landscaping. Department of Natural Resources, Olympia, Washington.

PART FOUR
Integration: Tradeoffs and Benefits

16

Sustainability in Landscaping

ROBERT C. PERRY

ABSTRACT The goal of developing ornamental landscapes that are safe, attractive, and functional for urban dwellers is pursued with great interest, and vast amounts of energy and material resources are used in this effort. But direct and indirect energy consumption, the need for supplemental water, and the concerns about soil and groundwater contamination raise serious questions regarding the long-term sustainability of urban landscapes. Sustainability in landscaping can be improved through a number of actions, such as planning and managing landscapes to function more like natural environments through cycling of resources and managing energy costs; integrating efforts to conserve water and energy, reduce green waste, improve soils, and increase wildlife value into comprehensive guidelines; and reducing the demand for energy and material resources in other sectors of the urban environment through microclimate mitigation and habitat restoration.

Over the past twenty years, the planning, development, and management of many urban landscapes have emphasized aesthetic and functional goals, resulting in landscapes maintained either for their visual character and recreational uses or to mitigate erosion, microclimate, and fire hazard conditions. Many of these landscapes include the extensive use of turf grass and assorted types of exotic trees, shrubs, and ground covers. Both the construction and long-term maintenance of these ornamental landscapes are dependent on resources and services that are most often measured in economic terms. More recently, there has been interest in assessing the short- and long-term demands on resources such as water and energy, and for increasing the environmental benefits of these landscapes in terms of carbon storage, oxygen production, microclimate mitigation, wildlife benefit, and species diversity. As a result, there is a growing effort to develop a balance of visual, functional, and environmental goals. This paper discusses a number of the environmental goals, with the aim of clarifying policies and practices that can improve the long-term sustainability of landscapes.

From an environmental point of view, landscapes that require excessive subsidies of energy, water, and other resources cannot be sustained indefinitely. Such landscapes clearly lead to a depletion of oxygen and energy resources, and contribute more carbon dioxide to the atmosphere and chemicals to soil and water resources than the landscape can mitigate. This view is based on data from case studies of several public landscapes in southern California that evaluated the use of direct and indirect energy associated with providing water, fertilizer, and pesticides, and also fuel to operate service vehicles and lawn equipment.

GOALS OF SUSTAINABILITY

Sustainability in urban landscapes can be improved when environmental benefits are clearly identified and the demands for energy and other resources are addressed on a long-range basis. The principal goal of sustainability is to provide for the survival of all species within the biosphere while not diminishing future options.

Case study data on urban landscapes help us focus on planning and management guidelines that can increase the efficiency of our landscape practices and optimize environmental benefits. In essence, the planning goal is to conduct more of a cost-benefit analysis of urban landscapes with greater understanding of resources and environmental impacts, thus promoting a consistent and integrated framework of participation.

Natural environments can serve as models for sustainable systems. They are highly complex and interconnected, and demonstrate principles of energy flow and resource cycling. Planning for sustainability should begin with a program of policies and guidelines that can fit these principles of natural environments into the structure and functioning of urban landscapes.

PROPOSED LANDSCAPE POLICIES

Efforts to achieve higher levels of sustainability in landscaping require a range of policies, standards, and guidelines. Outlined below are a number of key landscape goals that are proposed, requiring various levels of legislation, in order to develop and maintain sustainable systems.

- Landscapes that conserve, recycle, and reuse resources to achieve optimum levels of sustainability.
- Landscapes with increasing levels of conservation and efficiency in energy use.
- Landscapes based on principles of water conservation and optimal use of reclaimed water resources.
- Landscapes that achieve optimum levels of biomass storage, thus providing increased storage of carbon and production of oxygen.
- Landscapes made up of associations of plants having similar climate, water, soil, sun exposure, and maintenance needs.
- Landscapes with optimum levels of microclimate benefits to reduce urban heat buildup and energy demand for heating and cooling.
- Landscapes that incorporate organic soil management practices and can accommodate composted landscape trimmings.
- Landscapes that make minimal use of inorganic fertilizers, herbicides, and pesticides.
- Landscapes that are supportive of wildlife, biotic diversity, and significant biotic resources.
- Activities and programs to educate people on the benefits of sustainable landscapes.

RECOMMENDED OBJECTIVES AND ACTIONS

A series of objectives and actions are outlined below in an effort to illustrate the various types of activities that can lead to improved conservation, efficiency, and benefits in landscaping. A key aspect is the cross-referencing of actions among the various objectives to achieve greater integration and produce better results because all areas are working together.

Productivity

Objective: Increase the productivity and standing biomass of landscapes. Increased productivity leads to greater storage of carbon, production of oxygen, and air pollution mitigation. This productivity offsets the release of carbon and pollutants to the atmosphere through direct and indirect use of organic fuels in the development and long-term maintenance of the landscape.

Actions: Landscapes should be designed to achieve greater levels of planting scale and density, with the goal of producing more standing biomass consistent with energy, water, soil, plant, and wildlife considerations.

Plant Species

Objective: Develop landscapes made up of associations of plants that fit the region and microclimate conditions and have a high level of compatibility, in order to improve the productivity and vigor of the landscape, promote reduced use of energy, water, and fertilizer, and increase maintenance efficiency.

Actions: Plants should be organized into associations having complementary cultural preferences and tolerances for moisture, soils, and microclimates within the site conditions. Landscapes should include a diversity of plant species, thus enabling the landscape to adapt to site conditions, contend with pests and diseases, and fix nitrogen to reduce the use of water and fertilizers.

Energy Consumption

Objective: Achieve landscape designs that reduce levels of direct and indirect energy consumption. Direct energy consumption occurs with the use of mechanical equipment requiring fossil fuels. Indirect energy use occurs through the use of electricity to supply irrigation water, to manufacture chemical fertilizers and pesticides, and to cool buildings.

Actions: Landscapes should be designed to reduce direct energy use. Trees, shrubs, ground covers, and turf grass should be proportioned in a manner to reduce the frequency and volume of pruning, shearing, mowing, and service vehicle operations. Landscapes should be designed to reduce indirect energy use. Trees, shrubs, ground covers, and turf grass should be organized into associations and in proportions requiring less water, fertilizer, herbicides, and allowing for the composting of trimmings. Landscapes should also help reduce indirect energy use in buildings. Trees, shrubs, vines, and ground covers should be used to reduce direct solar heat load and ambient air temperatures.

Water Conservation

Objective: Increase conservation and efficiency in the use of water. Water conservation practices result in less indirect energy use, less runoff onto pavement, and increased effectiveness of water supplies.

Actions: Landscape plantings should be closely adapted to the climate and soil conditions of the site, organized into compatible plant associations and hydrozones, and efficient to irrigate. Landscape areas should be designed to capture and infiltrate irrigation water and seasonal rainfall. Irrigation design practices should provide systems that lead to the efficient application of water to root zones with consideration of hydrozones, soil infiltration rates, and topography. Water-saving products including heads, emitters, rain guards, and check valves should be used where appropriate.

Water application management should consider local climate conditions in estimating supplemental water applications to hydrozones on a seasonal basis. And water conservation should be increased through soil preparation and maintenance practices, including use of composted organic humus during the soil preparation process, and ongoing surface mulching and application of composted organic humus to the soil.

Microclimate Mitigation

Objectives: Incorporate passive solar design principles regarding configuration of lots, orientation of structures, and layout of roads which allow plants to optimize the conditions of sun and wind. Use landscape plants to manage solar incidence up to two stories in height on structures to reduce indirect use of energy and to provide for optimum levels of summer cooling and winter heating. Use landscape plants to reduce heat gain from paved surfaces and provide pleasant, shaded pedestrian areas. And use landscape plants to reduce levels of particulate air pollution along major roadways, within residential developments, and in open space links.

Actions: Trees should initially be located to shade west facing windows, walls, and outdoor living spaces to provide heat reduction benefits. Additional heat load reduction is achieved through shading of east facing windows, walls, and living spaces during summer months. Shrubs should also be located to shade west, south, and east facing walls for heat reduction, and can be used in place of trees when space or visual restrictions exist. Trees with open canopies or deciduous habits should be used along south and east facing walls of structures to provide winter sun exposure on wall surfaces while providing overhead shade during summer months. Deciduous vines should be located on east and south walls and evergreen vines on west and north walls.

Species Diversity/Biotic Resources

Objectives: Permanently protect and enhance significant biotic communities of native plants and wildlife within transition zones, open space spines, riparian corridors, and parks. Increase the habitat potential for indigenous wildlife—primarily birds—within ornamental landscapes. Encourage the restoration and rehabilitation of channelized riparian corridors to create greater value for native plants and wildlife.

Actions: Communities of indigenous plants and wildlife should be inventoried by a wildlife biologist to provide site-specific data and guidelines. Guidelines should address species type and diversity, fuel modification, interface between domestic pets and wildlife, and habitat management.

Soil Management

Objective: Prepare and maintain soils for landscapes in a manner that reuses composted landscape trimmings and achieves the minimum use of chemical fertilizers and herbicides. Composting and reuse of landscape trimmings can further reduce indirect energy use and increase water conservation efficiency.

Actions: Plan and design landscapes to have tree and shrub areas that can receive annual applications of composted landscape trimmings and surface mulch. Fertilizers specified for use in these and all landscape areas should be 100 percent organic.

CONCLUSION

The goal of planning, designing, and managing urban landscapes to achieve higher levels of sustainability requires a good working knowledge of natural environments. These environments provide a model for increasing the efficiency and benefits of urban landscapes through resource conservation, recycling, and reuse. These concepts can be applied to urban landscapes when addressing many needs—from water and energy conservation to microclimate and habitat improvement. When the foundation of sustainability is integrated into urban landscape practices, there will be a greater level of environmental value and integrity to their functioning.

17

Net Benefits of Healthy and Productive Urban Forests

E. GREGORY McPHERSON

ABSTRACT In California, urban forestry programs are facing new challenges due to dwindling municipal budgets, fewer trees, planting of smaller trees, and declining government support. However, changes in environmental policy, such as the use of market incentives to promote environmentally sound behavior, are providing new opportunities for urban forestry to broaden its base of support. Quantifying the benefits and costs associated with tree planting and care is fundamental to the development of economic incentives aimed at sustaining healthy and productive urban forests. Use of benefit-cost analysis to evaluate the economics of urban forestry policies and programs is illustrated with an example from the Chicago Urban Forest Climate Project. The thirty-year annual costs and benefits associated with planting 95,000 trees were estimated using the computer model Cost-Benefit Analysis of Trees (C-BAT) and discount rates of 4, 7, and 10 percent. Net present values were positive, and projected benefit-cost ratios were greater than 1.0 at all discount rates. Assuming a 7 percent discount rate, a net present value of $38 million, or $402 per planted tree, was projected. Benefit-cost ratios were largest for trees planted in residential yards and public housing sites (3.5), and least for park (2.1) and highway (2.3) sites. Discounted payback periods ranged from nine to fifteen years. Strategies for strengthening connections between city residents and city trees, as well as maximizing return on investment in the urban forest, are presented.

Although urban forests are capable of supplying substantial economic, environmental, and social benefits (Akbari et al. 1992; Anderson and Cordell 1988; Dwyer et al. 1992; McPherson and Nowak 1993; Rowntree and Nowak 1991; Sampson et al. 1992; Sanders 1986), local governmental support for city and county programs appears to be declining. Dwindling budgets are prompting community officials to ask if trees are worth the price to plant and care for over the long term. Urban forestry programs must now prove their cost-effectiveness. Similarly, some residents wonder if it is worth the trouble to maintain street trees in front of their homes or in their yards. Certain species are particularly bothersome due to litterfall, roots that invade sewers or heave sidewalks, shade that kills grass, or sap from aphids that fouls cars and other objects. Branches broken by wind, ice, and snow can damage property. Thorns and low-hanging branches can be injurious. These problems are magnified when trees do not receive regular care, or if the wrong tree was selected for planting.

This chapter highlights disturbing trends affecting urban forestry, but also looks at changes that provide new opportunities to broaden its base of support. Benefit-cost information for evaluating the economics of urban forestry policies and programs is discussed with reference to the Chicago Urban Forest Climate Project (CUFCP), a three-year study to quantify some of the environmental effects of urban vegetation in the Chicago area (McPherson et al. 1993, 1994). Based on findings of this study, strategies for increasing net benefits are considered. The chapter concludes with several ideas for strengthening the support of residents for their city trees.

THE STATE OF URBAN FORESTRY

Public attitudes about community forests are ultimately reflected in the health and productivity of city trees. Declining support for street tree management may show up first in the form of fewer replacement plantings and increased numbers of dead and unhealthy trees. Longer pruning cycles can result in a greater amount of tree cover being removed each time trees are pruned, as well as progressively shorter rotations due to increased mortality caused by larger wounds and inadequate care.

A 1992 survey of urban forestry in California focused on the changes in city and county tree programs since 1988 (Bernhardt and Swiecki 1993). Among the findings: (1) the average percentage of city operating budgets that goes to tree programs has dropped to less than 1 percent, thus declining over 18 percent between 1988 and 1992; (2) about 38 percent of the cities reported that they care for fewer trees now than in 1988; (3) there is a continued trend away from planting large-scale trees (90 percent of the street trees and 80 percent of the park trees planted are of small or medium stature); and (4) 20 percent of the respondents, compared to about 15 percent in 1988, report that government support is less than citizen support.

Given these trends, it is not surprising that when respondents ranked their three most pressing needs, 48 percent of the first-place votes were for increased program funding; second place went to improved tree maintenance. Although first-rate urban forestry programs abound in California, data from this survey suggest that municipal budgets for urban forestry are dwindling. Results from two similar independent surveys now under way will help determine if this trend is confined to California or is larger in scope.

NEW DIRECTIONS IN ENVIRONMENTAL POLICY

Timothy Duane recently (1992) addressed the policy and planning implications of emerging trends in environmental problems. Several of these trends pertinent to the field of urban forestry are summarized below.

- *Pollution is a transboundary issue.* The impact of acidic deposition in New England from air pollution generated in the Midwest is a prime example. It is no longer acceptable to export pollution. How would planting trees along all streets in the Los Angeles basin affect pollution concentrations and human health on those streets? The health of ecosystems in the nearby mountains? Air quality and visibility at the Grand Canyon?

- *Pollution control is shifting to nonpoint sources.* The easy gains in pollution abatement have been made through traditional technology-based, centralized command and control procedures. Now pollution control is shifting from industrial smokestacks to individual behavior (such as automobile use, or the use of lighter fluid for backyard grills). Water quality regulations have traditionally addressed end-ofpipe treatment, but runoff prevention is beginning to gain attention under section 31a of the Clean Water Act amendments of 1987. How would increased tree cover affect runoff volume and quality? Would incorporating landscape mulch into urban soils and collecting rainwater on individual properties have a beneficial effect on water quality and the demands for landscape irrigation?

- *Life-cycle analysis is important.* Recycled products may be cheaper than products using virgin materials if their prices capture all environmental externalities associated with production, utilization, and disposal. Corporations are beginning to take "cradle-to-grave" responsibility for their products, and electric utilities are incorporating environmental externalities into their resource planning process. Conserving energy through some demand-side management programs is proving to be less expensive than purchasing power from other sources or constructing power plants. Partly because of their cost-effectiveness, shade tree programs for energy conservation are now sponsored by utilities in Washington, D.C., Maryland, Texas, Arizona, Utah, and California (McPherson 1993).

- *Market incentives are emphasized.* Approaches that modify consumer behavior by offering economic incentives are receiving greater support by planners. For example, sulfur dioxide emission permits are now being traded in the marketplace, and this is expected to reduce the annual cost of compliance by over a billion dollars nationwide (Alm 1992). Urban forestry can offer one means for meeting policy objectives aimed at improving environmental health. The extent to which environmental planners use economic tools to this end will be related to their ability to identify connections between the economics of urban forest management and its environmental and social impacts. Quantifying benefits and costs associated with tree planting and care is a first step toward developing new market incentives aimed at sustaining healthy and productive urban forests.

CHICAGO BENEFIT-COST STUDY

Current efforts to determine the value of greenspace do not include a broad range of important benefits and costs or how they vary across time and location. Nor do they allow comparison of future cost-benefit relationships associated with alternative management scenarios (McPherson 1992). In response to these limitations, the Cost-Benefit Analysis of Trees (C-BAT) computer model was developed to quantify various management costs and environmental benefits. C-BAT as applied here quantifies annual benefits and costs for a thirty-year period associated with the establishment and care of 95,000 trees in Chicago. Contact persons from organizations responsible for much of the tree planting and care in Chicago were interviewed to estimate the number of trees to be planted annually over a five-year period (1992 to 1997), growth and mortality rates, and planting and management practices and costs (Table 17-1).

Quantifying benefits and costs associated with these plantings provides initial answers to the following questions: (1) Are trees worth it? Do their benefits exceed their costs? If so, by how much? (2) In what locations do trees provide the greatest net benefits? (3) How many years does it take before newly planted trees produce net benefits in Chicago? (4) What planting and management strategies will increase net benefits derived from Chicago's urban forest?

Table 17-1. Typical locations, planting sizes and costs, tree growth rates, and organizational roles in a Chicago computer modeling study (C-BAT).

Location	Planting size (caliper), cost per tree	Average annual growth rates: tree height, dbh	Organization and tree planting/care activity
Park	4-inch, $470	0.8-ft, 0.4-inch	Chicago Park District plant and maintain
Residential yard	2-inch, $250	0.8-ft, 0.4-inch	Residents plant and maintain small trees; arborists maintain/remove large trees
Residential street	2-inch, $162	0.67-ft, 0.33-inch	Bureau of Forestry plant and maintain
Highway	3-inch, $250	0.67-ft, 0.33-inch	Gateway Green, Illinois Department of Transportation, and arborists plant and maintain
Public housing	2.5-inch, $150	0.8-ft, 0.4-inch	Openlands, treeKeepers, and residents plant and maintain while young; arborists maintain larger trees

dbh = diameter at breast height.

Although Chicago's urban forest is planted with many tree species (Nowak 1994), the scope of this analysis is limited to planting and caring for a single typical species, green ash (*Fraxinus pennsylvanica*), in each of five typical locations: parks, residential yards, residential streets, highways, and public housing sites. Locations were selected to represent the types of trees, management approaches, socioeconomic situations, and growing conditions that influence tree health and productivity in Chicago. Green ash was selected because it is one of the most widely planted and successful tree species in Chicago.

C-BAT estimates annual benefits and costs for newly planted trees in different locations over a specified planning horizon. It is unique in that it directly connects tree size with the spatial-temporal flow of benefits and costs. Prices are assigned to each cost (e.g., planting, pruning, removal, irrigation, infrastructure repair, liability, waste disposal) and benefit (e.g., heating/cooling energy savings, absorption of air pollution, reduction in stormwater runoff) through direct estimation and implied valuation of benefits as environmental externalities (Chernick and Caverhill 1991). C-BAT incorporates data on different rates of growth and mortality as well as different levels of maintenance associated with typical trees. Hence this greenspace accounting approach "grows trees" in different locations and directly calculates the annual flow of benefits and costs as trees mature and die (McPherson 1992).

In this computer modeling study, trees were "planted" during the first five years and their growth was assumed to follow an S-shaped curve that incorporates a slow start after transplanting. As trees aged, their numbers decreased. Transplanting-related losses occurred during the first five years after planting, and age-independent losses occurred over the entire thirty-year analysis period. Transplanting-related losses were based on annual loss rates reported by local managers and other studies (Miller and Miller 1991; Nowak et al. 1990). Age-independent losses were assumed to be equally likely to occur in any year (Richards 1979). Tree growth (Table 17-1) and mortality reflected rates expected for the green ash on each type of site.

C-BAT directly connects selected benefits and costs with estimated leaf-surface area or, as in the case of carbon sequestered and "other" benefits, the tree's annual trunk diameter growth. Because many functional benefits of trees are related to leaf-atmosphere processes (e.g., interception, transpiration, photosynthesis), benefits increase as leaf-surface area increases. Similarly, pruning and removal costs usually increase with tree size. To account for these time-dependent relationships, benefits and costs are assumed to vary with leaf area (LA) and trunk girth.

For most costs and benefits, prices were obtained for large trees (assumed to be 20 inches in dbh or about 45 feet tall and wide) and estimated for trees of smaller size using different functions (e.g., linear, sine, cosine). These prices were divided by the tree's leaf area to derive a base price per unit LA for different tree size classes (e.g., $20 per 10,000 square feet LA = $0.002 per square foot LA). C-BAT multiplied the base price by the total LA of trees in that size class to estimate the total annual nominal value of each benefit and cost. Once the nominal values were calculated for each year into the future, they were discounted to a present value. Discount rates of 4, 7, and 10 percent were used to account for the different costs of capital faced by tree managers. Thus both tree size and the number of live trees influenced the dollar value of each benefit and cost. More detailed information on assumptions and pricing for each benefit and cost can be found in McPherson (1994).

This analysis was complicated by incomplete information on such critical variables as tree growth and mortality rates, the value of social, aesthetic, and economic benefits that trees produce, and costs associated with infrastructure repair, litigation, and program administration. When data from local sources were not available, it was necessary to use the best available data. As a result, some variables were excluded from this analysis (e.g., costs of litter cleanup, and health care benefits and costs). Estimating the value of social, aesthetic, and economic benefits—called "other benefits" in this study—is uncertain because we have yet to identify the full extent of these benefits or their implications. Additional problems emerge, since many of these benefits are not exchanged in markets and it is often difficult to estimate appropriate dollar values. Therefore, this study provides an initial approximation of those benefits and costs for which information is available. As our understanding of urban forest structure, function, and values increases, and we learn more about urban forestry programs and costs, these assumptions and methods used to estimate benefits and costs will be improved.

Mortality and Leaf Area

Mortality rates reflect the anticipated loss associated with growing conditions, care, and likely damage from cars, vandalism, pest/disease, and other impacts. Loss rates were projected to be greatest along residential streets (42 percent), where trees are exposed to a variety of human and environmental abuse (Table 17-2). A 39 percent loss rate was projected for trees planted in parks, on public housing sites, and along highways. About 18 percent of the trees planted in residential yards were expected to die. Of the 95,000 trees planted, 33,150 (35 percent) were projected to die, leaving 61,850 trees alive at the end of the thirty-year analysis (Figure 17-1).

The total amount of leaf area varies according to tree numbers and size. Although twice as many trees were projected to be planted along residential streets than in yards,

Table 17-2. C-BAT results.

Planting location	No. trees planted	Mortality rate (%)[a]	New tree cover[b]	NPV in $1,000[c]	Benefit/ cost[d]	Per planted tree (dollars)[e] PV benefit	PV cost	NPV
Park	12,500	39	190	5,592	2.14	840	393	447
Yard	25,000	18	433	14,637	3.51	818	233	585
Street	50,000	42	489	15,160	2.81	471	168	303
Highway	5,000	39	58	1,606	2.32	564	243	321
Housing	2,500	39	34	1,155	3.52	645	184	461
Total	95,000	35	1,204	38,150	2.83	621	219	402

[a] Percentage of trees planted expected to die during thirty-year planning period.

[b] Estimate of new tree cover in acres provided by plantings in thirty years (2022) assuming listed mortality and no replacement planting after five years.

[c] Net present values assuming 7 percent discount rate and thirty-year analysis period.

[d] Discounted benefit-cost ratio assuming 7 percent discount rate and thirty-year analysis period.

[e] Present value of benefits and costs per planted tree assuming 7 percent discount rate and thirty-year analysis period.

total leaf area for both was about 100 million square feet at year 30 because yard trees were faster growing (i.e., larger trees) and had a lower mortality rate. Because relatively few trees were projected to be planted in highway and public housing locations, thirty years after planting their projected total leaf area was about one-tenth that of street and yard trees.

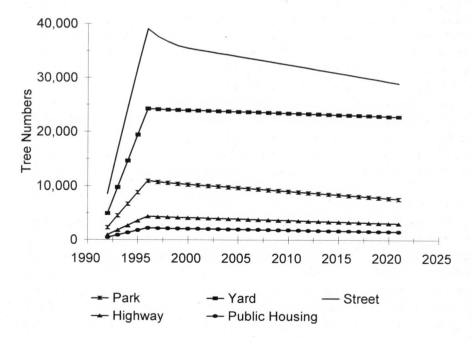

Figure 17-1. Projected number of live trees at each location, assuming planting and replacement during the first five years only.

Net Present Values and Benefit-Cost Ratios

The net present value (NPV) reflects the magnitude of investment in tree planting and care at each location, as well as the flow of benefits and costs over time. The projected NPVs were positive at all discount rates, ranging from $638,153 at public housing sites with a 10 percent discount rate to $30.6 million for street trees with a 4 percent discount rate. At a 7 percent discount rate, the NPV of the entire planting (95,000 trees) was projected to be $38 million, or about $402 per planted tree (Table 17-2). This means that on average the present value of the yield on investment in tree planting and care in excess of the cost of capital was $402 per tree. The NPV of street and yard trees was projected to be about $15 million each, while the NPV for park tree plantings was $5.6 million. The NPVs were lower for planting and care of trees along highways ($1.6 million) and at public housing sites ($1.2 million), because fewer trees were projected to be planted than in the other locations.

The discounted benefit-cost ratio (BCR), or the present value of benefits divided by the present value of costs, was greater than 1.0 at all discount rates. The BCRs ranged from 1.49 for park trees with a 10 percent discount rate, to 5.52 for residential yard trees with a 4 percent discount rate. At a 7 percent rate, the BCR for all locations was 2.83, meaning that $2.83 was returned for every $1.00 invested in tree planting and care in excess of the 7 percent cost of capital (Table 17-2). BCRs were projected to be greatest for residential plantings (3.5 for yard and public housing at 7 percent) and least for park trees (2.14), although actual BCRs will vary with the mix of species used and other factors influencing growth, mortality, and tree performance.

Although NPVs and BCRs vary considerably with discount rate, these results indicate that economic incentives for investing in tree planting and care exist, even for decision makers who face relatively high discount rates. While the rate of return on investment in tree planting and care was less at higher discount rates, benefits still exceeded costs for this thirty-year analysis. Given this result, a 7 percent discount rate is assumed for the findings that follow.

Present Values of Costs and Benefits per Planted Tree

Differences in return on investment can be understood by examining the present value of costs and benefits per planted tree at different planting locations (Figures 17-2 and 17-3). Even though trees of similar size and wholesale price were projected for planting in all locations, the present value of planting costs varies markedly, ranging from $109 per tree at public housing sites, where volunteer assistance kept costs down, to $341 in parks, where costs for initial irrigation added to the planting expenditures. Participation by residents of public housing in tree planting and care can reduce initial tree loss to neglect and vandalism. Similarly, initial watering of park trees can increase survival rates by reducing tree loss to drought.

The present value of pruning costs was only $12 per planted street tree, even though trees were assumed to be pruned more frequently along streets (every six years) than at other locations. In fact, the present value of total costs was only $168 per tree for street trees (Figure 17-2). Cost-effective planting and care of street trees is important because they account for about one-third of Chicago's overall tree cover (McPherson et al. 1993).

The present value of removal costs was projected to be highest for trees planted in parks and public housing sites ($16 to $22 per tree). Costs for infrastructure repair, pest and disease control, and liability/litigation were relatively small. The present value of

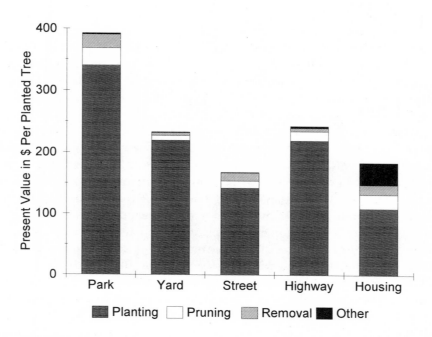

Figure 17-2. Present value of costs per tree planted at each location, assuming a thirty-year analysis period and a 7 percent discount rate. "Other" includes costs for sidewalk and sewer repair, liability/litigation, program administration, and pest/disease control.

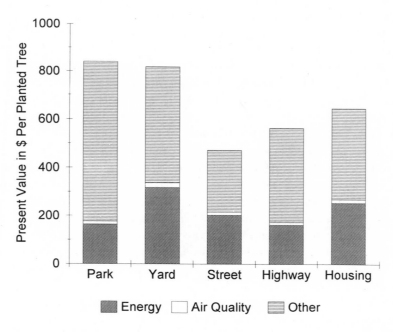

Figure 17-3. Present value of benefits per tree planted at each location, assuming a thirty-year analysis period and a 7 percent discount rate. Air quality benefits are totals for PM10, ozone, sulfur dioxide, nitrogen dioxide, carbon monoxide, and carbon dioxide. Hydrologic benefits from reduced stormwater runoff and avoided water consumption at power plants are small and included with the "Other" category, which also includes benefits such as scenic beauty, wildlife habitat, outdoor recreation, stress reduction, noise abatement, and soil conservation. These other benefits were calculated as the total compensatory value minus explicitly valued energy, air quality, and hydrologic benefits. See McPherson (1994) for additional information on benefit estimation.

program administration costs for tree plantings by Openlands and trained volunteers was $35 per planted tree. Generally, nonprofit tree groups have higher administrative costs than municipal programs using in-house or contracted services because of their small size and the expense of organizing and training volunteers. These additional expenditures somewhat offset savings associated with reduced labor costs for planting and initial tree care compared to municipal programs.

The projected present value of benefits per planted tree was $471 and $564 for street and highway plantings respectively, $645 for public housing sites, and more than $800 for trees planted in parks and residential yards (Figure 17-3). Lower benefits for street and highway trees can be attributed to their slower growth, smaller total leaf area, and relatively smaller energy and other benefits, due to locational factors.

The amount of annual benefits the typical tree produces depends on tree size and the relation between location and functional performance. Larger trees can produce more benefits than smaller trees because they have more leaf-surface area. Because yard trees exert more influence on building energy use than highway trees do, they produce greater energy savings per unit leaf area. To illustrate how these factors influence benefits, nondiscounted annual benefits were estimated for the typical tree at year 30 in each typical location (Table 17-3). Estimated savings in annual air-conditioning energy from the 36 foot (14 inches dbh) yard tree were 201 kWh (0.7 GJ) ($24 nominal) compared to 102 kWh (0.4 GJ) ($12 nominal) for a 34 foot (13 inches dbh) tree along a highway. Differences in benefits from the uptake of air pollutants by trees, including carbon sequestered, were assumed to be solely due to differences in tree size, because little is known about spatial variations in pollution concentrations that influence rates of vegetation uptake. However, location-related differences in cooling energy savings translated into differences in avoided emissions and water consumed in the process of electric power generation. For instance, trees were projected to intercept more particulate matter and absorb more ozone and nitrogen dioxide directly than in avoided power-plant emissions. But energy savings from the same trees resulted in greater avoided emissions of sulfur dioxide, carbon monoxide, and carbon dioxide than was gained through direct absorption and sequestration. Street trees were projected to provide the greatest annual reductions in avoided stormwater runoff: 327 gallons (12.4 kl) for the 32 foot tree (12 inches dbh) compared to 104 gallons (3.9 kl) avoided by a park tree of larger size. More runoff was avoided by street trees than by trees at other sites because street tree canopies intercept rainfall over mostly paved surfaces. In the absence of street trees, rainfall on paving begins to run off quickly. Trees in yards and parks provided less reduction in avoided runoff because in their absence more rainfall infiltrated into soil and vegetated areas; thus less total runoff was avoided. Assumed differences in economic, social, aesthetic, and psychological values attached to trees in different locations were reflected in the projected value of "other benefits" (Table 17-3).

Discounted Payback Periods

The discounted payback period is the number of years before the benefit-cost ratio exceeds 1.0 and net benefits begin to accrue. Assuming a 7 percent discount rate, projected payback periods ranged from nine years for trees planted and maintained at public housing sites to fifteen years for plantings in parks and along highways (Figure 17-4). Yard and street trees were projected to have thirteen- and fourteen-year discounted payback periods, respectively. As expected, payback periods were slightly

Table 17-3. Projected annual benefits produced thirty years after planting by the typical green ash tree at typical locations in Chicago.

Tree location and benefit categories	Park	Residential yard	Residential street	Highway	Public housing
Tree size (height in feet)	39	36	32	34	37
dbh (inches)	16	14	12	13	14.5
Energy					
Cooling (kWh)	116	201	152	102	179
Heating (MBtu)	5.1	8.3	6.5	4.5	7.7
Total dollars	39.42	65.62	50.74	34.74	59.98
PM10 (lb)					
Direct uptake	2.19	1.8	1.41	1.67	1.93
Avoided emissions	0.02	0.30	0.02	0.01	0.02
Total dollars	1.44	1.37	0.93	1.09	1.27
Ozone (lb)					
Direct uptake	0.79	0.65	0.51	0.60	0.70
Avoided VOC emissions	0	0.01	0.01	0	0.01
Total dollars	0.19	0.16	0.13	0.15	0.17
Nitrogen dioxide (lb)					
Direct uptake	0.55	0.45	0.36	0.42	0.48
Avoided emissions	0.15	0.26	0.19	0.13	0.23
Total dollars	1.54	1.56	1.21	1.21	1.56
Sulfur dioxide (lb)					
Direct uptake	0.51	0.42	0.33	0.39	0.45
Avoided emissions	0.79	1.37	1.03	0.69	1.22
Total dollars	1.07	1.47	1.12	0.89	1.37
Carbon monoxide (lb)					
Direct uptake	0.04	0.03	0.03	0.03	0.04
Avoided emissions	0.08	0.13	0.10	0.07	0.12
Total dollars	0.06	0.07	0.06	0.05	0.07
Carbon dioxide (lb)					
Direct uptake	112	94	77	87	49
Avoided emissions	166	271	212	145	241
Total dollars	3.06	4.02	3.18	2.55	3.19
Hydrology (gal)					
Runoff avoided	104	177	327	132	187
Water saved	69	120	91	61	102
Total dollars	2.20	3.75	6.70	2.75	3.92
Other benefits (dollars)	196.46	233.82	247.69	231.07	190.2

Prices used to estimate benefits: $0.12/kWh, $5/MBtu, $0.65/lb PM10, $0.245/lb ozone and volatile organic compounds (VOC), $2.2/lb NO_2, $0.82/lb SO_2, $0.46/lb CO, $0.011/lb CO_2, $0.02/gal runoff avoided, $0.00175/gal water saved, $27/inch dbh for other benefits (Neely 1988). See McPherson (1994) for additional information on benefit estimation.

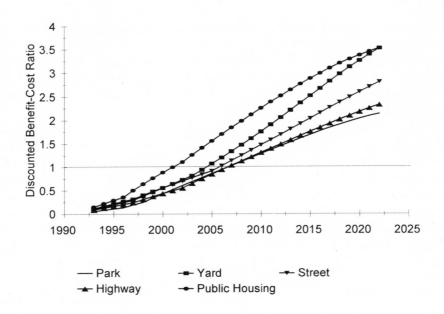

Figure 17-4. Discounted payback periods depicting the number of years before the benefit-cost ratio exceeds 1.0. This analysis assumes a thirty-year planning period and a 7 percent discount rate.

longer at the 10 percent discount rate (eleven to eighteen years), and shorter at most locations with a 4 percent discount rate (nine to thirteen years).

Early payback at public housing sites can be attributed to several factors. Trees were projected to add leaf area at a relatively rapid rate due to low initial mortality and fast growth compared to trees at other locations. These trees were relatively inexpensive to plant and establish due to participation by residents and volunteers. Thus the payback period was shortened because up-front costs, which are heavily discounted compared to costs incurred in the future, were low.

Summary

Are trees worth it? Energy savings, air pollution mitigation, avoided runoff, and other benefits associated with trees in Chicago can outweigh planting and maintenance costs. Given the assumptions of this analysis (thirty years, 7 percent discount rate, 95,000 trees planted), the projected NPV of the simulated tree planting was $38 million, or $402 per planted tree. A benefit-cost ratio of 2.83 indicates that the value of projected benefits was nearly three times the value of projected costs.

In what locations do trees provide the greatest net benefits? Benefit-cost ratios were projected to be positive for plantings at park, yard, street, highway, and public housing locations at discount rates ranging from 4 to 10 percent. Assuming a 7 percent discount rate, BCRs were largest for trees in residential yard and public housing (3.5) sites. The following traits were associated with trees in these locations: relatively inexpensive to establish, low mortality rates, vigorous growth, and large energy savings. Because of their prominence in the landscape and existence of public programs for their management, street and park trees frequently receive more attention than yard trees. By capitalizing on the many opportunities for yard tree planting in Chicago, residents can gain additional environmental, economic, social, and aesthetic benefits. Residents on whose property such trees are located receive direct benefits (e.g., lower energy bills, increased property value), yet benefits accrue to the community as well. In the aggregate, private trees improve air quality, reduce stormwater runoff, remove atmospheric carbon dioxide, enhance the local landscape, and produce other benefits that extend well beyond the site where they grow.

How many years does it take before trees produce net benefits in Chicago? Payback periods vary with the species planted, planting location, and level of care that trees receive. C-BAT findings suggest that discounted payback periods for trees in Chicago can range from nine to eighteen years. Shorter payback periods were obtained at lower discount rates, while higher rates lengthened the periods.

What tree planting and management strategies will increase net benefits derived from Chicago's urban forest? Findings from the C-BAT simulations suggest several strategies to maximize net benefits from investment in Chicago's urban forest. These concepts are not new and most of the following recommendations have application in communities besides Chicago.

- *Select the right tree for each location.* Given that planting and establishment costs represent a large fraction of total tree expenditures, investing in trees that are well suited to their sites makes economic sense. Matching tree to site should take advantage of local knowledge of the tolerances of various tree species (Ware 1994). Species proven to be well adapted should be selected in most cases, though limited testing of new introductions increases species diversity and adds new horticultural knowledge (Richards 1993).

- *Weigh the desirability of controlling initial planting costs with the need to provide growing environments suitable for healthy, long-lived trees.* Because the initial investments in a project are high, ways to cut up-front costs should be considered. Some strategies include the use of trained volunteers, smaller tree sizes, and follow-up care to increase survival rates. When unamended growing conditions are likely to be favorable, such as yard or garden settings, it may be cost-effect to use smaller, inexpensive stock, thus reducing planting costs. However, in highly urbanized settings, money may be well spent by creating growing environments that improve the long-term performance of trees. Frequent replacement of small trees in restricted spaces may be less economical than investing initially in environments conducive to the culture of long-lived, vigorous shade trees.

- *Plan for long-term tree care.* Benefits from trees increase as they grow, especially if systematic pruning and maintenance result in a healthy tree population (Miller and Sylvester 1981). The costs of providing regular tree care are small compared to the value of benefits forgone when maturing trees become unhealthy and die (Abbott et al. 1991). Efficiently delivered tree care can more than pay for itself by improving health, increasing growth, and extending longevity. A long-term tree care plan should include frequent visits to each tree during the first ten years after planting, to develop a sound branching structure and correct other problems; thereafter less frequent but regular pruning, inspection, and treatment should be carried out as needed. Mature trees in Chicago provide substantial benefits today. Maintenance that extends the life of these trees will pay dividends in the short term, just as routine maintenance of transplants will pay dividends in the future.

CONCLUSIONS

Clearly, a healthy urban forest can produce long-term benefits that all city residents can share. The Chicago benefit-cost study illustrates the value of some of these benefits, as well as the costs. Improving the health and increasing the productivity of America's urban forests will require increased support from local residents, planners, and policy makers. Benefit-cost information can be part of public education programs designed to make residents more aware of the value their trees add to the environment in which they live. Also, it can be used by environmental planners to develop economic incentives for increased investment in urban forestry.

In summary, greater support for urban forestry programs will be predicated on stronger connections between city residents and city trees. Opportunities to strengthen these connections include:

- *Research and sound economic analyses that quantify the benefits and costs of trees.* If decision makers are asked to invest substantial amounts of money in the urban forest versus other investment opportunities, they must be provided with the best available information regarding the potential return on investment. Future analyses should consider who will bear the costs and who will receive the benefits, and how these will shift over time. For example, local investment in trees that reduce power plant emissions could benefit communities many miles downwind of the power plant.

- *Demonstrations of successful tree planting and management projects.* Numbers do not drive all decisions. A policy maker may be more influenced by experiencing the cooler temperatures and beauty of a shaded parking lot, compared to one with no trees, than by an exhaustive comparison of surface energy budgets and cost-benefit ratios.

- *Public awareness of the multiple benefits trees produce.* People are less aware of the environmental benefits trees produce than the aesthetic contributions of trees to community attractiveness (Gangloff 1993). More information regarding all benefits needs to be communicated to the public. A professionally produced television piece might reach a large segment of the general public, while children can be taught through science curriculums that include more materials on urban ecosystems.

- *"A bigger tent for urban forestry"* (Willeke 1994). New partners are needed to share the work of nurturing our urban forest resources. A key to creating a bigger tent lies in recognizing the urban forest as a community resource. Trees produce multiple benefits that extend well beyond the site where each tree grows. Our challenge lies in achieving a better understanding of these benefits and how the self-interests of new partners can advance the common interests of all residents through increased participation in stewardship of the urban forest resource.

ACKNOWLEDGMENTS

I wish to thank Paul Sacamano, Steve Wensman, Scott Prichard, Marcia Henning, and Lisa Blakeslee for their assistance with data collection and C-BAT modeling. Information on tree planting and care programs in Chicago was provided by Geri Weinstein and

Robert Megquier (Chicago Park District), Larry Hall (Hendrickson The Care of Trees), Steve Bylina (Bureau of Forestry), Vince Pagone (Chicago Gateway Green Committee), Rick Wanner (Illinois Department of Transportation), and Suzanne Malec-Hoer (Openlands). Helpful reviews of early versions of this manuscript were provided by Tim Duane (University of California, Berkeley) and Ray Aslin (Kansas State Forestry), and all errors of fact or interpretation are the responsibility of the author.

LITERATURE CITED

Abbott, R.E., C. Luley, E. Buchanan, K. Miller, and K. Joehlin. 1991. The importance of large tree maintenance in mitigating global climate change. Research Report. National Arborist Association, Amherst, New Hampshire; International Society of Arboriculture, Urbana, Illinois. 7 p.

Akbari, H., S. Davis, S. Dorsano, J. Huang, and S. Winnett. 1992. Cooling our communities: A guidebook on tree planting and light-colored surfacing. U.S. Environmental Protection Agency, Washington, D.C.

Alm, A.L. 1992. A need for new approaches: Command-and-control is no longer a cure-all. EPA Journal 18(2):7-11.

Anderson, L.M., and H.K. Cordell. 1988. Influence of trees on residential property values in Athens, Georgia (U.S.A.): A survey based on actual sales prices. Landscape and Urban Planning 15:153-164.

Bernhardt, E., and T.J. Swiecki. 1993. The state of urban forestry in California, 1992. California Department of Forestry and Fire Protection, Sacramento. 61 p.

Chernick, P.L., and E.J. Caverhill. 1991. The valuation of environmental externalities in energy conservation planning. *In* Energy efficiency and the environment: Forging the link, pp. 215-228. American Council for an Energy-Efficient Economy, Washington, D.C.

Duane, T.P. 1992. Environmental planning and policy in a post-Rio world. Berkeley Planning Journal 7:27-47.

Dwyer, J.F., E.G. McPherson, H. Schroeder, and R. Rowntree. 1992. Assessing the benefits and costs of the urban forest. Journal of Arboriculture 18(5):227-234.

Gangloff, D. 1993. Thinking cool: From attitude to action. Urban Forests 13(6):6-7.

McPherson, E.G. 1992. Accounting for benefits and costs of urban greenspace. Landscape and Urban Planning 22:41-51.

——. 1993. Evaluating the cost effectiveness of shade trees for demand-side management. Electricity Journal 6(9):57-65.

——. 1994. Modeling benefits and costs of tree planting and care in Chicago. *In* E.G. McPherson, D. Nowak, and R.A. Rowntree, eds., Chicago's urban forest ecosystem: Results of the Chicago Urban Forest Climate Project. General Technical Report NE-186. USDA Forest Service Northeastern Forest Experiment Station, Radnor, Pennsylvania.

McPherson, E.G., and D.J. Nowak. 1993. Value of urban greenspace for air quality improvement: Lincoln Park, Chicago. Arborist News 2(6):30-32.

McPherson, E.G., D.J. Nowak, P.L. Sacamano, S.E. Prichard, and E.M. Makra. 1993. Chicago's evolving urban forest. General Technical Report NE-169. USDA Forest Service Northeastern Forest Experiment Station, Radnor, Pennsylvania. 55 p.

McPherson, E.G., D. Nowak, and R.A. Rowntree, eds. 1994. Chicago's urban forest ecosystem: Results of the Chicago Urban Forest Climate Project. General Technical Report NE-186. USDA Forest Service Northeastern Forest Experiment Station, Radnor, Pennsylvania.

Miller, R.H., and R.W. Miller. 1991. Planting survival of selected street tree taxa. Journal of Arboriculture 17(7):185-191.

Miller, R.H., and W.A. Sylvester. 1981. An economic evaluation of the pruning cycle. Journal of Arboriculture 7(4):109-111.

Neely, D.N. 1988. Valuation of landscape trees, shrubs, and other plants. 7th ed. International Society of Arboriculture, Urbana, Illinois.

Nowak, D.J. 1994. Urban forest structure: The state of Chicago's urban forest. In E.G. McPherson, D. Nowak, and R.A. Rowntree, eds., Chicago's urban forest ecosystem: Results of the Chicago Urban Forest Climate Project. General Technical Report NE-186. USDA Forest Service Northeastern Forest Experiment Station, Radnor, Pennsylvania.

Nowak, D.J., J. McBride, and R. Beatty. 1990. Newly planted street tree growth and mortality. Journal of Arboriculture 16(5):124-129.

Richards, N.A. 1979. Modeling survival and consequent replacement needs in a street tree population. Journal of Arboriculture 5(11):251-255.

——. 1993. Reasonable guidelines for street tree diversity. Journal of Arboriculture 19(6):344-349.

Rowntree, R.A., and D.J. Nowak. 1991. Quantifying the role of urban forests in removing atmospheric carbon dioxide. Journal of Arboriculture 17(10):269-275.

Sampson, R.N., G.A. Moll, and J.J. Kielbaso. 1992. Opportunities to increase urban forests and the potential impacts on carbon storage and conservation. In R.N. Sampson and D. Hair, eds., Forests and global change, vol. 1, pp. 51-72. American Forests, Washington, D.C.

Sanders, R.A. 1986. Urban vegetation impacts on the hydrology of Dayton, Ohio. Urban Ecology 9:361-376.

Ware, G.H. 1994. Ecological bases for selecting urban trees. Journal of Arboriculture 20(2):98-103.

Willeke, D.C. 1994. A bigger tent for urban forestry. Urban Forests 14(1):20.

18

Bellevue, Washington: Managing the Urban Forest for Multiple Benefits

LEE SPRINGGATE and ROGER HOESTEREY

ABSTRACT Across the country it is common for local parks and recreation departments to be the largest landowners within the city limits. It is quite uncommon for city or county governments to have active land stewardship programs. Bellevue, Washington has been developing a comprehensive urban forestry and land stewardship program for several years. This case study presents a model for how communities on the urban edge can conduct active natural resource management based on ecological principals. Specific project examples show how many of the special purpose landscapes discussed in this volume can be integrated to provide the public with a broad set of environmental, recreational, social, and aesthetic benefits. Cities can expand their land management roles and concepts of urban forestry to include greenbelt management, wildlife enhancement, use of native plants, and ecological resource management.

Bellevue, Washington is a city of 90,000 residents just east of Seattle. It is known regionally for having a comprehensive greenway program that blends open space acquisition, sensitive area protection, long-range planning, community involvement, and natural resource management from an ecosystem perspective. The unique mosaic of water, forest, and mountains makes the Puget Sound basin of Washington State one of the most desirable areas of the country in which to live and work. Greenways help to create a healthy and aesthetically pleasing environment, thus contributing to economic and cultural vitality. Trees growing from the shoreline of Lake Washington and Lake Sammamish to the top of Cougar Mountain form an urban forest that softens the rough edges of man-made structures.

The greenway is clearly an old idea with exciting new applications to urban living in the United States. From the storied Vienna Woods to the rolling English countryside, greenways have historically provided a spectacular natural contrast to urban density. Increases in population, coupled with the depletion and exploitation of the natural resource base, have triggered a renewed interest in urban greenways. Rather than viewing open space predominantly as a privately managed and manipulated commodity, the perception shifts to that of treasuring the diminishing open space as a vital public good. But given the extraordinary competition for the available public dollar, it is imperative that urban open space systems be sensibly created and carefully managed. Urban greenways are enlightened responses to the realities of the 1990s because they provide multiple benefits at an affordable price to a wide array of citizens.

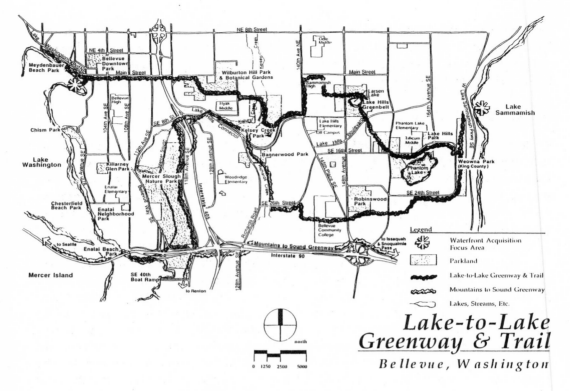

Figure 18-1. Lake-to-Lake Greenway and Trail.

OLMSTED REVISITED

Frederick Law Olmsted and his contemporaries developed an extraordinary series of open space plans for cities throughout the United States, from New York and Boston to San Francisco and Seattle. These plans emphasized the concept of a park "system" in which significant parklands are connected by boulevards, trails, and greenbelts. Many of these plans were faithfully implemented around the turn of the century by elected and appointed officials who had both the vision and courage to act aggressively on behalf of present and future generations. They left a magnificent legacy that should serve to inspire the current park leadership in this country.

The idea of linkages is crucial. By connecting disparate sites via boulevards, trails, and open space, parklands become more usable, accessible, and visible. The park and open space system achieves a sense of integration and completeness. It begins to affect our daily lives, where we work, live, and play. The system interacts with us as we walk to school, look out our living room windows, drive down the local arterial, recreate and move through our normal living routine. In short, it becomes a part of the community fabric, a source of pride and identity. The system connects neighborhoods, commercial areas, parks, schools, and other points of public interest in a very special way.

Emerging urban centers such as Bellevue should view these Olmsted systems as excellent historical precedents. We are grateful that some farsighted people were able to so convincingly demonstrate the value of park and open space systems within the urban context. Bellevue is in the process of acquiring and linking an exciting variety of park sites between Lake Washington and Lake Sammamish. This system, referred to as the Lake-to-Lake Greenway and Trail, was inspired by a unique blend of the Olmsted philosophy, environmental degradation, rampant growth, and the mandate to squeeze multiple benefits from scarce resources (see Figure 18-1).

NATURAL RESOURCE MANAGEMENT

To ensure that the greenway benefits continue for many generations, a comprehensive management program must be in place. The natural resources must be managed with the same skill and commitment as any other community resource. Six key objectives of the natural resource management program are: (1) ensure safety of citizens, (2) improve forest conditions, (3) protect and enhance wildlife habitat, (4) provide recreation opportunity, (5) buffer land uses and separate developments, and (6) protect water quality.

A key component of managing greenways in western Washington is managing the urban forest. Historically, urban forestry has focused on the management and maintenance of planted street trees and individual tree management. Our forestry activities have expanded on this approach to include all community trees, not only as individuals, but as a forest community of plants and animals. The ecosystem strategy analyzes the interrelatedness of the different components of natural systems, as well as the human impact on their functioning. We must understand the natural parameters of climate, soil, water, sunlight, and other components that provided the foundation of our ancient forests. Just as important, we must understand the past and present human influences that have shaped the type of forests we see today.

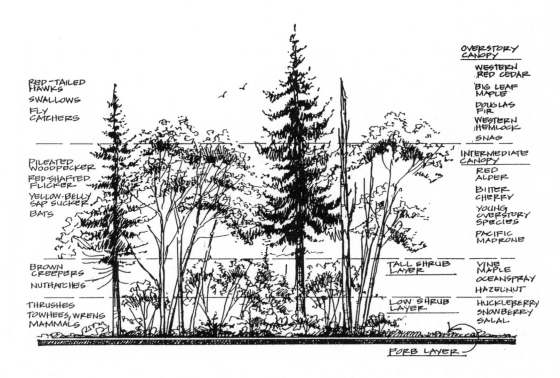

Figure 18-2. Four layers of a mature forest, with the birds that typically inhabit each.

For example, in Bellevue the ancient conifer forest stood intact just a hundred years ago. We know that the climax forest was subject to localized forest fires and windfall that opened the canopy to pioneer species creating beneficial diversity. Today, due to human influence, the forest canopy is a mix of second-growth conifers and overmature pioneering species of red alder (*Alnus rubra*) and bigleaf maple (*Acer macrophyllum*). One of our goals is to restore the forested greenbelts and parklands to conditions as close to natural (premodern era) as possible. This includes the selective removal of pioneering and introduced species and replanting of trees, shrubs, and ground covers characteristic of a Puget Sound lowland forest. Snags, dead trees, and fallen logs are often retained for their exceptional wildlife value (see Figure 18-2).

Street landscaping is a part of this overall goal. We make a transition from the formal, more ornamental planting of the central business district to landscaped corridors along arterials that are wide enough to accommodate native plantings. Environmental regulations protect steep hillsides, forested wetlands, and significant trees on private property. Plant and animal communities do not acknowledge political boundaries or delineations of ownership. For us to be wise stewards of the natural resources, our planning must look beyond artificial, man-made boundaries and consider the entire ecosystem.

Program planning is based on the following assumptions:

- Natural features improve over time. Man-made structures deteriorate.
- Nature is the ultimate landscape architect. In greenbelts and forested parkland we seek to preserve and restore natural conditions.
- Ecosystems and human impacts on ecosystems are complex. We seek to understand the interrelatedness of all factors.
- A community's forest canopy consists of all the trees—tree cover on private property, parks, greenbelts, and streetscapes.

Specific forestry and habitat enhancement activities are prescribed only after a careful review of individual site conditions, development of a specific management plan, and consultation with local residents. We are willing to use more labor-intensive techniques such as hand falling, slash removal, and planting to minimize disturbance to understory vegetation and soils.

Pruning is required to remove dead and damaged limbs, to balance crowns, and to provide light and air circulation to understory vegetation. On each site the trees are evaluated and may be removed if they are diseased, present a hazard, or interfere with the optimal health of other trees. Quick removal restricts the spread of disease and reduces the possibility of human injury or property damage. In western Washington, it is common for the forest in early successional stages to be overcrowded with dense stands of young trees competing for air, light, and nutrients. The health of individual trees and the forest as a whole can be greatly improved through well-planned thinning operations.

RECREATIONAL ENHANCEMENT

Recreation amenities such as trails, scenic overlooks, picnic tables, and benches are all planned and developed in conjunction with the natural resource management activities. The goal is to plan and maintain trails that can be enjoyed during all seasons. A trail standard has been developed that allows two people to walk side by side. Socially, this

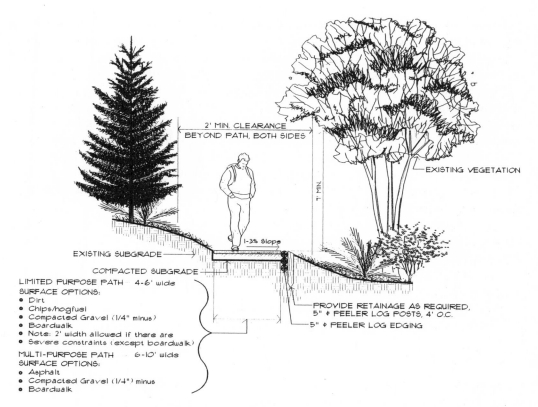

Figure 18-3. A typical section of a two-person recreational trail.

is a far more enjoyable experience than walking single file. Our experience has shown that trails that are properly designed and sensitively constructed have little impact on the environment. In fact, such trails can be used to minimize impact on sensitive landscapes like wetlands, by channeling human impacts away from fragile areas and keeping human disturbance to limited areas (see Figure 18-3).

The key to wildlife management is habitat management. The most important component of habitat for most species of native animals is vegetation. Proper management of the wildlife enhancement areas will increase wildlife diversity, improve the aesthetics of the site, and provide passive recreation and educational benefits. Wildlife enhancement activities focus on specific areas where the habitat has been degraded by human activities. For example, a previously farmed area may be covered with a monoculture of introduced plant species. By removing the invasive plants and restoring the site with the correct structural and species diversity, wildlife habitat will be improved. Grant funding and volunteer labor are readily available for well-conceived wildlife enhancement programs.

PUBLIC EDUCATION AND INVOLVEMENT

Public education and involvement cannot be overlooked if we are to develop and maintain sustainable programs. Policy makers, regulatory staff, and of course the local residents must all clearly understand our goals, objectives, and operational practices before work can begin. Tremendous public support can be generated by involving individuals, school groups, conservation organizations, and local businesses in hands-on natural resource management projects. There is a tremendous sense of personal fulfillment that can be gained by engaging in projects to improve the health of our environment. A key secret of the success of Bellevue's program is public education and involvement.

Public education is an important component of the urban forestry program, particularly with the public's sensitivity to any tree removal. Urban forestry issues are discussed in numerous public meetings with the Park Board, Planning Commission, Environmental Commission, and City Council. Prior to implementing on-site operational activities, the staff conducts community meetings to explain long-term goals, operational techniques, and landscape improvements.

It is difficult for people unfamiliar with resource management techniques to visualize the benefits of enhancing forested landscapes. As a result we have developed a brochure entitled "Bellevue's Urban Forest" that explains our long-term forest management objectives. Ranger personnel conduct environmental education programs for school children. The community forests are excellent outdoor classrooms. Youth and adult volunteers actively participate in enhancement projects. This hands-on involvement is critical in building public support for future urban forestry programs.

CONCLUSION

The public awareness of environmental issues is at an all-time high. As professionals and dedicated citizens, we have a tremendous opportunity to be leaders in solving many of the environmental problems facing our cities. It is time we expand our concept of urban forestry to include greenbelt management, wildlife enhancement, use of native landscaping, and ecological resource management. By employing a greenway strategy to urban forestry, we can provide the public with a broad set of benefits and significantly improve the character of our communities.

19

Tiger Mountain State Forest:
A Working Forest in an Urban Environment

DOUG McCLELLAND

ABSTRACT The Tiger Mountain State Forest, 20 miles east of Seattle, Washington, is an accessible outdoor laboratory where forest resource managers can demonstrate modern forestry techniques to the public. The idea of a working forest creates a partnership between the Washington State Department of Natural Resources and the public. This paper explores the integration of multipurpose landscapes in an urban working forest. The discussion includes the background history of the Tiger Mountain State Forest, how management philosophy has changed over time, and the benefits of attempting to integrate multiple forest purposes across a landscape.

Where does the Tiger Mountain State Forest fit into the urban forest landscape? It is certainly not an urban park with ball fields, meadows, and playgrounds. It cannot be considered a wilderness area similar to the adjacent Alpine Lakes. It is also hard to describe Tiger Mountain as a commercial tree farm. In reality the Tiger Mountain State Forest is a mixture of these purposes.

Located twenty miles east of Seattle and thirty miles northeast of Tacoma, the forest is situated within a triangle created by three major highways: Interstate 90, State Route 18, and the Issaquah-Hobart Road. Tiger Mountain is a working forest readily accessible to over 1.5 million residents of the Puget Sound region. The forest is made up of a cluster of lowland Cascade mountains; the highest peak is Main Tiger Mountain, at 3,004 feet. The entire forest encompasses 13,500 acres, with the northwestern corner dedicated as a Natural Resource Conservation Area. The first timber harvesting began in the 1920s and only 450 acres of forest remnant trees remain today. Tiger Mountain is a major recreation area, with the Highpoint Trailhead east of Issaquah competing with Mount Si as the number one trailhead in the state.

In King County's comprehensive plan and Growth Management Act, Tiger Mountain is on the western edge of the designated forest production district. The forest is surrounded by urban development on the west and industrial forest lands to the east. Forest land conversion may eventually encircle Tiger Mountain with urban development. If this happens, the forest will lose a critical wildlife link to the Cascade Range.

Tiger Mountain is a typical fire-based lowland coastal forest that contained some of the largest trees in King County and has very productive soils. In the 1920s the first commercial timber harvest was conducted on Tiger Mountain. Five mills surrounded the area and in a matter of twenty years the entire forest was harvested, leaving only a few patches of uncut trees. The forest reestablished itself and in the 1970s Weyerhaeuser Company began the second harvest on Tiger Mountain. The Washington State Department of Natural Resources began harvesting their lands there in 1980.

Population growth surrounding Tiger Mountain brought increased public interest in forest management. The department's South Puget Sound Region began studying ways to better coordinate land management within the forest, and in November 1981, Brian Boyle, commissioner of public lands, announced plans to create the Tiger Mountain State Forest. Weyerhaeuser traded its lands on Tiger Mountain to the state, and a state Forest Advisory Committee was created which developed recommended guidelines for management of Tiger Mountain. In 1986, utilizing the advisory committee's work, the Department of Natural Resources completed a landscape plan for Tiger Mountain. In 1991 the 4,400 acre West Tiger Mountain Natural Resource Conservation Area was created. With the addition of a conservation area and its unique resource protection responsibilities a new purpose landscape was created.

For eighty years the primary purpose of the forest was industrial forest land management. The goal of landowners was to produce maximum revenue by the sale of timber. Recreation was dispersed, uncontrolled, and lawless. Recreation users were in conflict with each other as well as with the forest landowners. Through the creation of the state forest, purposes were broadened throughout the landscape. Forest management now includes recreation, water quality, fisheries, education, wildlife, scenic, old-growth, and conservation values. The forest has become a self-supporting open space and a critical link in the Mountains to Sound Greenway.

VISUAL BENEFITS

From the scenic perspective, the forest is a key connector in the Mountains to Sound Greenway. It is the only undeveloped forest in the Interstate 90 corridor from Seattle to Snoqualmie Pass. This forest backdrop is the last green that motorists see before reaching the urbanized areas of Issaquah and Bellevue. Managing timber removals over time, by utilizing landscape design criteria, has enabled the forest to meet objectives of both generating revenue from state trust lands and maintaining scenic qualities. This is how the forest is able to remain a self-supporting open space. The addition of the West Tiger Mountain Natural Resource Conservation Area protects unique old-growth stands and the diverse forested background to Issaquah.

FOREST REMNANTS AND CONSERVATION

Forest remnants remaining from the first timber harvests in the early 1900s are a significant component of the forest ecosystem. The key to success in managing the older trees is to keep your options open. When Tiger Mountain was created as a state forest, the citizen advisory committee and the agency agreed not to harvest these trees for ten years. During that time the Department of Natural Resources would study the older forest stands to determine which were unique, which should be expanded, and which might be harvested. The department would also use this time to develop protection methods for the unique areas. In 1987 the Natural Resource Conservation Areas Act was passed by the legislature. From this new legislation the West Tiger Mountain Natural Resource Conservation Area was created.

Conservation areas are designed to maintain, enhance, or restore ecological systems, while protecting habitat of threatened, endangered, and sensitive plants and animals. If possible, these areas can also provide opportunities for environmental education and low-impact public use. By deferring harvest on the 450 acres of older trees on Tiger Mountain, a system was developed to protect these unique areas. In addition, as the entire conservation area moves through time, the older forest component will increase. In the future we should have an interconnected ecosystem of over 5,500 acres of old-growth forest habitat in the Tiger Mountain State Forest. The entire forest will have a mixture of young, mature, and old-growth forest habitat supporting a diverse wildlife population.

WILDLIFE HABITAT

From a wildlife perspective, Tiger Mountain is the key travel corridor for wildlife from the Cascade Range to more isolated areas such as Cougar and Squak mountains to the west. This connector system is critical for continuing a healthy wildlife population. If Tiger Mountain is severed from the 90,000 acre Seattle watershed to the east, over 20,000 acres of lowland forest will lose a valuable ecosystem component. The simple action of widening Highway 18 has the potential to isolate Tiger Mountain forever.

Within the forest, several management techniques are used to enhance wildlife. Roads are abandoned and gated to prevent wildlife harassment from motorized recreation. The goal of timber harvest design is to maintain wildlife diversity. Partial harvest, shelter-wood, and small groupings of selected trees create forest openings while providing vertical forest diversity for wildlife. Some critical old-growth forest characteristics can be created in fifty years' time through forest manipulation using New Forestry techniques. These techniques are not really new, but only a departure from the standard approach of clearcut, burn, and plant of the early 1960s. The objective is to maintain maximum biodiversity throughout the forest landscape, maximize the numbers of wildlife species, develop a coordinated forest habitat, and most of all provide a sustainable forest ecosystem.

FIRE, ENERGY, AND WATER

The threat of fire comes more from the adjacent urban lands than from the forest. Debris burning, structural fires, and land clearing have the greatest potential of causing a forest fire. With the restrictions required by the Clean Air Act, debris- and land-clearing fires will soon be eliminated adjacent to the forest. There is some threat from fires started by recreationists, although history suggests that this is a small component of all human-caused forest fires. Since the goal is to reduce smoke emissions in the region, the silvicultural use of fire will be limited on a case-by-case basis for research and habitat enhancement.

From the energy perspective, this lowland forest provides a major cooling effect on the natural and developed environment. The forest also provides a cool respite for the recreationist from urban heat and has an impact on the local weather. Annual rainfall varies from 45 to 80 inches, and nighttime downslope winds from the summits provide evening cooling for adjacent valley areas. Wildlife have certain habitat requirements within the managed forest, thus landscape planning considers the energy effect on wildlife created by large harvested areas.

The goal for the forest is to maintain sustainable, clear, and cool water. Considering the high level of urbanization surrounding the forest, Tiger Mountain is the largest undeveloped component of the Issaquah Creek drainage basin. The Issaquah Creek Salmon Hatchery, downstream from the forest, relies on Tiger Mountain for its unfiltered water supply. To predict the flow from the forest the Department of Natural Resources installed electronic water monitoring systems on major forest streams. These monitors provide flow, turbidity, rate-of-change, and chemical data on an hourly basis. To allow for collection of background information, water monitors were installed in 1985. From the data collected, management prescriptions can be designed to meet water quality needs. Adjacent urban areas cannot rely on the forest to offset their watershed impacts. The Issaquah Creek drainage basin has reached its limits in water flow, temperature, and turbidity. The forest and adjacent developed regions must maintain or enhance the water quality if the salmon hatchery is to survive.

HUMAN IMPACTS

The most critical impact on the forest is human. Increased recreational demands are causing damage to wildlife populations and natural plant communities. The Highpoint Trailhead has over 1,500 visitors per weekend, along with canine companions. Visitors damage fragile plant communities at the Talus caves, the summit of West Tiger 3, and the shore of Tradition Lake. The sheer number of users has already degraded the forest. To meet the ecological protection goals of a Natural Resource Conservation Area, the forest will require aggressive management of recreation.

Development adjacent to the forest has a significant effect on wildlife, water quality, and visual character. The forest has homes as well as manufacturing and commercial development on its perimeter. Forest production districts are usually buffered from urban development by a wide rural zone. On Tiger Mountain, urban lands are directly adjacent to the forest zone. And adjacent landowners have conflicting management objectives.

PUBLIC SUPPORT

There is strong public support for the development of New Forestry techniques within Tiger Mountain. The role of the forest is to be a laboratory where forest managers and the public can learn together how to manage a working forest in an urban environment. The West Tiger Mountain Natural Resource Conservation Area has enormous support. This approach combines the protection of native ecosystems with trust management in the remainder of the forest. These uses may seem in conflict, but in reality the forest now has an overall conservation overlay. Diverse management direction is an asset to the forest. The ecological research opportunities in the Conservation Area and the entire forest can be a model for other public and private forest lands. What we learn on the 13,500 acres of the Tiger Mountain State Forest can be readily applied to the entire 2.1 million acres of forest trust lands in Washington State.

INSTITUTIONAL OBLIGATIONS AND POLITICAL ISSUES

From the perspective of the institutional obligations of a trustee, Tiger Mountain must still meet the objective of revenue generation. The trust mandate for all state lands is receiving a wider interpretation than dollars alone. By the incorporation of a conservation area, a new wetlands policy, upland management areas, gene pool reserves, and sensitive area protection the forest has already diversified the trust mandate. Tiger Mountain should be a leader in pushing the envelope of change in trust land management.

Politically the forest has extremely active user groups. These groups are the support base which allows the agency to seek new directions. Organized groups are the checks needed to make sure we are still on track. Interest groups include the Issaquah Alps Trails Club, Washington Environmental Council, Society of American Foresters, Backcountry Bicycle Trails Club, and the Backcountry Horseman. Many other groups and organizations watch what is occurring on Tiger Mountain and help formulate change. The success of the Tiger Mountain State Forest is based on two things, trust and communication. It took over five years to develop a cooperative working relationship with the public. As an agency, the Department of Natural Resources had many things to learn through public involvement. The most important lesson is that the process of communicating and learning is a two-way street. Both the department and the interest groups learned through the development of a forest management plan. As the plan is implemented both parties will make mistakes and must adapt accordingly.

Politically you have the problem of holding onto the trust and lines of communication that you worked so hard to develop. To maintain effectiveness you need to make a long-term investment in public communication. As time goes by, the key players change and history is lost. Documentation, management plans, and geographic mapping systems record only the facts. Trust is based on your level of knowledge and its critical implementation. This is the one area that land managers need to continually work on. The continuity of management through open communication is critical to the success of the forest.

Even with the best efforts in communication and public involvement, you will always have new adjacent landowners moving in. Everything is great until an issue hits their backyard. The key to success is to keep in contact with organized groups and adjacent landowners. For example, our first timber sale within the forest prompted a negative letter to the editor in the *Issaquah Press*. Before we could call the individual to discuss his concerns, he had already been contacted by two of our citizen advisory committee members who took it as their obligation to defend the forest. Interest groups have an ownership in the process, and are as much a part of its success as the department staff. Developing public trust on Tiger Mountain results in political clout, support, money, and technical assistance from knowledgeable forest users.

During the past ten years, political battles have raged between competing recreation users. In 1980 the conflict was between off-road vehicles and hikers and horse riders. The eventual winners were the hikers and horse groups. For the next ten years the forest developed a good relationship between these two users. Occasionally there would be some trail damage by horses, but in general the two groups worked well together. In 1990 the arrival of the mountain bicycle revived old controversies. Mountain bikers became a new user group demanding access to all trails. Recreation uses change daily.

In the future, watch for the growth of the new sports of paragliding and rollerblading, the mountain bikes of tomorrow.

The problem with recreation user conflicts is not only safety and resource damage but also that resolving these issues can become very time consuming. New conflicts focus attention away from more critical issues. Environmental education and conservation efforts often are allocated little funding or staff time within the forest. When a recreational issue such as hiking versus bikes surfaces, you must divert your limited time and money to the crisis of the moment. Maintaining harmony in recreation is a key component of the total forest picture. The success of the timber sales program is directly tied to the success of the recreation program. Intense recreational use conflicts can burn out staff and user group leaders. These issues become very personal to the individuals involved. Protecting user safety and preventing resource damage are the primary concerns.

THE ECOLOGICAL SYSTEM

Ecological processes are affected by institutional programs. Originally the forest was a fire-based ecology. Every few hundred years, lightning strikes caused the entire forest to burn. Today, fire suppression has ended major wildfires and the Clean Air Act restricts burning in the area surrounding Tiger Mountain. The threat of a fire escape to adjacent property restricts the use of silvicultural burning. Harvest planning must take into account that fire will not be a component of the ecological system. In the future a nonfire-based ecological process will need to be developed.

The evolution of legislative conservation programs has made a dramatic change in the forest. Since 1989, changes in the Forest Practices Act have added the protection of wildlife trees, down logs, and snags, and the creation of upland management areas. Recent changes have included greenup requirements and size limitations for clearcut harvests. The 1992 Forest Resource Plan developed for state land management broadened the protection of critical habitats. This plan also directs the agency to use landscape planning as the design tool for the future. The Natural Resource Conservation Area Program of 1987 protects lands for their ecological values. Trust obligation is no longer the only criteria for management decisions. Ever-changing institutional directions, combined with an adaptive management philosophy, guide Tiger Mountain State Forest management.

THE FUTURE

The future for the Tiger Mountain State Forest look bright. Over the past ten years public opinion has varied as to the future of Tiger Mountain. Many have said it will become a state park, a subdivision, a wildlife island, possibly never return a penny to the trust, or just develop into a giant uncontrolled recreation area. With proper management, many positive visions are possible. The key to finding the right vision is in retaining options for the future. Tiger Mountain is the centerpiece of the Mountains to Sound Greenway. Forest lands need to be acquired now to complete the forest boundary before the potential of creating a self-sustaining greenway becomes impossible. The vision for the future of Tiger Mountain is of a demonstration forest that combines conservation, environmental education, and sustainable revenue production. That was the vision in

1983 when the Tiger Mountain State Forest was created. The vision is still possible. We are on the right track.

LITERATURE CITED

Forest Resource Plan, State of Washington. 1992. Policy direction for forest land management on State of Washington Forest Lands. Department of Natural Resources, Olympia, Washington.

Natural Resource Conservation Areas Statewide Management Plan. 1992. Guidelines for conservation area management. Department of Natural Resources, Land and Water Conservation Division, Olympia, Washington.

Tiger Mountain State Forest Citizens Advisory Committee Guidelines. 1985. Forest management recommendations from eighteen months of advisory committee work. Department of Natural Resources, South Puget Sound Region, Enumclaw, Washington.

Tiger Mountain State Forest Management Plan. 1986. Guides management in the Tiger Mountain State Forest from 1986 to 1995. Department of Natural Resources, South Puget Sound Region, Enumclaw, Washington.

Tiger Mountain State Forest Recreation Plan. 1991. Guides recreation management and capital improvements within the Tiger Mountain State Forest. Department of Natural Resources, Land and Water Conservation Division, Olympia, Washington.

West Tiger Mountain Natural Resource Conservation Area Management Plan. 1993. Site specific management plan. Department of Natural Resources, South Puget Sound Region, Enumclaw, Washington.

20

Some Thoughts on Integrating Multiple Objectives for Urban Forest Landscapes

GORDON A. BRADLEY

I was recently asked to advise on what to do with a five acre forest remnant located near downtown Seattle. The parcel has been the subject of community discussion for many years. In fact, a community open space committee has existed for about a decade, and during that time there has been much debate about the most appropriate action to take in restoring and managing the forest.

Most of the area is fairly steep, with slopes facing north, south, and west. A stream runs through about a third of the site, creating a ravine and relatively wet valley floor. The trees are approximately sixty to ninety years old and consist primarily of alder, maple, and madrona. English ivy and Himalayan blackberries cover much of the ground, and the ivy has climbed high into many of the trees. It is not a pretty site!

While this case is of immediate concern to me, it is only one of thousands of urban forestry scenarios that cry out for solution. In the course of addressing the complex issues that are the domain of urban forestry, the previous chapters in this book have provided many other examples of equally challenging problems.

And, as we look closely at the "domain" of urban forestry, we discover that in fact there is no such thing as "the" urban forest. Urban forest landscapes change as one moves from city center toward wildland settings. They change also with time and the different conditions that each setting presents. Given the wide variety of purposes for which urban forest landscapes may be created, they offer great flexibility and opportunities for innovative solutions.

How are such solutions to be crafted? How can the five acre forest remnant be managed effectively? This final chapter is organized in terms of three topics that serve to integrate the material raised in the previous chapters:

1. Opportunities and hazards in managing urban forest landscapes.
2. The "people factor" in planning and decision making.
3. Taking action in the face of uncertainty.

OPPORTUNITIES AND HAZARDS IN MANAGING URBAN FOREST LANDSCAPES

As Gary Moll noted earlier, just as the Eskimos have one hundred words for snow, we also have many ways to describe urban forests and urban forestry. Because of this, in managing urban forest landscapes it is easy to lose track of some factors as one focuses on others. The need to be aware of the diverse spectrum of opportunities and hazards is an important first step in the process.

This awareness is created by first deciding what purposes will be served by a particular urban forest landscape and then by making it explicit what is gained or lost by pursuing the development of a particular landscape type. The general purposes, as discussed by Henry Lawrence in a historical context, are social, natural, and aesthetic. These remain more or less intact today, although we may refer to them as social-political, ecological, and aesthetic. Also, these purposes are quite interdependent, and when we begin to get specific, conflicts may emerge. Thus the need to be clear in purpose.

Previous chapters have discussed in some detail what urban forestry attempts to achieve in creating urban landscapes that respond to the need for greenbelts, wildlife habitat, aesthetic satisfaction, fire safety, and energy and water conservation, among other things. In order to develop and maintain such landscapes, it is apparent that vegetation structure is a significant element and that there are "costs" associated with its maintenance. This being the case, it is necessary to know where conflicts may emerge regarding structure, and, as John Dwyer points out, what is gained or lost. An explicit analysis of tradeoffs is vital not only in developing and managing landscapes but also in promoting them in the social and political setting that supports them. Urban forests are not programs operating in isolation from other very worthy programs. They are competing for an increasingly sought after allocation of land, labor, and capital resources. It is critical to make explicit the range of choices and the social, ecological, and aesthetic consequences of those choices when creating urban forest landscapes.

The general opportunities for which an urban forest may be created are truly substantial. They are a major integrating factor across regions and a catalyst for action in our communities. Greenspaces can play an important role in bringing people, places, and programs together. A couple of recent events serve to illustrate these points.

The Seattle Parks and Recreation Department organized a meeting recently to discuss ideas for restoring Seattle's greenspaces. The turnout was in the hundreds, and the enthusiasm was contagious. People from throughout the city attended with stories to tell about their respective successful greenspace experiences. They and many others are excited about the prospect of making a difference in their community—a difference that has social, environmental, and aesthetic outcomes.

Each person who spoke obviously represented a particular community group, which in turn had a link to a specific place. In the meeting room about fifty posters illustrated the community projects, and it became apparent that there was hardly a greenspace in Seattle that did not have a constituency. There was "this" creek alliance, and "that" ravine committee, and the "whatever" jurisdiction land trust. These efforts bring people together and serve to create an important sense of place within each of the communities around Seattle. But I don't think Seattle is unique in this regard. This phenomenon is probably typical of communities throughout the country.

Although we usually associate urban forestry with street-tree, park, and open space programs, a recent effort by the Washington State Urban and Community Forest Council illustrates how urban forestry can be extended into other areas. Throughout Washington, cities and counties are preparing growth management plans in compliance with the state's recently adopted Growth Management Act. The Council developed a very useful booklet called "Community Forestry and Growth Management: A Toolbox for Comprehensive Management Plans," which provides sample goals and policies for several plan elements, including land use and urban design, transportation, housing, capital facilities, utilities, and energy use. In such ways, urban forestry cuts across many areas and achieves an effective integration of people, places, and programs.

THE "PEOPLE FACTOR" IN PLANNING AND DECISION MAKING

Urban forestry also provides many opportunities to involve, empower, and educate people. While there are several examples that effectively illustrate this point, I will rely on the "action mandates" provided by Rachel Kaplan in her chapter, for they do bear repeating.

Valuable information is not the exclusive property of those with expertise and status. The information held by local individuals is no less pertinent than the information held by those who wield power, money, or scientific "truths."

Humans are sensitive to signs of making a difference. Asking for information and promptly ignoring it is worse than not asking at all! The cumulative effect of such ill-fated participation is a demoralized citizenry.

People need to know what their choices are. They do better in providing information if they understand the context, the situation, the constraints. Hearing about or seeing some alternative solutions, for example, facilitates understanding at the same time that information is being shared.

Information in the hand is not information in the mind. The delivery of educational material is no assurance that it will be read, understood, or heeded. It is essential to invest considerably greater effort in determining what it is that leads to effective transmission of information. This is at the heart of affecting change. Good intentions have never been enough. The difference between what experts know and take for granted and what the public knows and holds dear is too often not examined.

TAKING ACTION IN THE FACE OF UNCERTAINTY

In the face of uncertainty, we seem more often than not to seek the definitive plan, the answer, or the solution to our problems. Our vocabulary almost prohibits us from admitting that we may be uncertain as to the outcome of a proposed action.

The idea of adaptive management, referred to be Rowan Rowntree in an earlier chapter, is an attempt to embrace uncertainty and take explicit action toward incorporating it into our problem solving strategies. The notion of developing testable hypotheses instead of goals is a way of saying, "We don't know exactly what the outcome will be, but by crafting a well-designed experiment, we can find out." Stephen Kaplan has given considerable thought to the idea of incorporating adaptive management into a societal context by suggesting small-scale experimentation as a way of averting environmental problems (DeYoung and Kaplan 1988).

There are many places where close monitoring of our activities, or "small experiments," can be utilized to deal with uncertainty. Some of those activities have been discussed in previous chapters—bond campaigns, regulatory strategies, educational programs, and recognition of the multitude of benefits that flow from urban forests. Our understanding of all these aspects of urban forestry could be increased substantially by pursuing each as an experiment rather than acting as if we were certain about the outcome of our proposed solutions.

In regard to the five acre forest remnant in Seattle that was in need of help, there were many questions to be answered. How do we deal with invasive plants? What should be done about the old trees and what areas should be replanted? And how do we counteract potential erosion problems on steep slopes? According to conventional wisdom we would expect to look for one plan to solve all of these problems. But why not consider an alternative? The site could be divided into more manageable units based on ecological factors, and then within each unit a series of experiments could be implemented to see what works under these specific conditions. Experiments could easily address plant removal, planting, and soil stabilization techniques. The forest remnant could become an experimental site in urban forest restoration and management. Each successful experiment carries the work forward and merits expansion. Each failed experiment is limited and is likely to suggest a better approach.

This approach avoids rushing into the unknown and risking error over the total site because of an uncertain plan. This is an opportunity to gain understanding, at little risk, from a set of well-crafted experiments. The involvement of the greenbelt committee only serves to strengthen the whole design—allowing opportunities for people to see what they like, how urban forest landscapes are created, and how they respond to change. The notion of small experiments allows for the generation of many possibilities to which people can respond. Thus, as noted earlier, success is linked to involvement, empowerment, and education.

This approach could just as well be taken for an open space bond campaign, a regional greenway project, or a specific treatment for testing a sustainability practice. The idea is to embrace uncertainty at the outset of the process and make it an explicit activity to resolve through experimental methods—or adaptive management—rather than trying to ignore its existence.

The successful creation of urban forest landscapes, while suggesting the need to integrate multidisciplinary perspectives, does not imply that their integration should be an exercise in comprehensiveness that overwhelms individuals and organizations. What it does suggest is that there are many considerations that are important when we are dealing with specific urban forests, large or small.

LITERATURE CITED

DeYoung, R., and S. Kaplan. 1988. On averting the tragedy of the commons. Environmental Management 12(3):273-283.

Contributors

James K. Agee is Professor of Forest Ecology at the University of Washington. He has a B.S. in forest management, an M.S. in range management, and a Ph.D. in wildland resource science from the University of California, Berkeley. His career with the National Park Service (fifteen years) and the University of Washington (five years) has focused on forest ecology research and the role of fire in natural ecosystems. He is the author of *Fire Ecology of Pacific Northwest Forests* and co-author, with D.R. Johnson, of *Ecosystem Management for Parks and Wilderness*.

Gordon Bradley is Professor of Forest Planning at the University of Washington and also holds faculty appointments in the Center for Urban Horticulture and the Department of Urban Design and Planning. His teaching and research interests include environmental policy and planning, urban forest program development, and organizational response to change. He has a B.S.L.A. in landscape architecture and environmental design from California State Polytechnic University, Pomona, an M.L.A. in environmental planning from the University of California, Berkeley, and a Ph.D. in urban and regional planning from the University of Michigan. He edited the book *Land Use and Forest Resources in a Changing Environment* and currently serves on the National Urban and Community Forestry Advisory Council.

James R. Clark is Vice President of HortScience, Inc., a horticultural consulting firm in Pleasanton, California. HortScience provides consulting services in landscape and tree management to public agencies, the development and design communities, and landscape managers. He is actively involved in tree retention programs, hazard tree evaluation, and development of landscape management plans. He earned his B.S. and M.S. degrees in horticulture from Rutgers University and a Ph.D. in plant physiology from the University of California, Davis.

Gene Duvernoy is an attorney and consultant in Seattle with a practice emphasizing land preservation and natural resource stewardship. He is retained by local governments, citizen groups, and nonprofit organizations to design and implement land preservation funding programs and campaigns and to resolve environmental and resource stewardship issues. Prior to entering private practice, he successfully managed the King County $50 million Farmland Preservation Program and led the development and implementation of the county's $116 million Open Space Bond Program. He has a master's in business administration, a law degree from Cornell University, and an engineering degree from Carnegie-Mellon University.

John F. Dwyer is research forester and leader of the research project Managing Forest Environments for Urban Populations at the USDA Forest Service North Central Forest Experiment Station in Chicago. He leads a multidisciplinary team of Forest Service scientists who work in cooperation with researchers from universities, and with public agencies, private groups, and forest managers and planners. Their research efforts are aimed at helping managers and planners understand how changes in the management of forest environments will affect urban people. He has B.S., M.S., and Ph.D. degrees from the State University of New York College of Environmental Science and Forestry at Syracuse, where his research focused on forestry economics and the influence of urbanization on forestry.

Roger Hoesterey is Assistant Director of the Bellevue Parks and Community Services Department. He oversees two divisions: the Resource Management Division, which maintains 2,000 acres of parkland, containing developed parks, streetscapes, gardens, golf courses, greenbelts, and wetlands; and the Enterprise Division, which conducts fee-supported services and programs. He serves on the Executive Advisory Committee of the Washington State Urban and Community Forest Council. He earned a B.S. in outdoor recreation from the University of Washington, College of Forest Resources.

Rachel Kaplan is Professor of Environmental Psychology at the University of Michigan. Her research has focused on the relationships between psychological well-being and the everyday environment, and has emphasized the role of the natural environment. She has also developed approaches for providing the public with alternatives to proposed environmental changes while at the same time obtaining useful feedback from citizens. Her current efforts focus on identifying psychological factors in sustainability, particularly noneconomic values central to human competence and identity. She has published widely in the area of environmental psychology and serves on editorial boards of several journals. She has an A.B. in philosophy from Oberlin College and a Ph.D. in psychology from the University of Michigan.

Stephen Kaplan is Professor of Psychology and Computer Science at the University of Michigan. He is a teacher and theorist whose focus includes the psychological benefits of nature, restorative environments, the kinds of environments people prefer, and how the mind's effectiveness is compromised by mental fatigue. His doctoral students have spanned a wide range of fields, including architecture, landscape architecture, psychology, geography, natural resources, nursing, and computer science. In addition to many articles, his publications include *Cognition and Environment*, *Humanscape*, and *The Experience of Nature*, co-authored with Rachel Kaplan. He has an A.B. in psychology from Oberlin College and a Ph.D. in psychology from the University of Michigan.

Henry W. Lawrence is Assistant Professor of Geosciences at Edinboro University of Pennsylvania. He received his B.A. in history from Yale University and his M.L.A. in landscape architecture and Ph.D. in geography from the University of Oregon. He has published articles on the history of American natural and recreational landscapes and of European urban vegetation as well as on specialized agriculture in metropolitan areas.

Konrad Liegel is an attorney with the law firm of Preston Gates & Ellis in Seattle, practicing in the areas of environmental, land use, real estate, and nonprofit law. He earned his B.A. in biology-philosophy from Carleton College and a J.D. from Cornell Law School. Prior to entering private law practice, he worked as a landscape ecologist in Wisconsin, where he wrote a land use and vegetational history of the Aldo Leopold Memorial Reserve, a national historic landmark.

Doug McClelland is the forest manager of the Tiger Mountain State Forest for the Washington State Department of Natural Resources, South Puget Sound Region. He oversees the efforts of an interdisciplinary team of foresters who manage a total of 30,000 acres of state trust land in urbanizing eastern King County. These lands are managed for revenue production, recreation, wildlife habitat, and conservation purposes. He earned his B.S. in forest management from the University of Washington.

E. Gregory McPherson is an urban forest researcher and Project Leader of the Western Center for Urban Forest Research, USDA Forest Service, University of California, Davis. His research focuses on the measurement and modeling of urban forest benefits and costs, with particular emphasis on energy and water use. He received a B.G.S. from the University of Michigan, an M.L.A. from Utah State University, and a Ph.D. in urban forestry from the State University of New York, College of Environmental Science and Forestry, Syracuse.

Patrick Miller is Professor and Head of the Landscape Architecture Department, Virginia Polytechnic Institute and State University, Blacksburg. As a landscape architect he has worked with a variety of public and private entities in the design and evaluation of the visual implications of various land alteration proposals, including timber harvesting, electric transmission lines, industrial development, and heritage preservation. He earned his B.S. in landscape architecture at the California State Polytechnic University, Pomona, an M.L.A. with a concentration in environmental planning from the University of California, Berkeley, and a Ph.D. from the University of Michigan. His scholarly interests lie in the area of design theory and landscape perception and assessment.

Gary Moll is Vice President of Urban Forests for the American Forests organization. He has worked as an urban forester for twenty years in the public, private, and nonprofit sectors. He started as a forester with a utility company in the Midwest, then moved to Maryland, where he coordinated the state's urban forestry program. He is a forestry graduate of the Michigan State University. At American Forests he is responsible for the editorial content of *Urban Forest Magazine* and numerous urban forestry articles and two books. He has also served as National Chairman of the Urban Forestry Working Group of the Society of American Foresters, President of the Mid-Atlantic Chapter of the International Society of Arboriculture, and Chairman of the National Urban Forest Council.

Robert C. Perry has been a professor in the Department of Landscape Architecture at California State Polytechnic University, Pomona, since 1972. His fields of instruction have included plant ecology and design, planting design, and senior design courses in the undergraduate and graduate programs. His research and consulting activities involve the ecology of landscape plants and their use in the urban environment. In 1981 he published *Trees and Shrubs for Dry California Landscapes* and recently completed *Landscape Plants for Western Regions*, which expands on ideas related to the sustainability of urban landscapes through water and energy conservation. He has a B.S.L.A. in landscape architecture and environmental design from California State Polytechnic University, Pomona, and an M.L.A. in environmental planning from the University of California, Berkeley.

Dorothy A. Milligan Raedeke is a Principal in the ecological consulting firm of Raedeke Associates, Inc., of Seattle. She is a practicing wildlife biologist with research and management interests in wildlife-habitat relationships in urban environments, with emphasis on all aspects of wetland ecology. She directs a staff of ecologists, physical scientists, and landscape design professionals in dealing with the issues of wildlife and wetland habitats in the urban and rural areas of the Pacific Northwest. She earned B.S. and M.S. degrees in wildlife ecology from the University of Washington, where her thesis research investigated the characteristics of urban wetlands that determined their value as wildlife habitat.

Kenneth Raedeke is a Principal in the ecological consulting firm of Raedeke Associates, Inc., and Research Associate Professor in the Wildlife Sciences Program in the College of Forest Resources, University of Washington. He is a practicing wildlife biologist, with research and management interests in large mammal ecology, population dynamics of exploited populations, wildlife-habitat relationships in forest environments, and wetland ecology. In addition to an active research program at the University, he directs a staff of ecologists, physical scientists, and landscape design professionals in dealing with the issues of wildlife and wetland habitats in urban and rural areas. He earned a B.S. in resource conservation from the University of Montana and a Ph.D. in wildlife ecology from the University of Washington.

Rowan A. Rowntree is Program Leader for the USDA Forest Service national research program in Urban Forest Ecology, which has scientists at Syracuse and Millbrook, New York, Albany and Davis, California, and Chicago, Illinois. Before forming this program in 1978, he was Associate Professor in Geography and Environmental Science at Syracuse University. His M.S. in forest ecology and Ph.D. in biogeography are from the University of California, Berkeley. He has written several dozen articles and edited three anthologies related to urban forest ecology, the last entitled

The Ecological City. He has been a Doctoral Fellow at Resources for the Future, a consultant to the President's Commission on the National Parks, Directorate Chairman for the U.S. Man and the Biosphere Program, and a visiting scholar at the University of California, Berkeley. In 1992 he received the USDA's highest award for distinguished research, and in 1993 American Forests awarded him their Urban Forestry Medal for Research.

Lee Springgate has served twenty-three years in the parks and recreation profession, the last sixteen as the Parks and Community Services Director for Bellevue, Washington. During his tenure, the city has used a variety of funding sources, including four voter-approved bond issues, to generate over $80 million for park acquisition and development. The department has received numerous awards, including the Gold Medal for Special Recreation. He has been Host City and Program Chairman for state conferences and has had speaking engagements at state and national conferences. He holds a master's degree in public administration from the University of Washington, teaches graduate courses at the University, and received the Outstanding Public Employee Award from the Municipal League of Seattle and King County in 1988.

J. Alan Wagar is Research Professor of Urban Forestry and Wildland Recreation at the University of Washington. He also runs a small business in Seattle to develop urban tree inventory and management software. He previously worked for the USDA Forest Service, most recently as project leader for landscape and urban forestry research at the Pacific Southwest Station, Berkeley, California, and prior to that as project leader for recreation research units in the Intermountain, Pacific Northwest, and Northeastern Forest Experiment Stations. His B.S.F. is from the University of Washington, and his M.F. and Ph.D. degrees are from the University of Michigan.

Index

Adaptive management, 57, 210-211
Aerial photography, 154
Aesthetic benefits, 6, 29-30, 90, 175, 192
Aesthetic values
    and decision making, 115
    of landscape designers, 116-117
    and science, 115
Afforestation, 44
Air-conditioning
    energy savings, 48, 53, 151-152, 156
    simulation studies, 152-153, 188
Airflow modification, 55, 151, 155, 156
Air quality, 26, 187, 188-189
Alder (*Alnus* spp.), 134, 135, 137, 144, 198
Alexander VII (pope), 31
Allée Buffon, 34
Allingham v. City of Seattle, 73
Alpine Lakes, 201
American Forests, 4, 14, 153-154
Amphibian and reptile habitat, 140, 142
Amsterdam, 18
Ann Arbor, 125
Antwerp, 18, 34
Arboriculture, 46
Arboriculture and Urban Forestry (IUFRO), 3
Area/perimeter ratio, 130
Arizona, 152, 153, 182
Arizona Corporation Commission, 153
Arson, 166
Atlas Peak fire, 167
Available growing space (AGS), 154-155

Backcountry Bicycle Trails Club, 205
Backcountry Horseman, 205
Ballot measures, 82-85
Bayer, Herbert, 116
Bear (*Ursus americanus*), 145, 146, 147
Bear Valley, California, 51-52
Beaver (*Castor canadensis*), 145
Beaux Arts school, 29
Bedford Square, 33, 35

Belgium, 18, 34
Belgrave Square, 35
Bellevue, Washington, 124, 195-200, 202
Benefit-cost analysis, 8, 10, 50, 51, 55, 92, 153
Benefit-cost ratio (BCR), 186, 190
Benefit-cost studies
    Bear Valley, 52
    Chicago, 182-192
Berkeley hills. *See* Oakland-Berkeley hills fire
Berkeley Square, 22
Berlin, 18, 23
Biodiversity
    components, 130, 140-141, 178, 203
    managing for, 141-143, 145-146, 147
    of wildlife, 203
    See also Patches
Bird habitat, 47, 140, 142-143, 145, 146, 178, 197
Birkenhead Park, 23
Blackberries, 137, 208
Blackheath, 24
Blacksburg, Virginia, 113, 119
Bloomsbury, 27
Blue Ridge Parkway, 120
Bois de Boulogne, 23, 29
Boston, 23, 153
Boulder, Colorado, 122
Boulevard de l'Hôpital, 32
Boundaries, 46-48
Boyle, Brian, 202
Broadway, 20
Buffers, 6, 129, 130, 147
Building construction, 155
Building density, 7
Byrne, Jane, 90

Caldwell, Lynton, 56
California
    areas of development, 164
    chaparral, 166
    evapotranspiration data, 162
    Golden Gate Park, 33
    landscape sustainability, 175

shade tree programs, 182
streetcar suburb, 25
survey of urban forestry, 181
wildfires, 165-166
California Department of Forestry and
Fire Protection, 166, 169
California Department of Water Resources,
162
Canopy stocking level (CSL), 154-155
Carbon dioxide emissions, 151, 153, 175,
176, 177, 187, 189
Carbon monoxide, 6, 187, 189
Cavendish Square, 27
Central Park, 23, 24, 26, 27, 28, 33
Champs Elysées, Avenue des, 18, 32
Charleston, South Carolina, 120
Chicago, 28, 29, 90, 94
Chicago Cost-Benefit Analysis of Trees
(C-BAT), 182-192
Chicago Park District, 183
Chicago Urban Forest Climate Project, 155,
181
Christiansburg, Virginia, 112, 125
Christo, 116
Churchyards, 20
Citizen advisory committees, 202, 205
City Beautiful movement, 29
Clean Air Act, 203, 206
Clean Water Act amendments, 182
Clearcutting, 143, 206
Climate in urban areas, 151, 156-157
Clinton administration, 154
Colorado, 122
Colorado Front, 53
Composting, 177, 179
Computer models, 182-192
Conifers, 134-135, 137, 140, 143, 144
Connectivity, 144
Conservation areas, 129, 202-206
Context of urban forest ecology, 44
Cook County, Illinois, 155
Cool Communities Program, 154
Core of urban forest ecology, 43-44
Corridors, 130, 144, 145, 146-147, 148
Cost-Benefit Analysis of Trees (C-BAT), 182-
192
Cottonwood (*Populus* spp.), 134, 144
Cougar (*Felis concolor*), 145, 146, 147
Cougar Mountain, 203
Council of Tree and Landscape Appraisers,
96

Cours la Reine, 18, 31
Courthouse squares, 22, 23
Coyote (*Canis latrans*), 47, 144, 145
Crime, 81, 145
Critical areas ordinances, 74

Daley, Richard M., 90
Deciduous trees, 5, 140, 151, 152, 153, 156
Deer (*Odocoileus hemionus*), 145, 146, 147
Deforestation, 44
Demographic information, 50
Demonstration forest, 201-207
Desert areas, 156
Development
building density, 7
laws regulating, 74
near state forest, 204
public attitudes toward, 112, 113
transferable rights, 75
Devil's club (*Oplopanax horridum*), 137
Discounted payback period, 188, 190, 191
Disease, plant, 135, 137, 145
Douglas-fir (*Pseudotsuga menziesii*), 5, 129, 135,
137
Drainage areas, 125-126
DuPage County, Illinois, 155

Earthworks, 116
East Bay hills. *See* Oakland-Berkeley hills fire
East Bay Municipal Utility District, 169, 170
East Bay Regional Park District, 170
Ecological processes, 8, 161-162
Ecological Society of America, 49
Economics
city budgets, 93
cost breakdown for urban trees, 15
fees, 92, 96
land preservation programs, 80-83, 86
maintaining urban landscapes, 35-38
marginal analysis, 93
net present value (NPV), 186, 187, 190
nonmarket benefits, 94-95
role in urban forestry, 10, 88-97
See also Benefit-cost analysis
Ecosystem concept, 54-56
Ecosystems
function, 45-48
management, 43-54, 56, 197-198
processes, 46
structure, 45-48
urban forests as, 12-13
Edge cities, 111

Edge effect
    animal species diversity, 142
    corridors, 130, 144, 145, 146-47, 148
    defined, 140
    in greenbelts, 129, 130, 133
    "wall" edges, 134-135
Electric energy efficiency, 152, 153, 154, 177
Elk (*Cervus elaphus*), 145, 146, 147
Elm trees, 26, 31
Emergent landscapes, 137
Energy conservation
    and fire safety, 5
    landscape applications, 6, 150-158, 177
    savings, 92, 95, 188-190
    simulated program, 188-190
Energy fluxes, 52-54
Energy Policy Act, 154
England. *See* Great Britain
Environmental Protection Agency, U.S., 153
Eucalyptus, 166
Euclidean zoning, 72
Europe
    detached housing, 25
    elm trees, 26
    Middle Ages, 18, 20
    parks, 23-24, 27, 29, 31-33
    private gardens, 18, 19, 24-26, 31-34
    public squares, 20-22, 23
    Renaissance, 20
    residential squares, 21-22, 23, 33
    suburbs, 24-25
    traditional use of urban trees, 17
    tree-lined streets, 18-20, 29, 31
    walled cities, 18, 31
    See also individual cities and countries
Evapotranspiration
    cooling effect, 151, 152, 153, 157
    process, 53, 54-55
    and water budgets, 162-163
Exotic species, 48, 52
Exurban area, 43

Farm Bill, 119
Farmland preservation programs, 81, 83
Fertilizer, 46, 176, 177, 179
Financial goals, 92-93. *See also* Economics
Fire
    effects on animal habitat, 144
    hazards, 165-68
    landscape continuous fuel, 130
    natural phenomenon, 206
    silvicultural use, 203, 206
    and stand development, 132, 134, 137

suppression, 206
    wildfires, 165-166
Fire risk meter, 168
Fire-safe landscapes, 5, 6, 125, 157, 164-171
Firs, 137
Fish habitat, 9, 147
Florida, 152
Food, Agriculture, Conservation, and
    Trade Act, 119
Forest Ecosystem Management Assessment
    Team, 57
Forest Park, 37
Forest Practices Act, 206
Forest remnants. *See* Greenbelts and
    forest remnants
Forest Resource Plan, 206
Forest Service, U.S.
    Chief quoted, 49
    ecosystem management, 49
    fire risk meter, 168
    forest inventory, 13
    research, 4, 49, 55
    State and Private Forestry branch, 55
    sustainability, 49
    wilderness program, 100
Forest succession, 51-52
France, 18-21, 24, 25, 28, 29. *See also* Paris
Frankfurt am Main, 19
Freeway Park, 37
Fuel ladders, 166, 170

Gaia hypothesis, 29
Gardening, 28
Gas Works Park, 37
Gateway Green, Illinois, 183
Geographical information systems (GIS), 16
Germany, 18, 19, 23, 25
Global Change Action Plan, 154
Global ReLeaf, 153
Global warming, 28-29
Golden Gate Park, 33
Golley, Frank, 55-56
Gradient concept, 6-8, 43, 47, 50-51, 145-146
Grand Boulevart, 31
Grand Canyon, 181
Grasses, 162-163
Grasslands, 140, 141, 143-144, 146
Great Britain
    parks, 23, 24, 32-33
    residential squares, 21-23, 33, 35
    suburban areas, 24
    See also London

Green ash (*Fraxinus pennsylvanica*), 183
Greenbelts and forest remnants
    corridors, 144
    ordinances, 74
    experimental site, 211
    public acquisition, 76
    remnant and emergent landscapes,
      128-138, 202
    size and structure, 130-131
    stand development stages, 131-133, 137
    traffic impact, 136-137
Greenways, 195-200
Growth management, 6, 78-87, 141, 201,
    209-210

Habitat. *See* Wildlife habitat
Habitat preservation or restoration, 141
Hampstead Heath, 24, 27
Hardwoods, 134, 135, 137
Harlequin Place (Denver), 116
Hayfork Adaptive Management Area, 57
Heating expenses, 150-158
Heat island effect, 4, 53, 94, 151, 153, 157
Highgate, 27
Highpoint Trailhead, 201, 204
Highway Bill, 119
Highway trees, simulated study, 183-191
Historical values in landscapes, 119-121, 125
History of urban landscapes, 17-38
Holme, the, 35
Hough, Michael, 111
Human considerations
    attitudes toward fire, 164
    impacts on environment, 44-45, 47-48,
      49-50, 54, 204, 211
    lack of connection with the land, 118
    need for information, 60-70, 210
    restorative effects of urban forests, 10,
      100-106
    safety, 144-145, 146, 147, 148, 198
    scenic values, 114-116
Hurricane-prone regions, 156
Hyde Park (London), 29
Hydrocarbons, 51, 53, 54
Hydrozones, 163, 178

Illinois Bureau of Forestry, 183
Illinois Department of Transportation, 183
Informational issues, 8-10, 60-70, 210
Institute for Ecosystem Studies, 47
Intermodal Surface Transportation
    Efficiency Act, 119

International Union of Forestry Research
    Organizations, 3
Irwin, Robert, 116
Island biogeography, 144
Issaquah Alps Trails Club, 205
Issaquah Creek, 204
Issaquah Press, 205
Issaquah, Washington, 201, 202
Italy, 18, 20

Jail House Garden, 117
James, William, 102
Jardin des Plantes, 34
Jensen, Jens, 29

Kensington Gardens, 31
Kent, Washington, 116
King County, Washington
    biodiversity, 140-141
    growth management act, 201
    farmlands preservation, 81, 83
    open space program, 84, 85
    sensitive areas ordinance, 141
    stream buffer, 147
Kitsap County, Washington, 82, 84
Kmart, 112

Lake Hills Greenbelt, 124
Lake-to-Lake Greenway and Trail, 196-197
Landowner incentives, 9, 75-76
Land preservation programs
    designing and developing, 80-85
    financing, 80-83, 86
    implementation, 86-87
    property selection, 86
    stewardship, 87
Landscape architects, 90, 111
Landscape design and aesthetics, 116
Landscape ecology, 111
Land use controls, 7, 9, 72-78
Land use planning, 49
Latin América, 25
Laws. *See* Land use controls
Leaf area, 53, 184-185, 188, 190
Le Pays, René, 27
Lightfooted clapper rail, 47
Linear promenades, 18-20, 29, 31
Liverpool, 23
London
    malls, 18
    parks, 23, 24, 32-33
    residential squares, 21-23, 33, 35

sheep, 27
  suburban areas, 24-25, 27-28
Los Angeles, 155, 162, 181
Los Angeles County, 81
Los Angeles Tree People, 4
Louis XIV, 20, 30, 31
Lucas v. South Carolina Coastal Council, 73
Lucca, Italy, 18
Luxembourg Gardens, 23

Mabry Mill, 120
Madrid, 23
Mammal habitat, 140, 142, 145-147
Management
  adaptive management, 57, 210-211
  greenbelts and forest remnants, 128-138
  greenway, 197-200
  state forest, 201-207
  urban forests, 91-92
  wildlife habitat, 140-148, 203
  See also Ecosystems; Growth management
Manchester Square, 35
Maple (*Acer* spp.), 52, 134, 137, 144, 198
Marguerite, gardens of ex-queen, 24
Marie de Medici, 31
Market incentives, 182
Market Street (Philadelphia), 20
Marginal analysis, 93
Maryland, 13, 182
McHarg, Ian, 111
Media, 85-86
Mencken, H.L., 104
Michigan, 125
Mill Creek Canyon Earthworks, 116
Minneapolis, 153
Mitigation banking, 147
Model Cool Communities, 154
Morgan, Elmore, 119
Morris Arboretum, 57
Mountains to Sound Greenway, 196, 202, 206
Mount Hood National Forest, 37
Mount Si, 201
Mulberry trees, 157
Mulching, 163, 178, 179
Mumford, Lewis, 31

Nancy, France, 21
Napoleon III, 19, 21, 31
Nash, John, 35
National Register of Historic Places, 119
National Scenic Byways Program, 119

Natural Resource Conservation Areas, 129, 202-206
Nest boxes, 146
Nested research, 51
Netherlands, 18, 27
Net present value (NPV), 186, 187, 190
New England, 23
New Forestry, 203, 204
New Jersey, 152
New York City, 20, 23, 24, 26, 27, 28, 33
New York State, 47
Nine Spaces, Nine Trees (Seattle), 116
Nitrogen dioxide, 187, 189
Nitrogen fixing, 137
North America
  detached housing, 25
  private gardens, 25
  traditional use of urban trees, 17, 19-20, 22-23

Oak, specimen tree, 120
Oakland-Berkeley hills fire, 8, 44, 165, 168-169, 170
Old-growth forest, 132, 143, 202
Old Salem Church, 121
Olmsted, Frederick Law
  linked parklands, 196
  social value of parks, 26, 27, 33, 38
  suburbs, 28
Openlands, 183, 188
Open space programs, 6, 7, 78-87, 141, 145
Our National Landscape, 118
Outdoor Challenge Program, 100
Ozone, 6, 51, 54, 187, 189

Pacific yew (*Taxus brevifolia*), 137
Pall Mall (London), 18, 26
Palm Springs, California, 163
Paris, 18-20, 21, 23, 24, 29, 31, 32, 34
Parking lots, 53
Park trees, simulated study, 183-191
Particulate matter, 188, 189
Pasadena, California, 25
Patches
  composition, 142-143
  corridors, 130, 144, 145, 146-147, 148
  dynamics and viability, 143-145
  size and shape, 142, 145, 147
Pennsylvania, 152
Pennsylvania, University of, 57
Peoria, Illinois, 22
Periurban area, 43

Philadelphia, 20
Pinchot, Gifford, 48
Place de la Carrière, 21
Plantable space, 154-155
Plants. *See* Vegetation
Poitiers, 29
Political issues, 9, 78-87
Pollutants
    air pollution mitigation, 177
    effects of urban forests on, 151
    mitigation in simulated program, 188-189
    nonpoint sources, 181-182
    regional planning, 52-54
    transboundary issue, 181
Poplar (*Populus trichocarpa x deltoides*), 135
Portland, Oregon, 37
Preferential taxation, 75
Presbytery of Seattle, 73
Private property, 49
Promenades, 18-20, 29, 31
Pruning, 134-135, 186, 187, 191, 198
Property values, 95-96
Psychological benefits, 10, 27, 60-70, 100-106
Public acquisition of land, 76
Public education programs, 75
Public housing trees, simulated study,
    183-191
Public opinion polls, 82, 84
Public policy, 44
Public support, 84, 126, 199-200, 204-205
Public utilities, 125-126
Puget Sound area, 140, 195-200, 201-207

Queen Square, 27

Raccoon (*Procyon lotor*), 145
Recreational uses of urban forests
    conflicts, 205-206
    hazards, 134
    impacts, 137, 198-199, 202
Recycled products, 182
Red alder (*Alnus rubra*), 135, 144, 198
Regent's Park, 23, 27, 31, 35
Regulatory controls, 72-77
Religious aspects of trees, 28
Remote sensing methods, 154
Research, 50-54, 55
Residential energy savings, 150-158
Residential yard trees, simulated study,
    183-191
Restorative environments, 103-106

Retiro (Madrid), 23
Right-of-way corridors, 141
Rio Shopping Center, 116
Riparian areas, 7, 140, 141, 146, 155, 178
Risk assessment, 65
Riverside (Chicago suburb), 28
Roman Forum, 31, 34
Roof composition, 166, 167, 168, 169
Root rot (*Phellinus weirii*), 135
Roses (*Rosa* spp.), 137
Running Fence, 116
Runoff, 54, 125, 187, 188, 189

Sacramento, 48
Sacramento Tree Foundation, 4
Sacramento-San Joaquin Valley, 53
Salmon hatchery, 204
Salt Lake Valley, 53
Sammamish, Lake, 196, 197
San Francisco, 33
Scenic byways programs, 119
Scenic value, 5, 8, 111-126
Schwartz, Martha, 116, 117
Science, 44, 50-54, 115
Scott, Frank J., 30
Seattle, 37, 81, 117, 129, 142, 195, 201, 202, 208-
    209, 211
Seattle Parks and Recreation Department, 209
Sensitive areas, 134, 141
Settlement patterns, 51-52
Sheep, 27
Shrublands, 140, 143, 146
Sierra Front Wildfire Cooperators, 170
Sierra Nevada, 48, 51-52
Sierra Nevada Ecosystem Project, 54
Simulation studies, 152-153, 182-192
Sitka alder (*Alnus sinuata*), 137
Smithson, Robert, 116
Snoqualmie Pass, 202
Social roles of urban forests, 26-34, 211
Society of American Foresters, 49, 205
Soil, 7, 179
Solar radiation, 52-53
South Carolina, 73, 120
Southwestern United States, 161
Spain, 20, 23
Species richness. *See* Biodiversity
Species selection, 4-5, 191
Spiral Jetty (Utah), 116
Spiritual values, 90
Spirn, Anne Whiston, 111

Splice Garden (Cambridge, Mass.), 116
Squak Mountain, 203
Standard Metropolitan Statistical Area, 46
Stand development stages, 131-133
State forest, 201-207
St. Cloud, Avenue, 30
St. James's Park, 31
Stormwater retention area, 125
Stormwater runoff, 92, 141, 188
Street tree ordinances, 74
Street trees, simulated study, 183-191
Subdivision regulations, 72, 74
Suburbs, 25-26, 27-28, 30, 36
Successional forest patterns, 143
Sulfur dioxide, 6, 182, 187, 189
Surveys of urban forestry programs, 181
Sustainability, 10-11, 49, 130, 175-179
SWA Group, 116

Talus caves, 204
Tansley, A.G., 48
Taxation, 75-76
Temperature in cities, 151, 157
Texas, 182
Thinning, 132, 134, 137, 198
Tiergarten, 23
Tiger Mountain State Forest, 38, 129, 201-207
Tradition Lake, 204
Traffic impact in forests, 136-137
Trails, 198-199
Transferable development rights (TDR), 75
Tree cover density, 51
TreeKeepers, 183
Tree-lined promenades, 18-20, 23-24
Tree maintenance programs, 191
Tree mortality rates (projected), 184-185
Tree planting potential (TPP), 154-155
Tree planting programs, 4, 5, 9, 55, 123, 152, 153-154, 182, 187-188, 191
Trees in urban areas
    canopy cover, 15
    cost breakdown, 15
    mortality, 14
    urban tree cover percentages, 15
Tree species selection, 191
Trees for Tucson, 153
Trust lands, 205
Tuileries, 23, 24
Turf, energy savings of, 152
Turf grass, 162-163, 175, 177

Ulrich, Roger, 89
Ultraviolet stress, 52, 53
Underplanting, 137
Understory, 46
United States history
    colonial times, 23, 25
    courthouse squares, 22-23
    detached housing, 25
    parks, 23-24, 32-33
    private gardens, 25-26, 32
    suburbs, 25-26, 28
    traditional uses of urban trees, 17, 19-20, 22-23, 32-33
United States Supreme Court, 73
Unter den Linden, 18
Urban forest ecology, 43-57
Urban forestry
    benefits, 4-5, 180-192, 209
    California survey, 181
    community aspects, 3-4, 8-9, 208, 211
    core and context, 43-44, 45-54
    professional aspects, 3-4, 8, 111-112
    in the United States, 12-16
Urban Forestry Center, 57
Urban landscape forms, 17-26, 34-38
Urban-to-rural land use gradient. *See* Gradient concept
Utah, 182
Utilities, public, 125-126

Vegetation
    in central areas of cities, 6-7
    effects of development on, 5
    effects on energy use, 155
    and forest structure, 4-5, 5-8
    hydrozones, 178
    introduced (alien), 128
    native, 128
    and regional planning, 52-54
    and risk of fire, 168, 169
    and sustainability, 177-178
    and scenic value, 122-124
    suitability to the landscape, 162
    understory, 137, 144-145
    and urban climate, 151
    and urban forest gradient, 6-8
    xeric (water conserving), 157
Versailles, 30
Vine maple (*Acer circinatum*), 137
Virginia, 112, 113, 119, 120, 125
Visual aspects of landscapes, 118-119

Washington, D.C., 182

Washington Environmental Council, 205
Washington, Lake, 196, 197
Washington State
    growth management plans, 6
    health and safety regulations, 145
    managed forest, 195-200
    working forest, 201-207
Washington State Department of Natural
    Resources, 202, 206
Washington State Department of Wildlife, 145,
    147
Washington State Supreme Court, 73
Washington State Urban and Community
    Forest Council, 4, 209
Water budget, 162-163
Water conservation, 6, 74, 125, 157, 161-163,
    178
Water distribution changes, 51-52
Water resource assessment, 204
Western hemlock (*Tsuga heterophylla*), 137
Western redcedar (*Thuja plicata*), 134, 137
West Tiger Mountain Natural Resource
    Conservation Area, 203, 204
Wetlands, 7, 74, 140, 141, 143, 146, 147
Weyerhaueser Company, 202
Wildfires. *See* Fire
Wildland Home Fire Risk Meter, 168
Wildlife habitat
    edge effects, 130

enhancement programs, 9
habitat management, 139-148, 199
inventories, 178
and land use regulations, 74
and patterns of land use, 47
and plant diversity, 162
and public acquisition of land, 76
and scenic values, 5, 124-125
in a state forest, 201, 204
urban, 27
See also Patches
Wind
    and developed areas in forests, 5
    effect on animal habitat, 144, 147
    effect on edges, 134-135
    as a recreational hazard, 134
    and residential energy use, 151, 152,
        153, 156
    and stand development, 132, 133, 134,
        137
    windbreaks, 52, 154, 156
Woodlots, 142-143, 155
Woodpeckers, 145
Working forests, 129, 201-207

Young, Arthur, 29

Zoning bonuses, 75

Urban Forest Landscapes

Integrating Multidisciplinary Perspectives
Edited by Gordon A. Bradley

The goal of urban forestry is to understand the ecological, institutional, and human issues at work in the urban landscape. Urban forestry is a comparatively new field within the academic discipline of forestry, and is closely allied to several scientific disciplines as well as the social sciences. Professionals in the field are called upon to provide scientific information and guidance, and to justify in economic, social, and environmental terms the value of the urban landscape in relation to other uses of the land and other needs of the city.

The multidisciplinary approach of this book recognizes the dilemma that in the attempt to solve problems by developing landscapes that address specific goals such as fire safety, energy and water conservation, and wildlife preservation, other problems are sometimes created because scientific knowledge is lacking or because not all aspects of the situation have been considered. *Urban Forest Landscapes* takes a critical look at the current state of knowledge and research in the field, and how available information is applied in the urban setting.

The book includes contributions by twenty specialists. Several articles outline the development of urban forestry in the United States and the use of trees in urban environments in the European and North American cultural tradition. Others consider the environmental setting: the level of scientific knowledge, public policy and perceptions of land management needs, human needs, land use laws and regulations, political and administrative issues, and economic approaches. Another group of articles discuss scenic value, management of greenbelts and forest remnants, wildlife habitat design, energy-efficient landscapes, water conservation, and fire-safe landscape. A final section focuses on sustainability of urban forest landscapes, both from a conceptual perspective and by presenting two practical case studies of managed forests in an urban environment.

Gordon A. Bradley is professor of forest planning at the College of Forest Resources, University of Washington. He also holds faculty appointments in the Center for Urban Horticulture and the Department of Urban Design and Planning.